The EVERYTHING.
Etiquette Book
SECOND EDITION

Dear Reader:

If you're like me, you've noticed that as our world has become more advanced in many things, communications included, our manners have become more backwards. Women wear clothing when they're out and about that they once would only wear in the bedroom; people have what sounds like private conversations on their cell phones in public places; and parents raise children without good manners. What has our modern world come to?

Obviously, you feel the frustration too, or you wouldn't have picked up this book. Think of *The Everything® Etiquette Book,* **2nd Edition,** as your soup-to-nuts reference book on how to act politely from birth to death, literally. Hopefully, you'll take my advice to heart, and little by little, people all over the planet will slowly become better behaved. Then years from now, when we talk about manners in the twenty-first century, we'll be able to highlight how nicely everyone has started to act.

Leah Ingram

The EVERYTHING® Series

Editorial

Publishing Director	Gary M. Krebs
Associate Managing Editor	Laura M. Daly
Copy Chief	Brett Palana-Shanahan
Acquisitions Editor	Kate Burgo
Development Editor	Michelle Chard Rizzo
Production Editor	Bridget Brace

Production

Director of Manufacturing & Technology	Susan Beale
Associate Director of Production	Michelle Roy Kelly
Series Designers	Daria Perreault
	Colleen Cunningham
	John Paulhus
Cover Design	Paul Beatrice
	Matt LeBlanc
Layout and Graphics	Colleen Cunningham
	Holly Curtis
	Erin Dawson
	Sorae Lee
Series Cover Artist	Barry Littmann

Visit the entire Everything® Series at *www.everything.com*

THE
EVERYTHING®
ETIQUETTE
BOOK
SECOND EDITION

A modern-day guide to good manners

Leah Ingram

Adams Media
Avon, Massachusetts

To my mother, Judy Watson Ingram, who taught me
that manners were what always mattered most.

An Everything® Series Book.
Everything® and everything.com® are registered trademarks of F+W Publications, Inc.

Published by Adams Media, an F+W Publications Company
57 Littlefield Street, Avon, MA 02322 U.S.A.
www.adamsmedia.com

ISBN: 1-59337-383-X
Printed in the United States of America.

J I H G F E D C B A

Library of Congress Cataloging-in-Publication Data
Ingram, Leah.
The everything etiquette book / Leah Ingram.—2nd ed.
p. cm. —(An everything series book)
Includes bibliographical references and index.
ISBN 1-59337-383-X
1. Etiquette. I. Title: Etiquette book. II. Title. III. Series: Everything series.
BJ1853.S44 2005
395—dc22
2005015478

This book is available at quantity discounts for bulk purchases.
For information, please call 1-800-872-5627.

Contents

Acknowledgments

For many years now, I've wanted to write a book on manners and etiquette. However, it never would have happened if it weren't for the brilliant agents at Sheree Bykofsky Associates, who brought this project to me when Adams Media needed someone to update *The Everything®️ Etiquette Book*. Thanks for giving me a real feather to put in my etiquette cap. I hope I've made you proud.

Thanks also to Kate Burgo, my tireless editor at Adams, who did a great job holding my hand through the learning curve process of understanding the unique method of writing an *Everything®️* book. "Youse" guys were great to work with.

I'd also like to give a shout out to Harry and Elaine Roberts who gave me a crash course in international etiquette and long ago helped me to learn that scotch is a drink, not a person from Scotland. And, of course, I must thank my husband Bill Behre, who was a great sounding board for all my manners-related questions when I was tired, writing late into the night, and not quite sure how to keep my polite wits about me.

Top Ten Faux Pas
That People Tend to Make on a Regular Basis

1. Forgetting to R.S.V.P. to an invitation.

2. Teaching their children that it's fine to call adults by their first names.

3. Omitting writing thank-you notes after receiving a gift.

4. Talking about inappropriate topics when someone is pregnant, such as the conception details or birth horror stories.

5. Deciding that disciplining misbehaving children isn't a priority.

6. Partaking of public displays of affection when everyone is thinking, "Get a room."

7. E-mailing incessantly at home and at work, including forwarding urban legends and insipid jokes.

8. Forgetting that cars are made for driving, not chitchatting on your cell phone.

9. Traveling to a foreign country and expecting everyone there to embrace the traveler's American-ness.

10. Letting their pets run amuck in the neighborhood.

Introduction

▶ FOR AS LONG AS MAN has been interacting with others, there have been unwritten rules of etiquette and manners that surrounded those interactions. From the caveman who likely let his cave "wife" eat the nuts and berries before he dug in, to the modern day commuter who lets another driver merge in front of him during rush hour traffic, there are common courtesies that likely make your everyday interactions that much more pleasant for all involved. The only problem is not everyone understands these inherent courtesies anymore, and that's why there's a need for a comprehensive book on all things etiquette.

Probably the biggest mistake that people make when it comes to manners and etiquette—besides not using any at all—is thinking that they don't apply to everyday occurrences. Most people think about manners in terms of white-haired ladies wearing pearls and gloves while enjoying a cup of tea. Obviously, this is an outdated picture of women and manners in general, which is why anyone who equates manners with these old-fashioned ladies is out of date himself in his belief about manners.

Sure, you need to act politely if your Aunt Clara invites you to join her at The Plaza Hotel in New York City for afternoon tea (yes, it still exists), but tea isn't the only time that manners matter. From the time you are born until the day you die, there is a place, somewhere in your life, for you to use good manners.

Children need to have their manners about them when they go to school or birthday parties, and grown-ups need them just as much when they go to the office or take a client out to eat. You also need manners whether you're commuting to work, taking a vacation to a foreign land, or are planning a wedding. In fact, if you were to pull out your appointment calendar and glance at any week in your life, you would see multiple opportunities and interactions where you would need good manners.

Studies have shown that people with good behavior go farther in life than those who act like clods. Obviously, you're interested in avoiding cloddish behavior at all costs, or you wouldn't have bought this book. By following the tips and instructions in the pages that follow, you're going to become one of those people whom your friends and family will always include in social occasions and want to spend time with. That's because, by brushing up on your manners and etiquette, you will always feel confident in knowing that you're well behaved. You will always know how to act appropriately and politely in each and every situation you find yourself in on a day-to-day basis, and the people around you are sure to appreciate just how well behaved you are.

Chapter 1

Being Proper During Pregnancy

It's hard to believe that just a few decades ago, showing a pregnant woman on TV, let alone saying the word "pregnant," was considered taboo (you had to say that she was "expecting" instead). Whether you refer to being pregnant as expecting or having a bun in the oven, no doubt you're going to be very excited when you find out that you're with child. You're probably going to want to share the news of your good fortune with anyone and everyone; but remember to do so with caution.

Announcing Your Pregnancy

While being pregnant and having a child is one of the most natural things that occurs in life, sharing the details of your baby's conception or how much weight you've gained might not be appropriate. Here's what you need to keep in mind so you come across as a proper pregnant lady—or know how to act politely should you run into someone you know and discover that she is expecting.

Once you find out you're pregnant, you may want to shout it from the rooftops. Your excitement is understandable, but there is a very good reason not to start spreading the news just yet—and it has nothing to do with manners. Most miscarriages occur before a woman reaches ten to twelve weeks of pregnancy. If you're not that far along when you discover that you're pregnant, it could be devastating to announce your pregnancy, only to have to follow it up with news of a miscarriage. Wait until you're at least twelve weeks pregnant to share your news.

Details of Conception

While you may think it's romantic that you conceived your first child with your spouse during the weekend of your high school reunion or while taking a romantic camping trip in the woods, not everyone may think so. Before you start sharing all the details of how you came to be with child, stop and think about how you would feel if someone gave you all the details of their bedroom goings on. That would make most people uncomfortable, and that's exactly what could happen if you share too much information about your child's conception.

ALERT!

When you use a home pregnancy test and discover that you're pregnant, you may want to save that test for a faraway scrapbook. That's a neat idea—sort of—but it's not exactly an appropriate item for a memory book. Instead, take a picture of the pregnancy test with the positive reading on it and place the photograph in your album.

It may be appropriate to talk about such intimate topics if you've been dealing with infertility and you're in a support group for couples in similar situations. Fellow group members may be used to the things that your friends may not receive well, and they may even benefit from hearing exactly how you were able to get pregnant successfully.

Morning Sickness

One of the telltale signs that a woman is pregnant is the onset of morning sickness. If you've ever been pregnant or talked to anyone who has, you know how pervasive morning sickness can be. In fact, morning sickness is really a misnomer, since for many women it turns out to be all-day sickness. While most doctors will tell you that morning sickness is a first trimester triviality, you may find that your morning sickness and nausea last well into your second or even third trimester.

Sharing the Details

No matter how ill you feel during your pregnancy, you should not share with your friends, commuting partners, or office mates exactly how sick you've been, how often, or even where morning sickness has overtaken you. Everyone knows that pregnant women feel nauseous but no one wants the details. Keep mentioning morning sickness to a minimum, unless you're going to be sick in front of them. In this case, politely (and quickly) excuse yourself and get to the restroom pronto.

Dealing with Morning Sickness

If your morning sickness is limited to mornings only, you may be able to deal with your nausea right away and start your day without delay.

However, if you're not so lucky and find yourself constantly saying, "Excuse me," because you feel morning sickness coming on, then you should prepare for these unexpected interruptions ahead of time. Talk to your boss, team members, or whomever you deal with on a daily basis, and let them know that you haven't been feeling well lately due to your pregnancy. Explain to them that you're not being rude intentionally by running to the restroom in the middle of a conference call or morning meeting. Hopefully, by your being upfront and honest, people will be more understanding of this temporary affliction.

If someone you know or work with is dealing with morning sickness, try to be as patient as possible with her. Don't point out how often she's had to run to the bathroom or for how long this has been going on. She's aware enough of this inconvenience, and she doesn't need anyone keeping watch over her.

Physical Woes

There are other physical changes that occur during pregnancy along with morning sickness. Some are very exciting, such as when your belly gets bigger, and some are less than wonderful. These are all private matters that you shouldn't broadcast to the world, and you'll do best to only share the details with your husband, your closest friends, your doctor, or your childbirth class.

By the same token if you work with a pregnant woman and you've noticed how swollen her feet are or how much weight she's gained, keep it to yourself. She's probably well aware of how much her body has changed, and she doesn't need you to remind her.

Swollen Feet

During the course of your pregnancy, your belly won't be the only thing to expand; your feet will swell too. Instead of constantly complaining about how your old shoes don't fit you anymore, be proactive and invest in a forgiving pair of shoes that you'll be able to wear for the duration of your pregnancy. These could be sandals, sneakers, or boots.

If your new, comfortable footwear is not appropriate for your work setting, talk to your boss and colleagues and let them know ahead of time why you need to wear such shoes. You'll be seen as much more polite if you address the issue now rather than spending the rest of your pregnancy being grumpy because your feet hurt.

Weight Gain

Weight gain is a normal occurrence during pregnancy. You have to put on pounds if you want your body to nourish your baby. Some people, though, may not understand that 25 pounds gained during a pregnancy is no big deal, so perhaps you would be best not to share those details.

ALERT!

It's one thing to refrain from complaining about the side effects of being pregnant. It's another to ignore aches and pains that could be cause for concern. If you experience anything that doesn't feel normal to you, such as severe abdominal pain, fever, or swelling in your hands and face, call your doctor immediately.

On the flipside, if a friend tells you that she's gained a lot of weight during her pregnancy, don't give her a shocked face or an exaggerated exclamation. Instead, smile, nod, and tell her what she wants to hear—that you're sure she'll have no problem taking off the weight after the baby is born.

The Baby Boogie

Sooner or later during your pregnancy, you're going to feel the baby move. You're sure to want to have friends and family members feel your stomach as the baby moves. That's great, if those people are comfortable with touching another person's stomach—not everyone is. Instead of grabbing your friend's hand and placing it on your stomach, ask her if she wants to feel the baby moving. If she says no, accept her answer but tell her to let you know if she changes her mind.

By the same token, if you run into a pregnant woman—one you know well or even a stranger on the street—don't automatically assume that you can invade her personal space and lay your hands on her belly. Always ask first before feeling a pregnant woman's belly, because not every pregnant woman is going to be comfortable with people's hands all over her.

Aches and Pains

As if weight gain, swollen feet, and a perpetually moving baby inside weren't enough for you to deal with when you're pregnant, you should also anticipate the general aches and pains that go along with pregnancy. These include sore hips and legs, as your body stretches to accommodate the baby, tender breasts, as they prepare for milk production, and an aching back.

If you have a friend who has recently gone through a pregnancy and you know she will offer a kind shoulder on which you can weep about your aches and pains, then by all means open up to her. If you can't find a way to relieve the pain through exercise or consulting your doctor, it's best to try to keep these problems to yourself.

Birth Horror Stories

It's natural for a woman experiencing her first pregnancy to be scared about the process of giving birth. Even women having second and third pregnancies may feel some trepidation as the big day draws near. If you've already had your children and you find yourself on the receiving end of your pregnant friend's questions about birth, try to be as helpful as you can in giving her answers. But whatever you do, don't share birth horror stories with an expectant mom. That's not to say that you should sugar coat the birth experience, but think about sharing constructive advice and tips with your friend so she can go into her birth experience better prepared. Avoid telling her how you thought you were going to die during labor, even if that's how you felt. She doesn't need to hear that.

If you're the pregnant woman and a group of people starts in with their birth battle stories, it's OK to tell them that you find their stories inappropriate. You may want to avoid those friends who love to share their battle (and C-section) scars before you give birth. That may be difficult, especially if they're close friends, but hearing birth horror stories will only heighten your anxiety.

Baby Showers

It's wonderful to shower a mother-to-be with a party that celebrates the impending birth of her child. While most women have one baby shower, it's perfectly OK if you want to have more than that for a good friend or family member. The only real etiquette to keep in mind is that holding a baby shower isn't truly appropriate in a work setting. That's not to say that you can't throw a colleague a baby shower—just don't do it in the conference room or during work hours. It's something you should plan to have when no one is working.

Planning a Pre-Baby Party

When planning a baby shower, you can choose to make it a surprise or you can tell the mom-to-be ahead of time that you've arranged for a celebration in her honor. Either option is acceptable. Just make sure that you give invited guests plenty of notice so that if they have to travel to attend, they can do so without experiencing any time or financial hardships.

If you've decided to make the baby shower a surprise, enlist a few friends who will be able to keep the expectant mom occupied on the day of the shower and get her to the party on time. Plan ahead of time for a good diversion, such as a morning at the spa together, and then a valid reason for her to visit the restaurant where the shower will occur. A ladies day out for lunch works well as a decoy.

ALERT!

First-time parents always need "starter" equipment for their home, some of which can be pricey. It's perfectly acceptable for a group of people to go in together on a big shower gift, such as a stroller, car seat, or crib. Just make sure that you check with others first before buying—no one wants to end up with two big-ticket items that need to be returned.

Since moms get so much of the attention before the baby is born, it may be a nice gesture to arrange for a second baby shower to be a couple's shower. That way the dads can be included, and you can ask guests to bring gifts that are appropriate for the new dad. You may even want to hold the dad's shower in a "manly" setting, such as at a backyard barbecue.

Registering for Baby Gifts

Baby showers have become just like bridal showers—with friends and family expecting a couple to register for gifts. Not only does this help the couple stock their nursery, but it also makes it easier for well-wishers to buy gifts.

Before you decide where you're going to register or what you're going to register for, consult any parenting books you may have picked up. They will give you a good sense of must-haves to include on your registry, such as diapers, wipes, and onesies. Then make sure that you devote enough time to registering, because it will take longer than you may anticipate—two to three hours is about average.

Unlike weddings, it's OK for people to share where the parents-to-be have registered in an invitation. If you're the person throwing a baby shower, you can feel comfortable including registry information in the invitation.

Keep in mind that your registry is supposed to help your guests buy your baby gifts, not frustrate them or make them feel inadequate. Restrict your registry selections to affordable basics, such as diapers and wipes, with only a few big-ticket necessities, like a crib or stroller. Even if you're dying to have the latest Louis Vuitton diaper bag, which retails for $1,000, resist adding it to your registry.

Attending a Shower Celebration

The first thing you should do when you've been invited to a baby shower is check your calendar and R.S.V.P. on time to the folks who are hosting the party.

If the invitation isn't specific about whether or not the shower is a surprise, call the host right away to find out. There would be nothing worse than ruining the surprise for the expectant mother. Find out from the host what time the mom-to-be is expected to get there so you can plan your arrival accordingly.

If the shower is a surprise, plan to arrive early or right on time, based on the party invitation. If you get delayed and know what time the expectant mother will be arriving, delay yourself even more so you don't show up when she shows up—that will give it all away, especially if you're holding a wrapped gift. Park somewhere discreet so you can watch for her arrival or just accept that you'll be getting to the shower fashionably late.

Gifts for Baby and Mom

Buying a gift for the new baby and the new mom is a snap, if you know that the person has registered somewhere. Do her a favor and buy a gift off the registry. Then you'll know you're getting her something that she wants and needs. If you find that there's nothing left on the registry in your price range, clothing, blankets, and diapering essentials are always a good bet. Another great gift to give in a pinch are note cards that she can use for her thank-you notes.

If you are expected to open presents at your baby shower, make sure that you practice your poker face ahead of time. You don't want to look dissatisfied if you open a gift that you don't like or that you believe is inappropriate. You should always smile and act graciously when you open presents in a group.

Finally, enlist a friend who can take notes as you open your gifts. Have her write down the name of the gift giver and what she gave you. Having a gift list like this will make it easier for you to write your thank-you notes later.

Showering Shower Guests with Appreciation

Your friends and family took the time to plan a baby shower for you and to buy you gifts. Now you've got to take the time to thank them for their good wishes and generosity.

Unless you go into labor immediately after your baby shower, there's no reason that you can't get your thank-you notes out immediately after the celebration. Don't worry about writing your version of *War and Peace* in each thank-you note. Instead, you can keep things simple if you follow this step-by-step process:

1. Start each note by greeting the person by name.
2. Thank her for the baby shower gift by name.
3. Tell briefly why this gift meant so much to you or how you plan to put it to good use once the baby is born.
4. Thank her again and maybe add something like, "We'll be sure to keep you posted on when the baby is born."
5. Sign your name.

Naming Your Baby

Naming your baby comes with great responsibility. You've got to choose a name that sounds good to you and your spouse and is meaningful as well. Only the two of you can determine which names qualify in both respects, and it's nobody else's business how you come to decide on your son or daughter's name.

Nevertheless, some people aren't shy about critiquing a baby's name when they hear what the parents have on their list, so you may want to hold off announcing your name considerations until after the baby is born. If you can't stand keeping that information in, be aware of the kinds of reactions you may get from people.

FACT

The Social Security Administration, which tracks popular baby names, reports that the top three names for boys are Jacob, Michael, and Joshua, and for girls, Emily, Emma, and Madison, respectively.

If you happen to hear a name that you personally dislike, react as politely as possible. It's rather rude to guffaw at a name choice or to offer your opinions on alternate name selections if you haven't been asked. However, if you hear a name that you don't understand, can't figure out how to spell, or just aren't sure where the parents came up with that idea, you could always politely ask if it's a family name.

Birth Day!

Congratulations. The baby is here. You must be very excited to hold your bundle of joy in your arms or, if someone you love just had a baby, you must be thrilled to be in your new role as father, grandparents, aunt, or uncle. Most parents are beyond ecstatic when their baby is born so they call or e-mail everyone they know with the good news—even before they come home from the hospital.

Labor Day Stories

Now that you've been through giving birth, you may want to recount, contraction by contraction, your labor and birth experience. That's fine to do with a sister, your mother, or at your Lamaze class reunion. Your friends and family may not be as interested in hearing about your water breaking, episiotomy, or what it felt like to get an epidural. Err on the side of being proper, and only share your labor stories with those who seem genuinely interested, and ask first if you have any doubt about this. If you really have to get the details out of your system, start a new journal and write everything down there.

Complications at Birth

The birth of a baby is always an exciting event, but sometimes things don't go as planned, and there are complications at birth. Some babies are stillborn; others are born with a birth defect. If you find yourself dealing with one of these situations, you should know that it's perfectly OK for you not to play the part of the happy new parent whom everyone expects you to be. Something sad has happened, and you have every right to mourn or to be upset that your expectations of a healthy child have been replaced with the reality that you're going to be dealing with a disabled child.

Of course, friends and family who know you're in the hospital giving birth will be waiting anxiously to hear about your son or daughter, and you should give yourself some time to gather your thoughts and deal with your grief about this unexpected turn of events. Then you and your spouse should put together a boilerplate, if you will, of what you're going to say when communicating the news to everyone.

If your child didn't survive birth, you or your husband can inform people of his time of birth but that he didn't survive. If your child was born with an unexpected birth defect or genetic anomaly, it's appropriate to share the details of time of birth and how much the baby weighed and mention that the doctor diagnosed the defect at birth.

People who receive news that a baby has died or was born with a defect may react in stunned silence. If you receive such information, you may not know what to do. It's best to share your compassion with the parents and not desert them. It's tough enough for parents to face difficulty during birth, but it's even worse when people don't know how to handle this kind of bad news and disappear. Be a good friend and support them.

Visiting Hours

Your first instinct when you learn that someone has had a baby may be to rush over and visit the new mom and baby in the hospital. While that's a nice gesture, it may not be the most polite thing that you can do. A woman who's just given birth is going to be exhausted, and she may want time alone to rest and to bond with her baby. Perhaps she's just giving breastfeeding a try and doesn't want to feel self-conscious about feeding the baby in front of others. Before you pack up the car with a welcome basket and make your way to the hospital, call first. Ask if the mom and dad are up for seeing visitors in the hospital. If they are, then great. You can go ahead with your visit. But if they're not, respect their wishes and wait until they've settled back into their home before going over to meet the baby.

Coming Home

With hospital stays getting shorter for new mothers, you may find yourself packing your diaper bag within twenty-four hours of your child's birth and getting ready to go home. Your friends and family members are sure to want to greet your new bundle of joy when you get home, and if you're not up for visitors, you should tell them this ahead of time. It's perfectly acceptable for a new (and potentially overwhelmed) mother to cocoon at home for a few days or weeks after her baby is born, and everyone should respect your wishes.

Well-wishers who can't stand the suspense of meeting the new baby should always call first before showing up on someone's doorstep. Yes, it's a wonderful gesture to bring a new mother a cooked meal or a gift basket soon after her baby is born. But you may show up in the middle of a feeding session, the baby's bath, or a nap. Check ahead of time when it would be convenient for you to stop by, albeit briefly, and then make your plans accordingly.

And do make the stay brief. Hand over your gift, spend a few moments oohing and aahing over the baby, and then leave. The new mom is sure to appreciate your quick departure.

Baby Announcements

Everyone is going to be excited to learn of your child's birth, and you should share the good news within two to three weeks of the birth date by sending out announcements. Make sure you include all the details that people will be curious about, such as date and time of the baby's birth, height and weight at birth, color of hair and eyes, and, of course, his or her name. If you have older children, you may even have the big brother or big sister "announce" the arrival of the sibling.

You may not have time to choose your announcements right after your baby is born. Plan ahead and place your order so it will be waiting to be processed once the baby is born. That way you can just provide the details of the birth and get the announcements printed in no time.

Sending Gifts

Upon receiving your baby's birth announcement, most people will want to send you gifts. You should show your appreciation for their generosity by writing thank-you notes. If you're lucky some people gave you note cards at your baby shower, which you can use now for your thank-you's. Or if you're tech savvy, you can take a digital picture of your new child and use your computer to print cards. However you choose to thank people, make sure you do it. These folks took the time to welcome your child with a gift—you should take the time to thank them for their generosity, even if it takes you a few weeks to do so. (Most people are pretty understanding about how time-starved a new mom can be.)

Chapter 2

The Well-Mannered New Parent

When you have a baby, a new chapter in your life begins. You go from being a husband and wife to now also taking on the role of father and mother. But just because you've adopted a new title doesn't mean you can leave your manners behind. Sure, people will be a bit forgiving of your behavior during those first few months of sleepless nights. But overall you should try to follow some simple protocol when dealing with all the must-haves and must-do's of a new baby.

Coming Home from the Hospital

As soon as you step through the front door with your new baby, you're going to be faced with the demands of your home life. There will be laundry to do, meals to make, and other children to attend to. At the same time, you'll be dealing with the desire of friends and family to meet your new baby. In fact, some may have already called or e-mailed to ask when they can come over to see him or her.

It's always considerate to call before dropping in on new parents. The last thing you want to do is show up out of the blue and assume that they'll have the time or inclination to sit and visit with you. An impromptu visit might seem like a good idea, but think about what you might be interrupting before doing so (like a nap or feeding time).

New parents should feel entitled to take the first week or so with their new baby to themselves. If you don't feel like entertaining guests, no one will hold it against you. It's exhausting having a newborn, and you and your spouse should take care of each other and the baby first before taking care of your friends' and families' needs.

Speaking of needs, if anyone asks if they can get you anything or do anything to assist you, take them up on the offer. It will be a great help to you (and not seen as rude) if you let them throw in a load of laundry for you or run to the grocery store to pick up some diapers. Maybe you really need your lawn mowed or the dog walked.

FACT

When offering to help out the parents of a newborn, don't just assume you know what they need. Always ask first if and where they need help, and then honor their request.

You could keep track of chores that people might be able to do for you in the days and weeks after coming home from the hospital and offer up a choice whenever someone asks. You'll discover that doing so will achieve a dual benefit—you'll have a little extra help around the house, and people will quit bugging you about seeing the baby because they'll have time with him or her when they come over to help out.

Novelty of a New Baby

When you're finally up for visitors, you'll probably feel like the proud father or mother who wants his or her new child to meet the world. But before you get all excited about handing the baby around to everyone, you'll need to really be considerate of how interested people are going to be in your baby or whether it's a good idea to have so many strangers interacting with him or her.

Baby-Centric Life

Keep your relationships healthy by making sure that your conversations include topics of discussion other than your baby. Baby or not, you've got to include others in the conversation. If you're in a social setting where all you can say is, "Isn't he precious?" or "Can you believe how beautiful she is?" you're going to lose the interest of other people really quickly. Make an attempt to inquire about other people's lives; ask them what's going on with their jobs or their children or spouses. It may have been a long time since you've spent a considerable amount of time with them, and it's likely that they'll have some news for you. While your baby's birth was a significant change in your life, acknowledge that it most likely was not the major point of focus for most of your friends or coworkers.

Being Prepared

As a new parent, you'll find that there are some supplies you'll need to have with you at all times. You may not yet be used to the idea that you've got to bring a diaper bag and stroller with you everywhere you take your baby, or that your life may revolve around your baby's sleeping and eating schedule. Adjusting to these changes will take some time, and it might not be the easiest thing to get used to at first.

If you want to make time with your new baby enjoyable for all involved, make sure you pack enough clothes, diapers, and wipes for any quick changes you might need to do. Similarly, don't take your baby out when he's wet, tired, or hungry, because all he'll do is cry. If you think ahead of time of how you can structure your day so that you're out in public when your baby is happiest, you'll be happy, too.

If you're out and about with the baby and loaded down with baby equipment, don't be shy about asking someone to help you board the train or hold the door open at the mall. It is better to err on the side of asking for assistance than to try and juggle everything yourself and end up bumping into someone in the process.

Sharing Baby

As mentioned earlier, you don't want to be the parent who thrusts her baby at anyone and everyone she meets. You'll want to make sure that the people you encounter while you're with your baby are genuinely interested in meeting her.

New parents may have a hard time believing this, but not everyone loves babies. When you find yourself in a social situation and want to share your baby with others, don't just hand her over and say, "Here, hold her." What if the person is afraid he'll drop the baby? Or what if the person is uncomfortable with the notion of babies in general? You really haven't given the person a choice. Rather than force your baby on someone, ask instead, "Would you like to hold the baby?" While most people will say, "Yes," if the person answers, "I'm not sure," or, "Not right now," or, "No," then back off.

If you're on the receiving end of an overly excited new parent who is thrusting her baby at you, you can politely refuse with, "I'm just getting over a virus and don't want to get your baby sick," or "I'm such a klutz. I'm afraid I'll drop the baby." Hopefully, the parent will get the hint. If she doesn't, then you're going to have to be blunt and say, "Please don't make me hold the baby. I don't feel comfortable doing so."

Baby Announcements

You're probably going to be too exhausted to call everyone you know soon after your baby is born. That's where baby announcements come in. These nifty printed products get you off the hook of having to call and e-mail everyone about your baby's birth by providing all the birth details in one fell swoop. You should plan to send them out within two to three weeks of your child's birth, or if you know your baby's sex from an ultrasound, you can have an order on hold and ready to go as soon as you give birth. Then you can pop them in the mail as soon as they come back from the printer.

Printed and Proper

Many parents choose to announce their child's birth by having announcements printed. These announcements can take many shapes, forms, and colors, or they might not even be in paper form at all, depending on how tech-savvy your family is.

If you're going for a traditional look, stick with pink announcements for girls and blue announcements for boys. Many announcements include a pink or blue ribbon, type or some other colorful element that defines the baby's sex—especially if your child's name doesn't clearly state his or her sex. (For example, Morgan, Taylor, and Logan are names for both boys and girls.)

ESSENTIAL

Regardless of the paper stock or type color you choose for your baby announcement, you should make sure that it includes the following pertinent information: Your baby's full name, the date of birth, the time of birth, the baby's weight and height at birth, and the parents' name and address. Some families like to include the baby's hair and eye color as well.

For a more festive baby announcement, you might want to go with one that features child-like images, such as teddy bears or the animals of Noah's Ark. Most stationery stores offer hundreds of different designs to choose from. Additionally, you can visit stores like Kinko's to purchase baby announcement-like paper that you can use to design and print the announcements using your home computer.

Regardless of what color announcement you choose or where you go to buy it, try to get the news out about your baby's birth as soon as possible.

Expedient and E-Mail

For the plugged-in family with plugged-in friends, sometimes the easiest way to get the word out about your son or daughter's birth is to put together an e-mail announcement. This lets everyone find out instantaneously about your child's birth, and it saves you a ton of time by not having to phone everyone. However, to be a truly well-mannered parent, you should still send out printed announcements to everyone within three weeks of the baby's birth.

Involving Siblings

One of the most heartfelt baby announcements that you could send would be one where the big sister or big brother announces the arrival of their sibling. Instead of having a generic baby announcement that lists all the stats regarding the baby's birth, you could write an announcement like this:

Big sister Sally and big brother John are excited to announce the birth of their baby brother, William Michael, on Sunday, September 12, 2004, at 6:04 P.M. He was 8 pounds, 12 ounces and 21 inches long at birth, and has blonde hair and brown eyes like his brother and sister.

You can list the names of all of the people in the family (children and parents), along with their address, at the bottom of the announcement.

Baby Gifts

Upon receiving a baby's birth announcement, most people will want to send you gifts. However, you have to understand that by sending people a baby announcement, you aren't telling them, ever so subtly, that they ought to send you a baby gift. Doing so is a nice gesture, but it's not a must.

Registering

Registering isn't a must in this day and age, but if you already have a registry on record, it would be OK to update it now that your baby has been born. You'll have a better sense of what you need on a day-to-day basis, and the store should be able to accommodate any additions to the registry. Also, ask to see if the store offers a registry checklist. This will help you determine if you've left any necessities off your registry list.

How Soon to Send a Gift

There's no set rule on how soon after a baby's birth you should send a gift or what kind of gift you should send. Most people tend to choose baby clothing as a gift. Clothing is practical considering babies can wear and then soil a handful of outfits in one day.

Keep in mind that babies grow very fast, and even though in your mind the baby is still a newborn, she could be wearing clothing marked for three month olds or older. If you can't get a baby gift to the new parents right away, make sure you send something that's age- and size-appropriate for the baby's current age. (You can ask store personnel for their advice on size selections.)

The Rights and Wrongs of Returning Gifts

You should never feel that you have to keep a gift you don't like, don't need, or that doesn't fit your baby, just because you received it as a gift. Returning gifts is always OK to do, as long as you don't broadcast to the gift giver that you've done so. If you decide to return a gift but can't figure out which store it came from, you should not ask the person who gave it to you. If you can't return the gift, you can always keep it as a back up, recycle it to someone else, or donate it to a charity.

ALERT!

Always include a gift receipt with a gift (not the regular store receipt). That way if you misjudged the baby's size or development stage, you've given the parents an option for returning or exchanging the gift.

The Importance of Thank Yous

Whether you love the baby gift or need to take it back, you have to thank the gift giver. Do not take the easy way out and send a mass e-mail as a thank you or use preprinted cards. Handwrite each thank-you note to the people who were kind enough to send you a baby gift.

FACT

There's no rule that says only new moms can send thank-you notes. If your thank you "to do" list for baby gifts has become overwhelming, enlist the new dad in assuming some of the thank-you note writing responsibility.

Unlike weddings, you have a little bit of leeway in your turnaround time for thank-you notes. Most people understand that new parents are time starved, and if it takes you two months to get your notes out, at least you've gotten them out. You can even add something in the note that explains the delay, such as "Little Laura has been suffering from colic, so I haven't had a lot of free time lately. But I did want to thank you for the adorable baby blanket." If you've gotten around to taking pictures of the new baby, it would be a nice gesture to include a snapshot with your note so the person can see the baby.

Reciprocating

Gift giving should never be a quid pro quo arrangement. That is, it shouldn't be a case of doing something so you'll receive something in return. However, should any of the people who sent you baby gifts have a child in the near future, it would be the right thing to do to send them a baby gift as well.

A great way to send a meaningful gift is to choose something that your child loved as a baby or that you found extremely helpful as a parent. Then when you sign the card, you can write, "Laura loved this squeaky toy whenever she rode in her stroller, and I hope your new baby will enjoy the toy as much as she did."

Baptisms, Bris, and Baby Naming Ceremonies

Most religions have some kind of spiritual ceremony that welcomes a child into their faith, such as a baptism (also known as a Christening) in Christianity, a bris in Judaism (during which the baby is circumcised), or a baby naming ceremony held in a house of worship. While most of these celebrations are very meaningful for those involved, they aren't very formal.

Most new parents provide verbal invitations to these kinds of events, although a written/printed invitation is also an option. Most online and brick-and-mortar stationery stores offer invitations for all these ceremonies. It's acceptable to choose either cards in which you handwrite in the details or to have your invitations formally printed. If you're inviting a lot of people or folks need to travel from out of town, a formal invitation will likely be your best bet.

Explanation of Rituals

There's always the chance that someone attending your son's baptism or your daughter's baby naming isn't going to have the same religious background as your family, and this person may not understand the reasoning behind the ceremony or the rituals involved in it. Make people more at ease by creating a program, just as you would at a wedding, which explains everything that's going to occur during the ceremony. If necessary, include a glossary of terms so your guests have a better grasp of what's going on. It's a wonderful way to make everyone who is joining you for this special occasion feel included.

It's traditional to give a child a religious-oriented gift when attending a religious ceremony, such as a bris or baptism. A children's Bible or anything featuring Noah's Ark is always a good gift bet for religions that believe in the Old Testament.

Hosting Guests

When you've invited friends and family to share in your baby's religious ritual, you should do the right thing and host those guests for a meal after the ceremony. You can have a simple buffet set up at your home, or you can reserve a space at a restaurant. Either way make sure that you extend an invitation for everyone to join you afterward.

Visits to Friends and Family

Just as you don't want people dropping in on you unexpectedly to see your new baby, you shouldn't do the same when going out and about with the baby. It's equally rude for you to show up on someone's doorstep and expect that they'll be able to invite the baby and you in right away. What if your host is in the middle of cleaning? What if their children are napping? That's why you should always call first before planning to visit anyone, anywhere, in any situation.

E ALERT!

If your baby might need to eat during your visit, let your friend know ahead of time that you might need to feed your baby. Ask if it would be OK for you to use a bedroom or drape a blanket over your shoulder. If neither option works, then you might need to wait to see that friend until your baby doesn't need to eat so frequently.

One important issue to keep in mind when planning visits to your friends and family is how you're going to handle diaper changes. Of course, you're going to be coming bearing your own supplies—you do have that diaper bag, don't you?—but not every house appreciates having a stinky diaper in the garbage. Plan ahead to deal with any diaper disposal issues by bringing recycled plastic grocery bags that you can wrap the dirty diaper in and dispose of in your friend's garbage pail outside. If there isn't a receptacle you can use outside, then you should put the "package" back in your car and take it home with you to throw out.

Sleep Tight, Baby

Napping is one of the most critical requirements for your baby's growth and development, and that's why you shouldn't ever deprive your baby of his nap. Babies tend to fall asleep during car drives, so you should plan for this contingency on any visit you take. Find out beforehand if the person you're visiting will have a quiet, dark place for your baby to nap, if you have to bring him inside, already asleep in his car seat. It's not reasonable for you to expect someone to activate the cone of silence in their home, simply because you showed up with a sleeping baby. If your baby has fallen asleep and you've determined that now is a bad time for you to go visiting, pull over to the side of the road and call your friend to cancel, postpone, or reschedule your visit.

QUESTION?

What do I do if a child with dirty hands comes over and starts to touch my baby's hands and face?

You need to step in immediately and remove that child's hands from your baby. Since babies are always putting their hands in their mouth, you need to take out a wipe and get those hands clean immediately—your baby's, that is, if the child touched them, although wiping the dirty child's hands isn't a bad idea either.

Hygiene Habits

Little babies are especially susceptible to germs, and you're going to have to get used to asking everyone who wants to touch your baby to please wash their hands first. You aren't being rude or acting like their mother in telling them to wash up—you're just trying to protect your baby. If someone declines your request, you have to put your baby first and refuse to let that person hold the baby. If a new parent has planned to visit you with the baby and you come down with an illness, cancel the visit. You'll be doing that person and her baby a favor by keeping them away until you're no longer contagious.

Chapter 3

The Etiquette of Infants and Babies

When you're dealing with a young baby, there isn't much you can do to control his behavior. But as a parent you can work hard at being polite in two ways. You can make sure that your baby is well rested and well fed, he's not too hot or too cold, and his diaper isn't wet or dirty. Beyond that, you as the parent, should make an effort to be considerate of others when you have your baby out in public or you're entertaining people in your home. Read on for the rules of etiquette involving infants and babies and how best you can follow them.

Nursing Niceties

During your prenatal visits or your childbirth classes, you probably learned about nursing or breastfeeding—one of the most natural, healthy, and economical ways to feed a baby. Some mothers only nurse for a few weeks. Others do it for a year or more. Whether or not you nurse is entirely up to you. However, should you decide to join the legions of breastfeeding mothers, you should keep some common courtesies in mind.

Lactation, Location

If you're a breastfeeding mother, you may have to finagle a comfortable place to nurse your child. While nursing a baby is the most natural thing a woman can do, not everyone in society feels this way. Whenever you're out and about with baby, you need to scope out in advance a discreet place you can retreat to should you need to feed your baby. Most ladies rooms in department stores have comfortable chairs or benches available for nursing moms to use. In a pinch, the backseat of your vehicle would work, or, if you're at someone's house, a bedroom where you can nurse in private.

ESSENTIAL

If you're out somewhere or in a social situation where you come across a nursing mother who is being less than discreet, don't make a big deal out of it. It's not illegal to breastfeed in public but at the same time that doesn't mean that nursing mothers shouldn't show a little discretion when they have to feed their babies.

In Mixed Company

At your "mommy and me" class or in a play group, it's usually not a big deal for a nursing mother to feed her baby. Everyone in the room is in the same boat as you are, and it's probably one of the few public places where you can feed your baby at will, without worrying about offending others.

Of course, when you're in a less child-friendly locale, such as a restaurant, it's always polite to ask first if anyone minds if you nurse your baby in front of them. If someone says they do mind, you need to figure out what your Plan B is going to be. Yes, it's an inconvenience that you shouldn't have to deal with but at the same time you don't want to be rude by ignoring someone's answer.

Despite your best laid plans for discreet breastfeeding, you may end up having to find a place to feed your baby fast when a shopping trip runs a little late or you get delayed. That's because infants can eat between eight and twelve times a day, making you feel like an all-night dairy bar.

Covering Up

Despite your best intentions to keep your nursing private, there are some times when you must feed your baby in front of others. You should come prepared and include a large blanket or shawl in your diaper bag. Then you can drape this over your shoulder and create a private little sanctuary in which your baby can feed. This is the perfect option if you have to nurse on an airplane, at the mall, or in a restaurant. Often a blouse or baggy, button-down shirt worn over a t-shirt can serve the same cover-up purpose.

You may even want to use this cover-up option when you have guests in your own home, especially if you don't feel completely comfortable breastfeeding with others around. Covering up is also a good idea if you'll be nursing your child before a nap—the cover up will provide a cocoon-like environment that can help the baby fall asleep more easily.

One of the occupational hazards of breastfeeding is the risk of your breasts leaking milk. Stocking up on nursing pads and wearing them during the day may help avoid embarrassing situations.

Is It Best to Bottle Feed?

No matter how well you plan for a cover up, there are some women who simply do not want to breastfeed in front of others. In instances like this, you have two options: use a breast pump to express milk, which you can then feed to your baby in a bottle, or you can supplement with formula.

The only potential social faux pas in bottle-feeding your baby is assuming someone else wants to feed your baby when she doesn't want to. Just as you should always ask someone if she'd like to hold your baby before handing her over, you should do the same with giving your baby a bottle. Ask first if the person you're with is interested in giving your baby a bottle. If he is, great, he can do you that favor. If he's not, then you've got to accept his answer and just feed the baby yourself.

Non-Nursing Mothers

There are plenty of women who for whatever reason can't or do not choose to breastfeed their babies. It is their right to make this decision, just as it is your decision to breastfeed your baby. Never force your views on someone who doesn't see breastfeeding in the same light that you do. Even if you feel very strongly that breastfeeding is best, the only thing you'll accomplish in becoming a vocal breastfeeding zealot is rude behavior.

Delicately Dealing with Diapers

Until your child knows how to control his bodily functions, you'll be dealing with diapers. You'll be buying them, changing them, and discarding them multiple times a day for many years. During that time you need to do your best to handle all your diapering situations as delicately as possible.

If you don't change your baby's diaper frequently, you'll make her more susceptible to urinary tract infections and other discomforts—and she'll be unhappy more often. To keep your baby healthy and happy, get rid of a diaper as soon as it seems full.

When to Change

Your nose may tell you right away that your baby needs to have her diaper changed. And it's a good idea to change her right away, because keeping your baby clean will help her be a happy and healthy baby. It's also the polite thing to do, because no one wants to be around a baby who smells as if she's been wallowing in toxic waste.

Sometimes parents can get overwhelmed with the everyday tasks associated with taking care of a baby. If you're holding a friend's baby or are nearby when you sense (read: smell) that the baby has just filled her diaper, it's perfectly polite to let the parent know. If you're adept at changing diapers, you may even want to offer to do the diaper change for her. It would be an awfully gracious gesture on your part.

Some studies suggest that a baby will go through more than 6,000 diapers in the first few years of his life, which may make an environmentalist's head spin. If you feel that diapers are bad for the earth, don't start lecturing every mother you meet. Until (and even if) you've had to make a decision between cloth or disposal diapers, you should keep your thoughts to yourself.

Being Discreet About Diaper Changes

Sometimes you've got to get that dirty diaper off your child's bottom, and it doesn't matter where you are—you've got to do a quick change. Even though there is an urgency to your mission, that doesn't mean that you can push politeness to the side.

Instead of setting up a diaper-changing shop on a friend's dining room table or on an expensive rug in her living room, you should ask first if there's a better place you can change the diaper. You may have to retreat to a friend's kitchen floor or a diaper-changing caddy in a restroom, but at least you know that by asking first, you haven't overstepped anyone's boundaries.

Also, keep in mind that most diaper bags these days come with a diaper-changing pad. Using these pads will not only protect the surface on which you're changing your baby, but it will also protect your baby's skin from coming into contact with any surface that's less than clean.

Dirty Diaper Disposal

Unless you're visiting a home with a baby or a store with diaper changing facilities in it, you can't just assume that you can drop your baby's dirty diaper in the nearest garbage pail. A full diaper can wreak havoc on a person's senses, and you shouldn't put that olfactory offense upon anyone even unintentionally.

Try to find an outdoor trash can in which you can dispose of your dirty diaper. If that's not possible, always have extra plastic bags on hand that you can wrap the diaper in and then dispose of when you get home.

Discussing Diaper Contents

One of the ways that new parents can assess whether their baby is eating and drinking enough is by counting the number of wet diapers the baby has in a day or how many bowel movements the baby has. This is the kind of conversation that mothers and fathers have all the time, and that's perfectly all right. However, the contents of your baby's diaper does not make for polite dinner conversation and is not something that you should chat about openly. Keep these kinds of chats to yourself. Your friends and family will be eternally grateful if you show good manners in this regard.

Bathing Baby

Your pediatrician may tell you that it's best for your baby's skin not to be bathed daily. But if your little boy is covered in food or just had a messy diaper that no amount of baby wipes can clean up, you would do best to give him a bath. Everyone appreciates a clean and sweet-smelling baby more than a stinky one.

Many parents choose to give their young babies a bath in the kitchen sink. It's easier on your back (no bending over a tub), and it's safer since you have to keep your hands on the baby at all times. This makes you more cognizant of your baby's whereabouts.

Should you find yourself needing to give your baby a bath in someone else's kitchen sink, don't automatically assume that it's OK. The thought of a baby's bottom in their kitchen sink might make some people cringe, and you'll maintain better relations with your friends and family if you check with them first.

A portable tub is a great way to bathe your baby without sticking her in the sink, and if you keep one in the back of your car, you'll never overstep your boundaries when you have to give your baby a bath on the run. You can find these kinds of tubs at toy stores and mass merchandisers.

Also, don't assume that someone else's home should have all the things that you'll need for the bath. It's fine to ask to borrow a towel or facecloth, but if they don't have any baby shampoo on hand, don't roll your eyes in response. Instead, always come prepared by keeping a travel-sized bottle of baby shampoo with you in your diaper bag.

Cry Babies

The only way your baby can communicate with you, beyond coos and smiles, is crying. You know how dogs have different barks in reaction to different situations? It's the same with babies. Soon enough you'll be able to understand how the "I need to go to sleep" cry differs from the "Ouch, I just hurt myself" cry.

Crying communications aside, it's never a good idea to let your baby cry for extended periods of time, especially when there are others around. In public places, such as a restaurant, movie theater, or mall, you should do your best to calm your child's cries as soon as you can. Usually, babies cry when they're wet or dirty, tired, hungry, or uncomfortable. If you find that picking up the baby and walking him around doesn't do the trick, change his diaper. Then see if he's hungry. Is he too hot or too cold? Might something on his clothing be rubbing him the wrong way? Is it his naptime? No one will consider it rude if you must leave a social setting to allow your baby to sleep. If anything, they'll be grateful that you're being considerate and taking your baby home for a much-needed nap instead of keeping him there to cry.

Babies also eventually need to figure out how to put themselves to sleep. Many parents choose to let their child "cry it out." If you find yourself at someone's home and their baby is crying it out, respect their desire to do this and don't interfere. It may make you feel uncomfortable hearing the baby cry in his room, but you've got to defer to the parent's judgment on this issue and opt not to say anything.

The Necessity of Naps

Along with eating, one of the ways that helps your baby grow and develop is by getting sufficient amount of sleep each day. You can expect your baby to take two to three naps a day as an infant and eventually two naps a day as he gets to be an older baby. What this means is that you're going to have to schedule your day around his naps, and doing so would be anything but rude. That means no playdates, birthday parties, or lunch outings at a time when your baby should be sleeping. If you go out when he needs a nap, he'll be missing out on the sleep he desperately needs, and you'll be dealing with an exceptionally cranky baby who will cry incessantly because he's tired.

The best place for your baby to nap is in his crib or bassinet at home. If that's not possible, then a car seat will suffice. Just make sure that your child has a quiet, dark place to sleep so he can sleep as long as he needs.

If you're out and about when your baby falls asleep, it's unreasonable to expect that everyone else's life will come to a standstill so your little one can slumber. Don't be rude and ask someone else's kids to "keep it down" when you're at their house—it's not your home. When your baby needs to sleep, you need to make sure that he's in a place that's conducive to his sleeping. If not, you've got to politely excuse yourself by explaining that you really need to get your baby home for a nap.

If you're at someone's house as a guest and their baby goes down for a nap, now is not the time to turn the radio up or to talk in loud voices. You should be a polite guest and keep things quiet while the baby is asleep.

Car Seats and Strollers

With a baby in tow, you probably feel like your diaper bag has become an extra appendage. You're likely to feel the same way about your car seat and stroller soon enough. They will go with you everywhere you travel and by nearly every mode of transportation—car, taxi, bus or plane.

ALERT!

Using a car seat makes good sense. Making sure your car seat is properly installed makes better sense. A recent Safe Kids study showed that 85% of parents have improperly installed car seats. Always double-check your handiwork before buckling up your baby.

Courteous Car Seat Use

Placing a baby or young child in a car seat is the law, and you'd be wise to follow it. If you're responsible for taking someone else's child somewhere, make sure you know how to use that child's car seat—not only how to install it in your car but also how to strap the baby in. Ask for a quick lesson on what you need to know to make the car seat useful, and never assume that you can get away without using one.

If a friend asks you to take her baby or child for a ride and she doesn't use a car seat, it's perfectly OK to decline driving the child. You can tell her you're not comfortable having a child in your car without a car seat and, if you have an extra car seat, ask if she would like to borrow it. If your friend refuses, don't feel like you have to concede.

Smooth Strolling

Having a stroller at your disposal makes it much easier to get around with a baby in tow. But just because you're pushing a stroller, that doesn't mean that you can push aside your manners. Strollers can be a cumbersome piece of equipment to maneuver, and you'll want to be careful of how you'll maneuver in tight quarters, such as grocery store aisles and crowded stores. Most people don't take kindly to having their feet run over by stroller wheels or being bumped into by one. It's your responsibility to make sure that you respect other people's boundaries. Don't assume that just because you're the one with the stroller, people should get out of your way. Apologize immediately if you do happen to hit someone or run over someone's foot.

When you do go out to stores and restaurants with your stroller, you should always scope things out ahead of time. You want to make sure that the aisles are wide enough to accommodate the pram. If they're not, park your stroller outside and carry the baby in.

For this reason alone, it's always a good idea to bring an alternate carrier for your baby, whether it's a sling or Baby Bjorn-like strap-on harness.

Baby's Got a Fever

Without a sophisticated immune system, your baby is bound to get sick from time to time. Whether he goes to day care or just play groups in the neighborhood, you will be considered a polite parent if you keep your baby home whenever he's not feeling well or is potentially contagious. It's bad manners to get other people sick on purpose—or just because you really wanted to get out of the house.

By the same token, you should never medicate your child so he isn't feverish on a temporary basis, just so you can get out of the house. It's not fair to anyone involved, and if your friends or daycare provider find out about your dishonesty, it could potentially harm your relationships. You must always do the right thing and "suck it up" when your baby is sick. Keep him home until he's feeling better, and then a few days later, bring him back to the outside world.

Chapter 4

Raising Civil Children

The formula for raising well-behaved children is simple: define your child's boundaries and have set rules about behavior. When your child strays from either, rein him in. Unfortunately, many parents think that the easiest way to raise kids is not to discipline them at all. That's entirely the wrong tact to take. Instead, as a parent you've got to start when your kids are young by telling them right from wrong and making sure that they understand the consequences of their behavior.

Taming Toddlers

Toddlers got their name from the way they toddle around. Toddlers are also usually synonymous with those children in their terrible twos. Put toddling and terrible twos together, and you've got a recipe for disaster. If you know what to expect of your toddler's behavior, you'll know how to handle matters when he gets out of hand.

Most adults prefer it when children call them Mr., Mrs., or Ms. Get your toddler in the habit of using these titles, even if it's only using it with first names, such as Mr. Steve or Mrs. Gail.

Fewer Expectations

If you want your child to act well around others, you need to know what to expect. If your son doesn't like loud places, then he's never going to be well behaved in an arcade or raucous play group. If your daughter has music in her and prefers to listen to her favorite tunes whenever she's playing, you'd be wise to keep her entertained and placated by keeping plenty of tunes on hand.

At the same time, toddlers don't have a lot of self-control, nor do they understand the dangers associated with climbing stairs or playing in traffic. In addition, sharing is a concept they haven't quite grasped. What does this mean for you, the parent? To be the polite parent of a polite toddler, you need to be vigilant about watching him and making sure that he not only keeps himself out of danger but that he doesn't end up becoming a nuisance to other children as well. You can't expect him to behave more maturely than is reasonable for his age.

The Necessity of Naps

Now that your youngster is more active and interested in participating in the world, you may think that he has the stamina to handle many different activities in a day. While it's true that he's probably given up his morning nap by the time he's two, he still needs his afternoon nap. Even though you may be tempted to push him so he can have fun, you should make naps a priority in your plans as well. Just like the young baby who needs sleep to grow and develop, so too does your toddler need his naps for this reason.

FACT

A toddler needs, on average, a two-hour nap each afternoon. That means that in order to keep your child well behaved and his sleep on track, you're going to need to plan your day so that come afternoon naptime, you're back home and he's in bed.

Developmental needs aside your child will be much more pleasant to be around if he's well rested. If your little boy or little girl seems completely out of sorts and is acting badly, despite all of your good intentions, this is your loud-and-clear cue that it's time to bow out of whatever you're doing, and get him or her home for a nap.

Feed Me

Another cause of crankiness in toddlers is hunger. You've probably experienced fatigue or irritability when your own blood sugar is low. Your child is no different. If you stick to a regular meal schedule and keep light snacks on hand for when hunger strikes out of the blue, this will help ensure that your toddler is a pleasure for everyone to be around.

ALERT!

Some children's behavior gets worse when they eat certain foods, and the root problem can be a food allergy or intolerance. If you notice that your toddler seems excessively cranky or just "off" after eating the same food, speak to your doctor about having him checked for an allergy or intolerance.

Playdate Duration

Playdates should be planned for the morning. That's a great time to get kids together, because they'll be starting the morning fresh. But most toddlers start drifting toward naptime just before lunch. If you force a playdate or play group to go into the noontime-hour, you're going to be dealing with a bunch of cranky kids. That means that as the parent, you should keep a watch on the clock and your kid. Only you will know how long your child can handle playing in the company of others.

If you start seeing meltdowns happen over nothing, then your child is probably tired and in need of his nap. To avoid forcing your friends to deal with your less-than-well-behaved child, you should excuse yourself and take your child home for a nap. He's sure to wake up a few hours later the epitome of the well-mannered child.

Children in Public Places

Everyone has a story to tell about a child they saw ran amuck in a public place, and the parents were nowhere to be found. What did you think of those parents (or their lack of parenting skills)? Admittedly, they were probably not very nice thoughts. If you don't want your child to be seen as a nuisance but rather as a joy to be around, you're going to have to make sure that she behaves whenever you go somewhere. One of the best ways to ensure good behavior in public is practice.

Public Displays of Good Behavior

If you're in a place like a playground or park, then you can feel free to let your child burn off some energy—that is, as long as he's not mowing down smaller children in the process. However, if you're in a public place where running is discouraged, such as a restaurant or store, then you need to keep on top of your child and stop him from running.

Again, in a place where other children are acting like children, no one is going to notice if your child joins in with the yelling. However, if he decides to yell in the middle of a movie or the mall, you need to go over to him right away and tell him "Shhh."

You should never let your child "cry it out" in public. There's probably a very valid reason that he's started crying, such as he's hurt himself or maybe he lost sight of you and he's scared. Find out the reason and try to resolve it. You shouldn't subject strangers to your child's screams and crying, and just wait until he calms down. This is definitely bad behavior on your part.

In order to raise a polite child, you've got to be a polite parent. Teach good manners by example. Make "please" and "thank you" part of your everyday vocabulary, and your children will start using those words, too.

Respectful Restaurant Behavior

You can start practicing your respectful restaurant behavior at home. For example, at the dinner table, you can remind your child not to speak with food in his mouth, never to call out when he wants to participate in the conversation, and always to speak in a quiet voice. Again, lead by example. Make sure that your table behavior is as good as you hope your child's will be. Then from time to time you can take your child to a restaurant, and let him practice his good manners.

Besides practicing good manners at home and at restaurants, you need to be aware that sometimes distraction is the best way to keep a hungry child from acting out. Many sit-down restaurants have introduced child-friendly fare and activities to keep their youngest customers occupied before the meal, but you can't always count on there being a sufficient supply of coloring books and crayons available when you get to any given restaurant. Bring toys and coloring tools that will keep your child occupied from the time you sit down at the table until the time your food arrives. If you've forgotten your coloring supplies, you can always start an impromptu game of hangman on the back of a placemat or begin doing "I Spy" from your seat at the table.

Finally, no matter how tired and hungry you are, you can't let that get in the way of making sure that your child is well behaved throughout the meal.

If he starts to climb out of his seat or wants to begin a conversation with the couple sitting next to you, you must stop him immediately. You may think he's being cute but your fellow diners may not agree. If your daughter decides that she's done eating and wants to run around, you have to explain that a restaurant isn't a place for running around. One of you may have to take her outside for a walk, if she can't sit still. If that doesn't work, you're going to need to take the rest of your meal home in a doggie bag so that your daughter's growing impatience with sitting still doesn't start to annoy the other people in the restaurant.

When you go out to eat with a young child, you should know in the back of your mind that keeping your child's behavior in check has got to be your top priority—this is not the time to have a relaxing meal with your spouse. You'll have to save that for when you hire a babysitter so you can go out together.

The Well-Mannered Moviegoer

Practice begins at home for how to behave at the movies. When you're watching TV, you've got to be vigilant about watching your child and making sure that she isn't jumping around when a movie is on or talking loudly during the show. You can practice whispering to one another when you have something to say while you're watching a video together at home, and then when she finally goes to the movies with you, she'll have a better sense of why you need to whisper in a theater.

Here are the behaviors you want to practice with your child to ensure she doesn't ruin the movie-going experience for others in the theater:

Staying in her seat (except if she needs to go to the bathroom).
Whispering when she wants to tell you something.
Not kicking the seat in front of her.
Eating quietly and neatly.
Not yelling out at the screen.
Applauding when the movie is over.

Politeness at the Playground

If there's one place where kids should feel free to be kids, it's at the playground. Parents who take their kids to the playground should expect lots of energetic play. If you don't like screaming or running around, you're going to have an awful time at the playground.

One of the biggest bones of contention at the playground has to do with the sharing of toys and equipment. It's perfectly normal for a young child not to want to share, but that doesn't mean that your child can't learn to do so. Again, practice makes perfect, and your child shouldn't be exempt from practicing these skills. Every time your little tike is in a situation where sharing is required, guide him through his good manners. If he's been using the swings for a long time and another child wants a turn, tell your child that it's time to share the swing and then take him off. He may not like your decision—and react badly—but unless you do this consistently, he'll never learn to share.

QUESTION?

What do you do about young bullies at the playground who take your child's toys?
You've got to put a stop to this. The next time you see this bully go after your son's stuff, get up and tell the other child that his behavior is unacceptable. It's never rude to stand up for your child, and you shouldn't feel bad in doing so.

While it's important to teach your child to share, you shouldn't teach her to be a doormat. If she's just started playing with a toy or piece of playground equipment, and immediately another child wants to use it, don't be fearful of telling the other child, "No." Of course, you should do this delicately by saying something like, "Gee, Sally just started playing with the toys in the sandbox. Why don't you come back in five minutes, and we'll switch?" If there are plenty of buckets in the sandbox, you could offer a few to the other child, but don't go for gracious behavior at the detriment of your child. You may think that you're acting polite—and teaching your child to be the same—but in fact you will be neglecting her feelings in order to appear polite, and that's just not a good idea.

Consideration at Stores and Supermarkets

The reality of being a parent is that sometimes you have to take your kids along when you go shopping. There's no better place for a kid to develop a case of the "gimmes" than in the aisle of the supermarket or a store. Kids tend to want to have everything they see on a store shelf, but it's unacceptable when parents give in to these demands all the time. Setting limits helps your child appreciate privileges instead of taking them for granted.

If your child has a meltdown in the middle of an aisle because you refuse to give in to him, you'll have two choices. First, you can try to reason with your child and get him to calm down. The younger the child, though, the less effective reasoning will be. Also, don't let "reasoning" turn into "negotiation" where you find yourself eventually giving in after all the whining and crying. That's not the point of this exercise. (Then all you will have taught your child is that the more he complains, the more certain it is that he'll eventually get his way.)

However, if reasoning doesn't work and the tantrum is getting worse, then you're going to have to leave the store. That means abandoning your shopping cart, and getting the heck out of dodge. Not only do you need to teach your child a lesson on good behavior—if you act badly, we leave the store—but you also want to avoid subjecting other shoppers to your child's behavior. You can try to take your child outside to calm him down. It's true that it might seem rude (to the store personnel) that you're leaving your cart in the middle of the aisle, but in the long run, leaving with a screaming child is better than continuing to shop with one.

Planes, Trains, and Automobiles

Ask any traveler what's the worst thing about being on a bus, train or plane with a child, and you're sure to hear about the kids who screamed nonstop, kept kicking the person's seat or ran amuck throughout the trip. Children need to learn the right and wrong way to travel with others. These lessons will start right in his car seat, in your automobile. That's when you can let your child know that kicking the seat and screaming are unacceptable behaviors.

Besides practicing how to behave when you need to travel somewhere—and making sure that you stay on top of your child's behavior throughout the trip—you should remember that the best way to have a well-behaved child on any road trip or flight is to make sure that he stays occupied. That may mean that you have to pack an extra backpack full of toys, games, and food, but the travelers around you will surely appreciate your doing so.

ALERT!

While it's a good idea to bring things along for your child to do during your travels, it's also good to consider that your fellow travelers may view certain activities as distracting. Your reading out loud to your child, helping him with his homework, or giving him a videogame to play will keep him occupied but all those activities could disturb the passenger sitting near you who is trying to work silently or, worse yet, sleep.

Behaving in School

One of the best tests of how well you've raised your child to be well behaved is when he goes to school. It's in a classroom where your child is going to be faced with all of the situations that he's likely to deal with in life (but on a smaller scale). These include getting along with others, making friends, sharing items, and behaving appropriately.

If you've practiced on the playground and in play groups about sharing toys, your child should have no problem transitioning to school. Most children quickly learn that there is a social benefit to sharing—if you share your toys, you get someone else to play with. However, if you hear from your child's teacher that your little girl isn't sharing as nicely as you'd like her to be, then you've got to start working on her sharing skills at home again.

No one wants a biter or a hitter in his class but the reality is that one way that young children show frustration is with biting and hitting. With a preverbal child, there's no reason to spend hours explaining why it's not good to bite or to hit friends. But whenever you witness this behavior or hear about it from a teacher, you must quickly and swiftly let the child know, "No. That's not OK," in a nonshaming way. Sooner or later he'll learn that biting or hitting a friend is no way to win friends and influence others, nor is it how to act politely in school.

Another skill your child should have picked up by now is the importance of inside voices—something teachers ask their students to use. If your child is constantly yelling or speaking in unacceptable tones of voice, take a hard look at how you behave at home. If you're always yelling or talking loudly, then your child will talk this way, too. If everyone works hard at home to use his or her "inside voices," your child will have a better time adapting his tone of voice to the classroom.

Never try to teach a hitter or a biter a lesson by hitting or biting him back. Showing the child how it feels doesn't help to improve his behavior—it only hurts him. It may seem like the perfect solution in the short term, but it can do long-term damage to your child. Never shame your child into improving his behavior.

Discipline Demeanor

On the face of it, it may seem counterintuitive that in order to raise polite children, you have to discipline them. But when you think about it, it makes perfect sense. How does anyone learn the difference between right and wrong? Someone points it out to them. If your child always acts selfish and you never correct it, your child will have a skewed view of socially acceptable behavior. On the other hand, if you correct your child whenever he doesn't share with others or when he does act disrespectful toward people, then he'll eventually realize that sharing is the way to go and acting disrespectful isn't.

Discipline comes in many forms, some of which are acceptable and others that aren't. Spanking your child will not get the message across about bad behavior. You should never act forcefully or in a way that hurts your child—or leaves you feeling guilty about how you scolded your child. Yelling at a child doesn't accomplish much, but sometimes you may find it necessary to raise your voice in order to make your point or to get your child's attention. Don't let your emotions get the best of you when you're angry with your child so that you end up doing something you regret, such as yelling at the top of your lungs or lashing out at him. Even adults can benefit from a time-out from time to time. If, as you're getting ready to discipline your child you feel your anger building, take a few minutes to compose yourself. This will allow you to address the situation with control.

Bad Words

Every parent can tell a story of how they thought their child wasn't listening when they used a bad word, only to discover that child repeating that bad word later in the day. Bad words can be like insidious viruses—they're nearly impossible to get rid of once a child's been exposed to them. But if you work hard to clean up your own language, that effort will go a long way toward keeping your children's language clean as well.

Defining

In some families, parents define bad words as the usual curse words you hear in an R-rated movie. In some other families, they consider the words "hate," "stupid," or "jerk" to be bad words. That means that the "s" word can mean two different things to two different families.

Before you scold your kids about what's coming out of their mouths, you need to figure out ahead of time what you would consider to be a bad word and what isn't. You also need to decide if context might affect your definition of a bad word.

ALERT!

It's a good idea to define bad words so your kids will know not to use them. However, there are times when you may need to redefine certain words for your kids so they know not to use them in the presence of others—especially when you'll be spending time with someone who might find certain words offensive even if you don't.

For example, if your child is frustrated because he can't get his zipper to work and he says something like, "Oh, this stupid zipper is stuck," you might not find that usage so heinous and not worth a scolding. However, if in the next breath he calls you or one of his siblings "stupid," then you might want to step in. Just as you have boundaries for acceptable and unacceptable behavior, you should have similar boundaries for good and bad words—and make sure that your kids know and understand them.

Finding Suitable Substitutions

There's nothing wrong with expressing yourself when you're angry, upset, or frustrated. But to be a truly polite person, you need to be able to tactfully express those feelings without offending anyone. Your kids need to behave the same way, too. If you find that your child is very verbal and needs something that he can say when he's feeling frustrated without fear of repercussions, work to find substitute words he can freely say. You can go with "real" words, like "sugar," "darn it," or "for Pete's sake," or you can make up funny sayings that won't offend, such as "cheese and crackers."

Fashion Faux Pas

To most people a fashion faux pas is wearing white after Labor Day or dressing in something that is completely out of style. When it comes to your children, fashion mistakes take on an entirely different meaning.

Acting Inconsiderately

One of the ways that your child can show bad manners when it comes to clothing is by pointing out when others are wearing clothing that isn't quite up to their standards or which they find offensive. Every kid wants to be accepted and often acceptance comes (unfortunately) with the kinds of clothing kids wear. If your child is aware that someone at school isn't wearing the right brand of sneakers or pants, you cannot let your child get away with pointing out this fashion discrepancy. Your child needs to understand that not every family can afford to purchase fashionable clothing and not every kid cares about what she's wearing. What's most important is for your child to treat everyone with respect and to like someone for whom she is, not what she's wearing. Labeling someone based on the labels in her clothing is a perfect example of bad manners. Don't let your child do this, ever.

E ALERT!

The best way not to have your child become a fashion diva is not to be one yourself. If you're constantly pointing out "labels" on other people, whether it's their clothes or car, then your child will follow your example and do the same with the people she sees.

Dressing Appropriately

Another way that your child can show bad manners is by how she dresses. If your school has a certain rule about what constitutes appropriate attire and what doesn't, then you need to set a good example for your child and make sure that you follow these rules. If your daughter's school's dress code says no halter tops, belly shirts, or flip-flops, then you can't let her get away with wearing them to school "just this one time."

There are other occasions where your child will have to wear her manners on her sleeve by choosing appropriate attire that doesn't offend others, although she may not be happy about it. Here are some ways to think about dressing appropriately for certain occasions and certain settings.

Church/Temple/Religious Settings

Part of showing respect in a house of worship is how you dress. That's why it's always wise to have your child (and yourself, for that matter) dress on the conservative side. That means no jeans, no tank tops—nothing too casual.

Holiday Get-Together

The only time it's acceptable to dress casually for a holiday celebration is if you're going to one that's casual by nature, such as a Memorial Day picnic or a Fourth of July barbecue. Otherwise, let the time and setting of the affair be your fashion guide. That is, the later in the day and the more formal the setting, the more formal everyone's attire should be.

School Pictures

Remind your child that a school picture is something that she's going to look back on for years to come. That's why she should make the effort to style her hair nicely and choose a neat, clean, and appropriate outfit to wear in the photograph. There's nothing wrong with choosing jeans for a school photo, but make sure they're not her pair that's full of rips and holes.

Shoes in the House

Do you take your shoes off as soon as you walk in the door of your own home? You might do it simply because you feel more comfortable not wearing them, or you may have been taught to do so to avoid tracking in dirt. When visiting someone else's home, it's a good practice to keep in mind.

If you notice that everyone there is walking around in socks, it's probably a good indication that they do not wear shoes in the house and that they'd appreciate your not doing so, either. If you've been walking around in the rain or you know that your shoes are muddy, do your host a favor and save them the trouble of having to clean up after you. Sometimes the "no shoes in the house" rule is more for the kids than the adults. When in doubt, ask the host what she prefers and then defer to her request. You may be allowed to keep your shoes on but your son definitely has to take his off. If you have a rule that everyone has to take their shoes off as soon as they enter the house, don't feel bad if your child has friends over one day and you have to gently remind the friend of this rule when he attempts to step into the playroom with his footwear still on. A child who visits should follow the rules of the home he is visiting.

When your children visit others' homes, they will be seen as very polite if they take their shoes off when they enter. It's a practice that does wonders for keeping floors clean, and other moms are sure to appreciate their effort.

Well-Behaved Birthday Celebrations

For children, birthday celebrations are usually the center of their social lives. Your child probably can't wait until his next birthday so he can have a party. He also probably can't wait to join in all his friends' birthday celebrations.

It's important to be as inclusive as possible when you draw up a guest list for your child's birthday. For a child in preschool or early elementary school, you should try to invite all the children in his class. As your child gets older and decides to have single-gender parties, he should include all the boys in his class or all the girls on her soccer team. The worst thing for a kid is to overhear others talking about a party to which he was not invited.

ESSENTIAL

If your son or daughter is only having boys or girls from the class for a party, send invitations through the mail, not the school. This way you don't run the risk of an uninvited child seeing an invitation to the party to which he or she was not invited.

On the day of the party, your child is likely to be excited about the festivities to come, and his behavior may be less than perfect. You might want to cut him some slack, due to the excitement. But by all means make sure that, once the party starts, he acts like a gracious host.

Similarly, once children arrive at your home for the party (or wherever you're holding the celebration), you need to make sure that everyone stays on their best behavior. As the parent hosting or paying for the party, you have every right to let a child know when he isn't acting appropriately or to step in when another parent doesn't. You are responsible for these children while they're at your child's birthday party, and they should behave by your rules, even if they have to be reminded of them throughout the party.

If your child chooses to open gifts in front of her friends, make sure that you coach her ahead of time how to react to each gift—graciously, even if she doesn't like the gift. She needs to be reminded that someone took the time to buy her this gift, and the least she can do is appreciate it when she opens it.

After the fact you need to make sure that your child writes thank-you notes for all the gifts she received at her birthday. With very young children or those who have just learned to write, you may have to write the actual thank-you note and then have the child sign it. An upper elementary school-aged or older child could certainly handle writing all her thank-you notes on her own, and it's your job to ensure that she does so on a timely basis.

Chapter 5

Manners at Home

It's one thing to teach your children to behave well when they're out in public, at school, or visiting a friend's house. It's another thing to make sure that your children continue to use their good manners when they're at home. Similarly, adults often need a timely tutorial on what constitutes polite or rude behavior (as the case may be) when entertaining guests at their home or when visiting someone else's home.

Everyone Pitches In

There are a number of ways that parents can teach their children good manners at home. One of the best ways is by example. That is, if you use polite language and behavior, your children are likely to mimic your good manners. Also, if you and your spouse continually help each other with household chores, then your children will learn the important lesson that everyone should pitch in.

Besides asking your children to bus their dishes or put their dirty clothes in the hamper, you can assign your older children chores as a way of teaching them responsibility. Think about it this way: if your children don't learn that they need to be responsible for things, they are going to grow up thinking that everything they want just comes to them. How rude!

You can start with simple things like asking your children to pick up their toys and books or empty the nonbreakables from the dishwasher every day. As your children get older, bigger, and stronger, you can assign them bigger tasks. These might include mowing the lawn, walking the dog, and taking out the garbage—all three are easy chores for children to take responsibility for.

FACT

The American Academy of Pediatrics (AAP) says that upper elementary school-aged children (eight through twelve) are old enough to assume chores around the house. The AAP also recommends giving children allowances as an incentive and a reward for doing chores.

Children at Parties

When you plan a family get-together, it's natural to want to include the children. They're a part of the family, so why shouldn't they be a part of a family celebration? This is fine, as long as the youngest guests are well behaved.

Seen But Not Heard

You may not have a choice, when visiting other adults, to not bring your own children along (especially if you're in a babysitting quandary) or to have their children near. However, if the point of your get-together is to entertain the adults and not the children, you'll want to make sure that you remind your children that they should keep interruptions to a minimum.

Maintain a well-stocked game closet and do an inventory of it before you invite parents with children over to your home for a party. This will ensure that the kids have plenty to do and play for the evening and that they'll keep to themselves as much as possible.

Staying Entertained

If you explain to your children that you want them to behave and give them ways to do just that, such as by supplying them with games to play, you'll likely be a lot more successful in your request. Do you have a finished basement filled with toys? Arrange it so the kids have their own space for a party down there. This will give the grown-ups upstairs the freedom to engage in adult conversation and the children the freedom to be, well, children, in a completely different area of the house.

If you haven't got a separate space where the children can play, consider sending them outside. Alert the parents ahead of time that they should bring their children dressed appropriately so they can partake of your playground or, if it's winter, so the kids can go outside and build snowmen. If playing outside is not an option, you should stock up on quiet games that the children can play together or at least invest in a couple of age-appropriate movies that the kids can watch for a bit while the adults eat or socialize in peace.

Table Manners

Speaking of eating—when it's time for the kids to have their meal, they should exercise all their best table manners—even if they're your own children in your own house. That means:

Placing your napkins in your lap.
No talking with food in your mouth.

No chewing with your mouth open.

Saying "please" and "thank you" when asking someone for something.

No reaching or grabbing for food but polite passing around instead.

Keeping comments about the food to yourself.

Asking to be excused when you're done eating.

Clearing your dishes from the table.

Before a big event at your house or someone else's home, practice all these good manners with your children. And make sure that you use your table manners during meals as well. Children learn best by example.

Adult-Only Festivities

There are times you may want to host family and friends in your home and have it be an adults-only party. Maybe you're planning a potentially raucous bachelor party for your best buddy or you'd just like to have a quiet dinner with friends without any youngsters around.

In instances like this, it's always a good idea to let your guests know ahead of time that the party is for adults only. You should also plan ahead to make sure that you've secured a baby sitter for your own children. As the guest in someone else's home, it's never polite to assume that your children have been invited with you to a get together. You should always call first and ask. If you find out that your little ones aren't welcome, you have two choices: you can hire a baby sitter, or, if you can't find someone to watch your kids, you can't go. Taking the kids along is not an option.

How-To on Hostess Gifts

Whenever you're invited to someone's home for a social occasion, you should always bring a hostess gift. When you R.S.V.P. to the initial invitation, you can ask, "What would you like me to bring?" If the host tells you something that you can contribute, then that item would double as your hostess gift. If the host tells you, "Oh, we've got it all covered," then you still need to find something to bring, because you should never show up at someone's house empty handed.

There are a number of stand-bys that work well in a pinch as a hostess gift. These include:

A bottle of red or white wine
A bottle of champagne if it's New Year's Eve
A box of chocolates
A dessert of some kind
A cadre of candles
Festive cocktail napkins
A plant or some kind of greenery

ALERT!

It's rude to demand that a hostess serve the bottle of wine that you brought along with you as your hostess gift. She is under no obligation to uncork that bottle right away, so don't ask her to do so.

Holding Your Liquor

The decision to serve liquor is entirely up to you as the host, although it's nice to always offer at least one kind of spirits when you have guests to your home. These may include the makings for mimosas at a brunch, a light wine for lunch or dinner, or beer for your weekly card game.

If someone who is joining you is an alcoholic, you shouldn't make it your mission to make sure that this person doesn't take a drink. But at the same time, if he abstains from drinking, you shouldn't make a big deal out of it and take it upon yourself to inform others about why he isn't drinking. It's not your place to reveal that personal information.

That's Smoking

If you're a smoker and you visit someone's home, you should assume that you need to take your cigarette breaks outside. These days even some who smoke don't do so in their own homes—they're aware of the negative effects of secondhand smoke and even what it does to their furniture, upholstery, and rugs (read: it makes them smell bad) so they step outside for a smoke.

Never light up without asking first—or without first checking to see if there are ashtrays and matchboxes on tabletops. These are usually clear signs that smoking inside is OK, but it's always better to err on the side of caution and to ask first. By doing so, you'll be seen as a very polite guest.

Food Fetishes

When you're invited to someone's house for a meal, it's your job as a guest to enjoy what's being served to you without being judgmental about their cooking ability or menu choice. If, unfortunately, you do not like what's been served to you, don't ask if you can go make yourself a sandwich in the kitchen. Instead, do your best to get through the meal. If the host asks why you haven't eaten much (which she shouldn't do—it's rude), you can say something like, "I'm not very hungry today."

If you're the host and you're inviting people over for a meal, it would be gracious to check ahead of time with your guests for any food allergies, likes, and dislikes. This will help you plan your menu accordingly. That way if you find out that some people are vegetarians, you can be sure to plan at least one nonmeat dish. Similarly, if someone has a nut allergy, you'll know to hold off putting almonds on the salad or mixed nuts out for an appetizer.

Religious Occasions

There may be times when you're invited to someone's home during a holiday celebration, and it's possible that the holidays they celebrate are not the same as yours. You would be a courteous guest if you did your best to respect whatever rituals this family follows. Likewise, as the host you should plan to explain what's going on or what's expected to anyone who is visiting during that time.

Respecting Other's Rituals

Every holiday, regardless of your religion, comes with certain rituals that everyone is expected to follow. These rituals range from putting on a yarmulke when attending a Jewish family's Passover Seder to bowing your head during a before-meal prayer at a Christmas dinner to forsaking food during daylight hours at a Muslim family's home during Ramadan. When you're a guest in another person's home, you should respect their rituals and participate as much as possible, and as much as you're comfortable doing.

Cultural Differences

Depending on a person's religion or culture, you may find yourself dealing with cultural differences at home that may catch you by surprise. If you're invited to someone's home and that person doesn't share the same religion or culture as you, you should know ahead of time about some of the social situations you may be facing. At the same time if you're inviting someone from a different cultural background over to celebrate with you, you may want to take certain precautions so you don't offend any of that person's customs or cultural obligations.

ALERT!

Generalizations about a person's religion or cultural customs, such as that Indian women only wear saris or that all Christians say grace before a meal, are never a good idea. When in doubt, ask first before committing a social faux pas, such as leading your host in grace without asking if, in fact, she wants to say it.

Jewish Families

Some Jewish families keep what's called a kosher home. That means that they only bring in food that is certified kosher. They usually have separate plates and utensils for dairy foods and for meat products. These are both ways of keeping a home kosher. If you've been invited to someone's home and you want to bring a hostess gift, make sure you choose something that has a kosher symbol on it, which could be a "U" or "K" on the label.

If you decide to help out in the kitchen, make sure that you ask first which dishes or silverware you should use. You don't want to choose the dairy flatware for serving meat or meat plates for a dairy meal.

If the Jewish family you're visiting is Orthodox or extremely conservative, they may have the men and women sit separately from one another. You should be prepared for this division beforehand, just in case.

Muslim Domicile

Like other religions, Muslims go to a house of worship to pray. But they also pray a number of times at home, in their living room, which requires them to bend down on the floor. For this reason alone, it is never a good idea to wear shoes in a Muslim family's home, and you should get in the habit of taking off your shoes as soon as you enter.

Also, Muslims forbid the physical interaction of nonrelated males and females. If you're a man, and the woman of the house greets you at the door, do not shake her hand or kiss her on the cheek. A wave hello or a nod of the head would suffice. And make sure that you come to the home in appropriate dress. Both men and women should avoid wearing anything that is revealing, such as shorts or tank tops. Many Muslims have very conservative views about how people should dress—at home and in public.

Similar to a kosher home, Muslim families often serve food, including meat products, that are considered to be halal, or that have been prepared in a way that follows Muslim tradition. If you're serving a meal to a Muslim family in your home, you'll want to buy your meat products from a halal grocer.

Hindu Homes

Probably the largest number of Hindus hail from somewhere in India. One of the most important things to remember when visiting an Indian or Hindu home is that there may be shrines to the various Hindu gods in the house. It is never a good idea to touch these shrines, as they are sacred.

FACT

As far as food goes, Hindus consider the cow a sacred animal, and they do not eat any meat from these animals. (They do, however, drink milk.) Leather is forbidden because it is a cow derivative. Avoid bringing a gift of something leather to a Hindu home.

Speaking of gifts, it is traditional for a Hindu host to offer the gift of tea and snacks to guests when they arrive. Always accept this gift of goodies, even if you only take one sip or nibble. If you don't, you risk offending the hostess.

Family Celebrations

It's always exciting to plan for your family to celebrate a special occasion at your home. It's wonderful when relatives can get together on a regular basis and enjoy each other's company. Sometimes, though, distance or dissolved marriages prevent you from having the ideal gathering you'd envisioned.

In the case of distant relatives, it's always a good idea to include them in any celebration you're planning. If they do attend, they may need some introductions to new significant others or younger children they may not have met before. Don't assume that your distant relatives will remember who everyone is. It's OK to remind them who certain people are by saying something simple, like, "You remember your cousin, Michael, I'm sure." It's your job as the host to make the introductions and get people reacquainted. You don't want to leave someone floundering to figure out people's names when all it takes is a brief introduction to ensure that everyone knows everyone else in attendance.

When it comes to dissolved marriages and family events, you can take two approaches to your guest list. You want your guests to feel as comfortable as possible, and this means being aware of any circumstances that may exist between a divorced or separated couple, or even between friends of yours who dated at one point. Nothing says you have to invite everyone, but if both people are good friends of yours, you should invite them both. You should let both of them know that you've invited the other and let them decide on their own whether or not they want to attend. If you happen to be closer to one person than the other, you can invite one person instead of the other and then let the person know that you've made the effort not to include their ex. This might help keep any unnecessary tension at bay. If the former couple is not on good terms, then this arrangement works best for everyone. If you do invite them both and they don't get along, you'll know in the future not to invite them to the same event.

Playing the Part of Good Host

You have certain responsibilities as a host whenever you invite people to your home. These responsibilities aren't designed to make you more stressed out or to add items to your to-do list. Rather, playing the part of the good host ensures that each of your guests feels welcome in your home.

Housecleaning

One of the best ways to prepare for having others over is to make sure that your home is clean. With everything you have on your plate as a host, you don't need the added stress of worrying if there are cobwebs in the kitchen or dust bunnies in the bathroom as your guests are milling about. Try to set aside time on the day of the event to do a quick run-through your home so you'll be sure that everything's neat and tidy. Not having time to get your house in order doesn't get you off the hook. Consider hiring a service to do the cleaning for you.

Inviting Others Over

One of the best ways to develop good relationships with your neighbors or to get to know them better is to invite them to your home. You can have them over for a meal, or maybe you can ask them to join you for your regular poker night with your buddies.

When entertaining in your home, you should try to be as inclusive as possible. Always make sure that if you're part of a social circle, such as a play group or supper club, that you include everyone in that circle whenever you have people to your house. If you can't include everyone, invite no one from that group.

Dietary Do's and Don'ts

While you can't be responsible for how much people eat when they come to your home or how much they like your cooking, you can act responsibly by making sure that you don't serve anything that offends anyone's customs or affects their allergies. When it comes time to invite folks over, ask them if they have any food preferences or allergies. Base your shopping on the answers you hear, such as making sure you have one meatless dish for your vegetarians or avoiding anything with seafood in it for those who are allergic to it.

For those with finicky food needs, they may offer to bring their own food to the party, such as the family that needs to eat gluten-free or follows a kosher diet. You should accept their offer to bring these items along and save a space on your table to put them out.

Introductions

The gracious host never lets one of her guests feel left out of the dinner conversation or the cocktail chatter. That's why as your guests arrive, you should greet them at the door and make sure that you bring them around to meet others at your party.

A good way to spark connections between strangers is to point out any common interests two people might share. A proper introduction might be, "Jane Smith, this is Lisa Jones. Lisa Jones, this is Jane Smith. Jane, Lisa went to Wellesley, and Lisa, Jane went to Radcliffe."

It's perfectly acceptable to ask the host of the party to introduce you to someone specific, even after she's made the general introductions in the room. You may notice someone who looks familiar but may feel shy about approaching that person on your own. It's fine to enlist the host in this respect.

If you'll be too busy working in the kitchen when your guests arrive, designate one of your friends or family members to be the party greeter. Instruct this person on your desire to make sure everyone gets introduced to one another, and that way you can feel confident that there will be plenty of mixing and mingling at your soiree.

Becoming the Social Butterfly

Even though the host of the party may have introduced you around when you arrived, you may not know how to move yourself from one conversation to another. Yet you don't want to spend the entire evening speaking to the same people. Here are some ways you can mingle effortlessly.

1. Excuse yourself at some point to get a drink or something to eat, but ask first if anyone you're talking to wants something. The bar or food table is where many people tend to congregate.
2. Don't feel shy about eavesdropping on a conversation as a way of moving yourself into that conversation. If you overhear someone saying something of interest, you can say that you apologize for eavesdropping but you couldn't help yourself—and here's what you think about that topic.
3. Compliments will get you everywhere. If you notice someone wearing a piece of jewelry, a pair of shoes, or with a hairstyle you admire, go over to him or her and say something.

Regardless of what tactics you use in starting conversations with strangers, always remember to introduce yourself and to do your best to remember the name of the person you've just met. Then if you happen to see someone you know enter the room, you can call her over and introduce her to the new person you've just met. Everyone will be so impressed with your social skills.

Chapter 6

E **The Social Graces on Being Social**

The proliferation of media and the across-the-board acceptance of less-than-perfect behavior (ad-hoc cursing, sloppy dress in public, etc.) have led many people to behave in a way that's too casual in nature when they're out and about in the world.

If you want people to think highly of you and your children, then you've got to take a refresher course on some basic social graces. By doing so, you'll ensure that you and your children will go quite far in school, at work, and in life.

Addressing Forms of Address

In a perfect world, everyone's children would refer to adults as Mr., Mrs., and Ms. as is expected in school. Unfortunately, you do not live in a perfect world, and too many parents allow their youngsters to call adults by their first names.

FACT

You can call someone with an advanced degree doctor (Dr.) instead of Mr., Mrs., and Ms. as a form of address but understand how etiquette dictates the use of this title in print. If you're inviting someone to a social occasion and the "Dr." has a Ph.D., then you wouldn't use the title Dr. (that's for academic use only). However, medical doctors of all kinds are always referred to as Doctor.

If you want to teach your children to respect their elders—an old-fashioned notion, to be sure, but one that's rooted in sensibility—then you've got to teach them that one of the first ways to show respect is to use Mr., Mrs., Miss, or Ms., along with a person's surname.

Using Titles with Surnames

When you introduce yourself to one of your children's friends, refer to yourself as "Mr. Smith" or "Mrs. Smith." When you talk about another child's parents, refer to them in the third person—"Mr. Jones will be coming by at 4:00 to pick you up from your playdate." This reinforces the importance of addressing adults properly.

For laid-back adults the idea of referring to your fellow grown ups by their surnames may feel a little weird. But it's really best for you to put aside your discomfort so you can teach your children the proper way to address adults.

Using Titles with First Names

Proper etiquette dictates that you always use someone's title with his surname, such as Mr. Smith, and it would be best not to try to circumnavigate the formality of forms of address by attaching a title to a person's first name, such as "Miss Jane" instead of "Mrs. Smith." This really does nothing to teach your children the importance of referring to adults in a proper way. However, if "Miss Jane" really doesn't want to be called "Mrs. Smith," then using "Miss" in front of her name is better than no title at all.

From Title to First Name

Some polite children grow up to be proper adults who continue to refer to the parents of their childhood friends as Mr. and Mrs. While it's fine to err on the side of being good mannered, at some point it's fine to let your older child know that she is now old enough to refer to adults as her equal. A good rule of thumb is this: when your child is old enough to vote or is seen as an adult in society's eyes, she is old enough to be given the option of calling an adult by her first name. Of course, you don't have to let your children know this upfront—you can wait until another adult says something like, "Oh, we're both adults now. You can call me 'Jane' instead of 'Mrs. Smith.'"

QUESTION?

How do I handle a form of address with a married woman who has kept her maiden name?

Many married women do not change their name after saying, "I Do." If you're unsure what form of address your child should use with this adult, ask. Some women don't mind being called Mrs., even if they didn't take their husband's last name. Others prefer Ms.

Common Courtesies

In today's busy world, you may have forgotten some simple courtesies. For starters it's still best to wait your turn. It can be frustrating when you see a long line or your child needs to hold off playing with a toy because others are using it. Also, in this world of instant messages and always-on communications, it's sometimes difficult to accept that there are still things you must wait for. But that old adage "Patience is a virtue" really is true. By reminding yourself and your kids to be more patient, you'll all become more polite people.

Besides waiting your turn to do something, you need to wait your turn to speak—which is where the saying "speaking out of turn" comes from. In school your children learn that they must raise a hand to contribute to class discussion. You should revisit your elementary-age self and remember why it was that people had to raise a hand to speak when others were talking—it's impolite to interrupt. One of the most common ways that folks communicate these days is through e-mail. Be careful how you use your e-mail, because it could blow up in your face. Never send an e-mail when you're angry, and always double check that you're sending an e-mail to the proper person. It's never a good idea to badmouth others in an e-mail, because it's possible that that person could get a copy of the e-mail.

Finally, whether on e-mail or in daily conversation, do not gossip or call others bad names—and teach your children this lesson as well. Sticks and stones may hurt your bones, but name-calling can harm a person way more than you'll ever know. Just put yourself in that person's position and think about how you'd feel if someone gossiped about you or made fun of you in one way or another. You'd feel pretty horrible, wouldn't you? Well, if you avoid this behavior at all cost, you won't hurt anyone's feelings, and your manners will always be at the top of their game.

If you discover that you've sent someone an e-mail that was not intended for him or her, immediately send a follow-up, mea culpa e-mail that apologizes for your mistake. This is especially important if your e-mail contains information that could upset the mistaken recipient.

Visiting Hours

There's nothing as homey feeling as living in a town where you can call on your neighbors at any time of the day or night. Whether it's your kids riding around the neighborhood looking for someone to play with or your taking a walk across the street to share a cup of coffee with a friend, there's something to be said for the freedom that living in close proximity to others offers. However, there's always room for good manners when you feel like acting neighborly.

Planning Ahead

There's a reason that "go outside and find someone to play with" has evolved into scheduled playdates. Most often, you plan ahead for your child's fun time together with a friend as you would a date with your significant other.

Calling ahead to arrange a playdate for your child means planning ahead, not calling the morning of and expecting someone to be free. While you may think you're being polite because you're calling first, what you're really doing is putting the person on the spot, which is rude.

In today's world it isn't always safe to send young children outside, unsupervised, to find someone to play with. In addition, many of today's modern families have two parents who work outside of the home. Or if these families don't have working parents, they do have afternoons filled with soccer practices, swimming lessons, and other extracurricular activities. That means that if your children want to get together with others, you've got to plan ahead. By the same token, you need to remember that just because a parent is home during the day doesn't mean that she isn't busy. That's why regardless of whether you're trying to schedule a playdate for your child or an impromptu coffee klatch with a girlfriend, you should always call ahead before showing up on someone's doorstep or ringing her bell and expecting to be invited in.

Even when you make plans sometimes things can go awry. Here's how to handle some of those social snafus:

- If you arrive earlier than expected, you need to kill time until your scheduled get-together.
- If you get delayed and won't get someplace on time, always call and let the person know that you're running late.
- If you can't make a date at the last minute, call as soon as you know you need to cancel and make sure you apologize profusely for backing out of your appointment.

Bringing a Gift

You know that you should always bring a gift when you're invited to someone's house for a weekend stay or for a meal. Well, the same rule applies when your girlfriend invites you over for a glass of wine or your son is going to a friend's house after school for a playdate.

You don't have to offer the host an elaborate gift, such as a bunch of flowers or a homemade dessert. However, your bringing the bottle of wine that you're going to share with a friend or picking up a quick snack for your son to enjoy during his playdate would be a truly wonderful gesture.

ESSENTIAL

Because impromptu playdates or poker games can and do occur unexpectedly, always keep your pantry or refrigerator stocked with a couple of items you can grab at the last minute to bring with you. These might include a few bottles of your favorite wine for a grown-up gathering, or a multipack of chips that you can use at a spur-of-the-moment play group.

The Body Politic

The freedom to express your political views is one of the things that makes the United States a great country—it's a right that's a part of the country's main governing doctrine, the Constitution. However, just because you have the right to speak your mind about politics or anything else related to elections or which candidate you favor, that doesn't give you carte blanche to toss good behavior out the window.

There are appropriate ways to express your political views that are less likely to offend others' sensibilities. If you keep your language clean and you don't point fingers at any one person or in someone's face as you're disagreeing with them, then you probably can enjoy political banter without ending up in a fistfight. Other inoffensive ways to express your political views include:

Bumper stickers
T-shirts
Lapel pins
A letter to the editor of your local newspaper

Keep in mind that many workplaces may have rules that prohibit employees from wearing politically motivated clothing or buttons in the workplace. Even if you're passionately involved in a current political campaign, you're going to have to consider your workplace off limits for such things. You should apply the same thinking to other places where people of all ages might be offended by your strong views. These include houses of worship and schools. If you feel strongly about an issue that could be confusing or upsetting to children, don't broadcast your views on a sign on your lawn. By the same token try to avoid wearing any offensive political clothing or insignia when you'll be dealing with children. It's one thing to express your civil rights. It's another to act civilly when doing so.

Dealing with Disagreements

When you've crossed the line from polite political discussion to disrespectful diatribes you run the risk of screaming at others, using inappropriate language to get your point across, or speaking in such a way that you've reduced someone to tears. Sometimes it's best, when you feel the heat rising, to take a deep breath and then a step back. Often, the best way to defuse a situation that's gotten out of control is to simply end the conversation. Agree to disagree; you don't need to share the same opinion with everyone.

Of course, just because you've decided not to let things get out of control doesn't mean that your verbal sparring partner feels the same way. If this person keeps coming at you, calmly repeat, "I think it's best to agree to disagree on this point," until the other person backs down. Either way, you've reached your goal of not blowing your top over a political discussion.

Political Debates

During election time, you're bound to run into someone whose views on the candidates don't agree with yours. Even when there's no election in site, it's possible to find yourself in a political debate with someone.

Debating the Point

One of the most important things to keep in mind when debating politics is this: you need to debate the point, not the person. It's fine to disagree with someone's views as long as you keep the conversation focused on the point of discussion—politics. It's when you start to insult one another over your differences of opinion that you can get into trouble.

One of the best ways to keep a political debate lively, interesting, and to the point is to think before you speak. If you find yourself wanting to call the other person names because you don't agree with his view, then you've got to edit yourself. You need to figure out a way to continue your conversation so that you can get back on topic. If that seems impossible, then you need to tell the person that you'd like to agree to disagree, and walk away.

Politics in the Workplace

It's wise to avoid talking politics in the workplace. It's possible that your views may differ from the people with whom you work and interact on a daily basis.

If you happen to find yourself at a political crossroads with a colleague, you may end up either leaving them with a bad impression or doing irreparable harm to your working relationship. Remember that edit function and use it wisely. You wouldn't want to lose out on a promotion at work, simply because you don't know how to hold your temper when it comes to politics.

Considerate Complaining

Just because you use good manners doesn't mean that you should be someone's doormat. It is perfectly reasonable to stand up for yourself or your children when necessary, and if you feel as if someone or some business has done you wrong, then by all means you should tell them so. There is an art to considerate complaining that not only keeps courtesy in mind but is also likely to get you the results you want.

Say Anything

How you say what's on your mind when something's gone wrong will go a long way toward getting your message across. While your first reaction may be to raise your voice and insult the person you're dealing with, you're more apt to get results if you take a breath and calmly express your reasons for being upset. Remember, the person you're talking to may not be directly responsible for the concern or issue you have. Attacking that person will only put him on the defensive and will do nothing to help you solve your problem. Think ahead of time how best to communicate your complaint.

One of the best ways to complain is to banish the "you" and "your" from your sentences—it's like verbal finger pointing, and it puts people on the defensive. Don't say to the bus company that drives your children to school, "Your bus driver keeps picking up and dropping the kids off at different times, and I'm sick of it." Instead, phrase it as a problem that the two of you need to solve: "I've noticed that bus stop times have been a bit erratic lately. What can we do to make things run a little smoother?"

If you feel so impassioned about your political views that you need to find a polite way to express your feelings, consider writing an op-ed piece for your local newspaper or becoming involved in politics yourself.

Even in business you can effectively complain—and get your point across—without using "you" and "your" in an accusatory fashion. If for instance you have a client who hasn't paid you for work completed, instead of calling and saying, "You jerk—you haven't paid me," you can say, "I'm concerned that sixty days have passed since I submitted my invoice. How can you help me figure out what's going on?" The same applies to dealing with any problems you face with a coworker or supervisor. The key is to come across as willing to work toward a solution and to appear collaborative.

Putting It in Writing

Sometimes you need to put a complaint on paper, especially if you're dealing with a long-running problem or need to prove your case to a manufacturer or company. While avoiding verbal finger pointing is important in this situation, what's especially key is making sure that you document the problem clearly and without emotion.

You need to recap any conversations you may have had with people at the company, and include documentation of the continued problem. This may include dates that you've talked to people about the issue at hand, what you discussed, and whom you spoke with. The more facts you can offer without sounding accusatory, the better. Again, you want to word your letter in such a respectful yet firm way so that the recipient can look past the rhetoric and understand your true message—that you want the problem fixed.

Following Up

There is a difference between being politely persistent about a complaint and harassing someone. If more than a week has gone by and the problem still hasn't been resolved, you should feel confident following up with another phone call, another letter or, if proximity allows it, an in-person visit. However, harassing someone until the problem is fixed will send a negative message and is not the way to go.

In business, sometimes you've got to get the legal system involved when dealing with an unprofessional client, especially one who owes you money. You may think that you can't be a well-behaved businessperson if you have to sue someone, but that's not true. As long as you behave in a professional manner throughout, from filing papers to settling the situation, you'll be the one who will have acted respectfully.

Chapter 7
Dining Out Decorum

Eating out in a restaurant is definitely one of life's little joys. You get a night off from cooking, serving, and cleaning up after the meal. Plus, if you plan things properly, you may also get to sample new cuisine or indulge in an old favorite that you can only get when someone else is doing the cooking.

Even though you're out of the kitchen, you're not off the hook when it comes to good manners. You still need to act respectfully and responsibly when you're eating in a restaurant—perhaps more so than when enjoying a meal at home or entertaining under your own roof.

Behave Yourself

It goes without saying that when you're eating out at a restaurant, you shouldn't slouch in your seat, take your shoes off, or put your feet up on the table. (Can't you just hear Mother Etiquette's voice in your head, asking, "What, were you raised in a barn?"?) Those seem like obvious foibles to avoid when dining out. However, there are other courtesies that you need to keep in mind when dining out.

Reservations, Please

One of the best ways to ensure your part as the gracious diner is to make reservations. Not only does this reduce your stress of wondering if the restaurant will be able to seat you but it also reduces the waitstaff's stress of suddenly having your unexpected and large party show up during a busy time at the restaurant.

Arriving on Time

Once you have your reservations, make sure you show up on time. If you don't think you'll be able to get to the restaurant on time, call ahead. Let them know you're running late, and if you won't be too delayed in your arrival, the restaurant should be able to honor your reservation. If not, remember: it's your fault if you got there late, and you shouldn't expect or demand that the world adjust itself just because you were running behind schedule.

If you want to make sure that you're never late for a restaurant reservation, set your watch ahead five minutes. Or set an alarm on your computer, PDA, or cell phone to help keep you on track time-wise.

When Plans Change

You should also call ahead if your party's size changes, or, if for some reason, you won't be able to honor your reservation after all. It's courteous to let a restaurant know that they can take away a seat or two, because fewer people will be joining you for a meal. Those unoccupied seats can go to other diners.

On the other hand, if your party has grown to a larger size, you must let the restaurant know this well before you arrive. It often takes careful finagling on the restaurant staff's part to accommodate a large party, and if yours just got bigger, you should give them fair warning.

Finally, if you will not be able to make your reservations as planned, you must let the restaurant know. Not only is this the right thing to do, but also if you tend to entertain at this establishment frequently—and don't treat them respectfully by calling ahead to cancel—you may find that the next time you need a reservation, they may not be able (or willing) to accommodate you.

Noises Off

The noise level at hopping eateries can get so loud that you need to shout to your dining companion in order to have a normal conversation. But at more subdued restaurants, you should do your best to keep noise to a necessary minimum. This can be hard to do when you're with a large crowd of people. If you control your own voice level, you might help other people keep their voices down, too. With children, you may need to remind them of this often, but that's much better than disturbing other people who are trying to enjoy their meal. Obviously, a fast food chain will have different protocol from a five-star restaurant, but if you're aware of the atmosphere and act accordingly, the other diners won't notice the difference.

ALERT!

Not every eatery is kid friendly, nor is it always appropriate to bring young ones along for a meal out. If you think your dining choice will be a bad fit for your family, find somewhere else to eat or hire a babysitter.

Keeping your voice down not only shows respect for the other diners, but it also helps you avoid sharing your private conversations with the world. Just because a topic might be relevant or of interest to you doesn't mean other people will want to (or should have to) listen to it. Keep in mind that restaurants usually don't space out tables and booths very far apart from each other, which means everyone's conversation becomes within earshot of other diners.

You should also keep all your technology quiet when dining out. Turn off your cell phones and pagers, or at least switch them to vibrate or lights only. If you do get a call, step outside to have your conversation. People who are trying to enjoy a meal may find it rude to be subjected to your telephone talk.

FACT

A National Restaurant Association survey showed that one-fifth of the nation's fine dining establishments put etiquette first and regulate their patrons' cell phone usage.

Appropriate Attire

Being dressed appropriately when dining out is important. You'd dress differently if you went to a sports bar than you would if you went to a classy steak house. Even though one spot might have numerous televisions broadcasting sports games and scores and the other might have soft music playing in the background with candlelit tables, there are still some basic rules of etiquette that should be acknowledged in both types of restaurants.

You may think you know what the appropriate attire is, but the only way you'll know for sure is when you show up (and discover that you're underdressed) or if you call ahead and ask. When in doubt consult a dining-out guide ahead of time—either a guidebook or your local newspaper's restaurant section—where you'll often find information about proper attire for certain establishments.

Table Manners

Having impeccable table manners is always a good idea—especially when you're dining out with colleagues and clients—but the truth is your table manners should begin the minute you walk into a restaurant.

For starters when the host tells you to follow her to your table, do so. Don't rush ahead to where she's gestured you should sit but instead walk behind her.

And even though we live in an age of women's liberation, men should always allow any females in your party to walk first to your table. Men should always bring up the rear.

Seating Arrangements

Once you've arrived at your table, you should always defer to the meal's host as to where everyone should sit. If you're the host and this happens to be a business lunch, you should direct people where to sit so that you can take a seat that's somewhat in command. If you're dining at a rectangular table, this seat would be at the head of the table. If you're sitting at another shaped table, you should sit in what some called the "gunslinger's seat." This is a centrally located seat that lets you see everyone at your table and the room itself—including the entrance. When you're entertaining clients, you never want to put them in this seat, because the activity of the room could distract them.

Those dining in mixed company should always let the women in the party sit down first. There's no need to pull out a lady's chair for her and then push it in, unless, of course, you're on a date and you want to impress her with your chivalry.

Manners at the Table

Once you take your seat, you'll need to remember another whole set of table manners—that is how to have good manners at the table. For starters, you should look at your menu immediately and decide what you're going to order. Not only will this help get your meal underway in a timely manner, it will also help you avoid delaying the waitstaff by having to ask them to come back again and again.

Ordering Etiquette

When it comes time to order your food, you should let your guests order first. Try to be as polite as you can when telling the waitstaff what you want by saying something like, "May I please start with the salad, and then I'll have the filet mignon? Thank you."

As far as ordering a bottle of wine goes, whomever ordered the wine is the person to whom the waitstaff or sommelier (the wine steward) will bring the bottle. Here's what you can expect to happen:

1. The sommelier will present you with the bottle of wine.
2. Don't take it from him. Instead, you should examine the label to confirm that this is indeed the bottle you ordered.
3. The sommelier will open the bottle and hand you the cork.
4. You should check to see that the innermost end of the cork is moist, which is a sign that the wine is still good and has been properly stored.
5. Once you nod your head at the sommelier, he'll pour a small amount in a glass for you to taste.
6. After you've tasted it, you can give him your approval (by nodding your head) that it's OK to pour wine for the other guests at your table.

If you're not satisfied with the wine, you can send it back during this taste test. That's exactly why restaurants do this—they want to ensure your satisfaction with the wine you've purchased. If you feel that the wine has spoiled, tell the sommelier. He should take it back without argument and offer to bring another bottle to replace it. Then you get to go through this tasting ritual again.

FACT

You should never be charged for an uncorked bottle of wine that you tasted and sent back because you found it to be unsatisfactory. If you notice a charge for that wine on your bill at the end of the evening, you have every right to dispute the charge.

Napkin and Utensil Use

Once you've ordered and the waitstaff has collected your menus, your next move should be to put your napkin in your lap. Do not tuck it into your collar or tie it around your neck, Western style. Napkins belong in the lap, so be sure to remove it from the table when you sit down. It doesn't matter if it's paper or cloth; the same rule applies for both.

Next, start your meal by using the utensils the farthest away from your plate, and then work your way in as you work your way through your courses. If you order an item for which there are no utensils already on the table, such as a soup spoon, your waitstaff will bring it to you before that course arrives. Make sure you use it for your soup only.

You may notice a spoon or fork that's laid out on the top of your plate—those are to be used for dessert and coffee. Your bread plate is to your left, and your drinking glasses are to your right.

ALERT!

You'll find clues about the proper way to use your fork and knife in how your place setting appears. You'll notice that the fork is on the left, so it should be held in your left hand. With your knife on the right, you should hold your knife in your right hand.

Don't let your manners slide once your food arrives. You shouldn't eat until everyone else has his or her food. Always offer to pass the bread, salt, pepper, butter, or other condiments nearest you to your dining companions.

Make sure you chew with your mouth closed, swallow before speaking, and eat at a slow pace. Try to remember to place your utensils down in between bites, and don't forget that napkin in your lap—use it to wipe your mouth if necessary.

Speaking of utensils, you should consider following European etiquette as far as signaling the waitstaff regarding your meal's progress. If you lay your fork and knife point to point (almost like a triangle with no bottom), that says, "I'm still eating." However, if you lay your fork and knife parallel to one another, on the side of the plate, that says, "I'm done, and you can take my plate away."

Treating the Waitstaff

When interacting with the waitstaff, be sure you return their greeting when they seat you or come over to introduce themselves. Initiate eye contact, make note of the person's name, and if you want to go for behavior bonus points, ask him how he's doing today.

Acting the Part of the Polite Patron

It bears repeating that when it comes time to order, you should be as polite as possible. Instead of saying, "I'll take the steak and fries," you might want to say, "May I please have the steak and fries? Thank you." Not only is this a wonderful way to communicate with your waitstaff, but also it sets a wonderful example if there are children present. Be sure to thank your server again once the food arrives and all the plates are on the table.

If you need the check in a hurry, don't wave your arms madly over your head as you try to get your server's attention. Either tell him as soon as you sit down that he should bring the check when he brings the food, or politely ask another server to send your waitperson over as soon as possible. Then when he gets there, ask for the check.

Excusing Yourself

There may be times during your meal when you need to excuse yourself. It could be to use the bathroom or because you sense that you've got a rather large piece of spinach stuck in your teeth. If it's the latter scenario, it's a good thing that you're getting up—you should never fish stray food out of your teeth in front of your fellow diners.

Simply announce to your table that you'd like to excuse yourself to go use the restroom, place your napkin on your chair, which signals to the waitstaff that you'll be right back, and then push your chair in. If the person with whom you're dining is getting up, you may want to stand up as the person exits the table. This is especially true for men when a female companion gets up to leave the table.

Tips on Tipping

Unless you've ever waited on tables, you may not realize how important a tip or gratuity is to a waitperson. The gratuity can sometimes make the difference between a good week at work and a bad week at work for a waiter or waitress.

An easy way to figure out a 20 percent tip is to look at the bill's total before tax, and double the first two digits for the tip total. If the first two digits are to the left of the decimal point, move the decimal point one space to the left for your tip amount.

Traditionally, people tip 18 percent in restaurants, and some establishments will automatically add on that tip for larger parties (such as six people or more at one table). Be sure to look over your check before bending your brain to figure out the tip—it may already be on there.

If you'd like to make the math easier on yourself and a make a waitperson's day, get in the habit of tipping 20 percent. You probably won't miss the little bit of extra money, and if you're a regular in an establishment, your reputation as a good tipper will help ensure good dining experiences in the future.

How to Handle Bad Service

First and foremost, do not start arguing with your server. If the kitchen is running behind or got your order wrong, and your waitress offered no apologies or didn't do anything to rectify the situation, she's in the wrong, but telling her that won't do you any good.

FACT

Nearly three-quarters of all restaurant-related complaints are about bad service (as opposed to bad food or crummy conditions).

Seek out a manager. Only a manager can adjust your bill or offer you a complimentary meal in the future to make up for things that went wrong today.

Also, keep in mind that even bad waitresses need to make a living. Even though you may be tempted to make your point by stiffing the waitress on her tip, don't stoop to that level. Instead, grab your calculator (most cell phones or PDAs have one on them), and figure out the 15 percent tip to the nearest penny.

Ethnic Restaurant Idiosyncrasies

In today's melting pot world, there are restaurants that serve food that's representative of nearly every country on the planet. It's exciting to expand your palette by trying different foods, but when you go to a restaurant whose culture is not your own, you need to tread lightly and carefully, lest you offend the restaurant owner, the waitstaff, or those around you.

For example, if you dine in an eatery where they require you to perform some kind of pre-meal ritual, such as taking off your shoes or washing your hands in a certain way, do it. Similarly, if there are specific rules about seating (on the floor or separated by sexes), do your best to follow along with the house rules.

Foreign Utensils

It's customary for you to have chopsticks in a Chinese, Japanese, or Korean restaurant, and if you feel comfortable using them, then by all means dig in. However, if you'll spend most of your meal fumbling with the chopsticks, quietly ask your server if she can bring you some traditional utensils. Most restaurants that cater to Westerners should have a couple of forks, knives, and spoons on hand.

While using chopsticks is an option in Asian restaurants, when you eat in establishments that have their roots in certain religions, you should always eat with your right hand—not both hands. Some religions see the left hand as the hand of the devil; others believe that your left hand should be used for washing yourself or keeping yourself clean after using the bathroom. This makes the left hand unclean, and you may risk insulting someone if you use both your right and your left hand to eat.

When in doubt, it doesn't hurt to ask. So if you visit a Middle Eastern restaurant where there's a chance the proprietor or waitstaff finds left-handed eating offensive, ask about this first.

ALERT!

Eating out is supposed to be a pleasurable experience. If you find yourself in an ethnic restaurant whose rules and regulations make your feel uncomfortable, then there's no reason to stay for a meal. Don't let your fear of being impolite put you in an uncomfortable situation.

Check, Please

Taking someone out to eat is a wonderful way to say thank you for a favor done or congratulations on a job well done.

If you know you'd like to treat someone to a restaurant meal, you can word your invitation to state your intentions. You can say something like, "I'd like to treat you for lunch at Joe's Crab House as a thank you for watching my kids last week." That should give your guest a pretty strong hint that she shouldn't go for the bill at the end of the meal. Of course, a great way to ensure that there's no confusion when the check comes is to fix the problem before it occurs. When you arrive, take the server aside and say, "I'm going to pay for the meal so please hand the check to me."

Good intentions will only get you so far if you end up arriving at the restaurant without sufficient cash to pay the bill or a credit card to cover the costs. Always plan ahead to go to the ATM, if necessary, so you can avoid sticking your guest with the bill.

Chapter 8

Dating Demeanor

Y ou can probably remember your first date, and it probably seemed like the most natural thing to do. And whether you eventually got married or kept on dating, chances are you didn't go for very long without having someone special in your life. However, despite the almost instinctual nature of people to seek out one another, there are certain things that may not seem as natural, such as knowing when to call, meeting someone's parents, or knowing how to act on a date.

Pleased to Make Your Acquaintance

There is no tried and true way or place to meet someone who you might be interested in dating. But if you talk to people who are in committed relationships or are happily married, you'll likely see a trend in how people met. It usually occurred through some shared interest (a hobby, membership organization or club they both belong to, etc.), a job, or a mutual acquaintance. Of course, there are exceptions to those rules, such as the couple who bumped into each other on the street and fell madly in love, or the couple who met in a bar and have been inseparable ever since.

Meeting New People

One of the best ways to find someone you're interested in dating is to put yourself out there. That means getting involved in some social activities or just doing more than sitting around your home, waiting for the phone to ring. Next, just be yourself. Someone who is interested in dating you is going to like you for who you are.

If you find it difficult to meet new people, ask for help from your friends and family. Many people enjoy setting someone up or trying to play matchmaker, and it's perfectly all right to ask someone to be on the lookout for a good match for you.

ALERT!

While friends and family may enjoy responding to your request to be set up on a date, you should never play matchmaker without someone's permission. Just because you've found someone that you think is perfect for a person, that doesn't mean that the other person is ready to date or is even interested in being set up.

Once you've met someone you're interested in, keep in mind that it's never good manners (or a good idea) to appear desperate, or to put on airs with others as a way of impressing him or her, because then you're not being genuine to that other person. A dating situation will evolve naturally when two people become attracted to each other or enjoy each other's company.

There isn't much else you can do to force things along, except to be patient and give it time.

List of Introductions

However clichéd they may seem, there are some tried and true "introductions" that help men and women meet one another, which is a nice way of saying that the following pick-up lines have been around so long because they tend to work. All of them, by the way, are perfectly polite to use:

"Have you got a light?"
"Is this seat taken?"
"May I buy you a drink?"
"Lovely weather we're having, isn't it?"
"How about those Red Sox?" (or whichever your favorite sports team is)

Asking these kinds of questions of someone you meet in a bar or on a bus can become your dating litmus test: how the person responds will tell you whether or not he or she is interested in you.

Asking Someone Out

It's a wonderful feeling when you meet someone with whom you'd like to spend more time, and one of the most natural next moves in a situation like this would be to ask that person out on a date. Thankfully, these days a woman doesn't need to wait for a man to ask her out, and men don't have to feel all the pressure of making that first move. It is perfectly acceptable for either of you to initiate that first date.

While modern roles may have changed, the way to ask someone out hasn't. Sure, it may be easier to send an e-mail or an instant message to the person you like, but you really ought to ask the person out in person or over the phone. This simply shows sincerity on your part, and the other person is bound to be impressed.

The best way to ask someone out is to be as specific as possible. Instead of asking, "What are you doing on Saturday night?" you should ask, "Would you like to go to the movies with me on Saturday night?" Asking the generic question seems, well, generic and may not impart your desire to take this person out on a date. For all he or she knows, you're simply making small talk. However, when you get specific, then your intentions are clear. If you're the person being asked out, it's best if you respond as directly and specifically as possible. If you're interested in this person and you have plans, don't say, "Let me think about it." This kind of answer may make the other person think you don't want to go out on a date. Instead, say, "I'm afraid I'm busy, but I'd love to see you another time," which clearly tells the other person that you do want to have a date, just not on that specific day.

Declining a Date

What do you do if you're not attracted to the person asking you out or you don't want to accept a date? Again, be as specific as possible. Saying, "Um, I'm busy that night," will only leave the door open for the person to ask you out again. A much better answer would be one that tells the person that you don't want to date him, but without being cruel: "Thank you for asking, but I'm dating someone else," or "Thank you for asking, but I'm taking a hiatus from dating right now."

Same-Sex Situations

Heterosexuals aren't the only folks who need dating advice. Those pursuing same-sex relationships may fall prey to social faux pas as well. This is especially true if you're interested in someone and not only aren't you sure if this person is single but you're also unsure whether he or she is gay or lesbian. The truth is unless you've met someone in a strictly gay environment, such as through a mutual friend, at a gay pride parade or in a bar that caters to same-sex couples, you may run the risk of asking someone out who isn't interested in a same-sex relationship.

So where do you start? In the same place where anyone looking to ask someone out would: by being direct with your question. If you meet a man or woman you're interested in, you can ask straight out, "Are you seeing anyone?" If the person answers, "No," then you can proceed with, "Would you like to go on a date with me?" Using the word "date" will help you determine upfront whether or not this person is interested in having a same-sex relationship.

If you're on the receiving end of a gay or lesbian date invitation—and you're neither gay nor lesbian—there's no reason to get indignant. A simple, "No thank you, I'm straight," will suffice in getting your message across.

Coming Out

If you haven't been truthful about your sexual orientation, then you may find yourself in a bit of a bind when you decide to ask someone of the same sex out on a date and you're not "out" with your friends or family yet. Sooner or later you're going to have to tell them the truth about who you are—and whom you prefer to date.

Obviously, this is a profound and emotional decision for a person to make—to declare his or her true self to the world—and when you communicate the news to people you love, care about, or work with, you need to do so in person and in a delicate fashion. You can get right to the point by saying something like, "You may have been wondering why I'm still single after all of these years," or "I have something important to tell you that I've been dying to get off my chest all of these years." Then you can say, "I'm gay," or "I'm a lesbian." It may seem uncomfortable to be so direct with this information but there's no reason to sugarcoat it.

Those who truly care about who you are as a person (not whom you date) will likely just shrug this information off or say something like, "That's OK." This is not to belittle what you've just told them but rather to let you know that it doesn't change how they feel about you. Others may not know what to do with the news or how to react to it, but the bottom line is this: you were honest and straightforward with them, and you did the right thing. How they react to your news is their problem, not yours.

First Dates

You're going on a first date with someone, and if you're like most people, you've probably got butterflies in your stomach. But before you let your nerves get the best of you, keep this in mind: If you're the person who did the asking out, then it's up to you not only to make all of the plans but also to pick up the tab.

There is no right or wrong "thing" to do on a first date. If the two of you met through a mutual hobby, you can find a way to work that hobby into your first date. If you're both food lovers, going to dinner at a restaurant would be a great way to spend time together.

It's sort of an unwritten rule that the person who initiated the date should make the plans for the date, but if you don't feel comfortable having all the control over your plans, it's fine to poll your date about what he or she would like to do. However, if you get a response that the person doesn't care or would like to leave it up to you, then by all means plan away.

While you may want to impress your date, you don't want to overwhelm him or her the first time you go out. Don't go over the top with any of your plans, and don't spend money wildly your first time out. Your intentions may be good, but your extravagance may have the opposite effect.

Sometimes it's best to have a first date on a weeknight. This option gives you an automatic ending time, since you'll both need to get up for work, school, or other commitments the next day. Of course, if you really like each other, you can always make plans to see each other again the next night or that coming weekend. However, not everyone works a nine to five schedule, so the weeknight rule doesn't always apply. Here are some considerations to keep in mind as you make plans for your date:

What are your respective work schedules? Might having a breakfast date make the most sense for you?

Do you have a mutual hobby that you can pursue together on your first date?

What's your financial situation? Do you need to plan something that won't cost a lot of money yet will still be fun?

How will each of you arrive at your first date? Do you need to make plans to pick your date up and take him or her home?

As mentioned earlier, it's never bad etiquette to run a date idea by someone before making plans. That way if any of the above considerations give you pause, you can always ask your intended date for his or her opinion and make your plans accordingly.

When picking someone up for a date, do not announce your arrival by honking the horn or calling your date from your cell phone. Show your consideration and get out of your car to meet your date at his or her door.

Picking Up Your Date

If you're the one who asked the person out, you should be the one to pick him or her up. Unless you and your date agree on other arrangements, you should pick him or her up or meet at a location that's convenient . You can either pick him or her up at home or at the office.

If the pick-up place is her home, then you should really do the right thing and meet any of the people she lives with—whether it's her parents or her roommates. This gives them the chance to check you out and may help her feel more comfortable because she's able to have the people she trusts and loves around before she goes out on a first date with you.

If you're the parent and your child is about to have her first date, then you should insist that the person taking her out pick her up at home. If they've decided to meet somewhere, such as at the mall or the movies, then it is your duty to make sure that you meet the lady or gentleman that your child is going out with, introduce yourself, shake hands, and state any clear boundaries about the date's duration or when you expect your child home.

Saying Goodnight

At the end of the night, you should always make sure that your date gets home safely, whether you drive that person home, share a cab, or walk him or her to the door. This is a must, even if you are not the person who initiated the date, the night didn't go well, or you have no intentions of going out on another date.

QUESTION?

How do I impress someone on a first date?
Use chivalry whenever possible. You can hold the door open, or you can open the car door when you get to your destination. When it comes to dating demeanor, chivalry never goes out of style.

Now what if things did go well and you're getting ready to say goodnight? There's nothing wrong with a kiss to say goodnight and then ending the evening. But what do you do if you want more than a kiss?

You've probably heard the line, "Would you like to come upstairs for a nightcap?" in movies or on television. Or perhaps you've even used it yourself in the past. This can be a catchall phrase to see if your date is interested in getting intimate with you on that first date, or it could be a completely platonic request to continue your conversation only.

If you would like to spend more time with this person but tonight's not a good night, ask for a rain check and mention a night that works for you. By giving the person a specific response, you're letting him know that you are interested in seeing him and that you're willing to commit to a second date on the spot.

ESSENTIAL

What do you do if your dating experience is dead in the water? Shake the person's hand when saying goodnight and offer something like this: "It was a lovely evening, but I think it would be best if we just remained friends."

Second Dates

The best time for you to bring up the subject of a second date is at the end of the first date. This helps you to avoid the whole "I'll call you" scenario, even if you have every intention of phoning that person the next day. That phrase leaves too many people hanging on, and to be a delightful date, you should never leave someone wondering, "How does he really feel about me?"

Instead, if you'd like to see that person again, bring up when you'd like to have that second date. You can firm up your plans with a phone call the next day or sometime soon, but don't end the night without something concrete in place: "Let me call you on Friday once I know my plans for the weekend" will be much more satisfying than your saying, "Let's talk at some point over the weekend."

ALERT!

Thanking someone after a date is always appropriate, especially if you really like that person and want to see him or her again. But unlike gift-giving occasions, you can get away with a phoned-in thank you to let the other person know how much fun you had on your date.

Going Steady

The term going steady is really a throwback to years gone by, but everyone understands what it means: when you go steady, you've committed to a monogamous relationship with another person. You usually can't expect some big pronouncement of your decision to go steady—unlike when you get engaged—but sometimes there are clear clues that, in fact, you have crossed this threshold in dating. These clues include when the other person refers to you as the "boyfriend" or "girlfriend" or when you're invited to share holidays and family gatherings at the other person's home—or you invite the person to yours.

Age Appropriateness

There is nothing wrong with two people deciding that they want to date each other exclusively, and if you're facing this reality with your teenager, you should handle the news as calmly as possible. You should also think of ways to welcome your child's boyfriend or girlfriend into your lives, not only because it's the right thing to do but also because then you can keep an eye on how the relationship is developing.

Timeline

You may know after your first date that you want to date this person exclusively, if not spend the rest of your life with him or her. Or it may take a few months before you decide that you're ready for a monogamous relationship with this person. Whatever timeline you set for yourself, make sure that you and the other person are on the same page when discussing how and when you're going to take your relationship to the next level. If you find yourself facing holidays and families—and neither of you wants to be apart when visiting the family—then now is the perfect time for the two of you to bring up the notion of how serious your relationship has become or what path it might be taking. You can bring this topic up for discussion the next time you're together, face to face, by saying something about how you would really like to be able to spend the holidays together and now might be a good time to decide if you're both interested in dating each other exclusively. This should be a mutual discussion, and there should be mutual agreement about how serious your relationship may become in the near future.

Picking Up the Tab

Once you've decided to go steady, you may find yourself at a crossroads about who pays for what. It's unfair for one person in the relationship to be constantly picking up the tab, but it may also feel weird for the two of you to split the bill.

The best way to deal with this situation is to figure out ahead of time how you want to handle things when you buy movie tickets, pay for meals, or take vacations together. You could alternate payment responsibility, or if one of you earns significantly more than the other, you may decide that it's best for the higher earner to pay for the lion's share of activities. Overall, it's best not to assume anything when it comes to money and your relationship. By talking things out you're sure to avoid any uncomfortable financial situations in the future.

Public Displays of Affection

Can you remember back to high school when couples that were going steady would walk each other to class, then "swap spit" or play "tonsil hockey" before saying goodbye to each other at their next class? If you were on the outside looking in, it was probably pretty gross. And even today it still is—especially when it's the grown ups who are doing the spit swapping.

No matter how much in love you two are with each other, you should try to keep your public displays of affection (PDAs) to a minimum. That means, hand holding, putting your arms around each other, a quick hug or swift kiss are all OK in public—and this is a lesson you should share with any teenage children you have who have started to date. However, once you start doing anything that could easily be done in a bedroom, such as groping or deep kissing, then you've crossed into disrespectful territory, and you need to stop.

Dealing with Public Displays of Affection

Probably the only time that people aren't going to notice or be offended by outright public displays of affection is at a fraternity party, where everyone has a little bit too much to drink. But let's assume that you're neither planning such an alcohol-soaked event nor are you a member of a fraternity, but you are hosting a get together at your home. Even if you and your significant other are feeling particularly amorous on the night of your soiree, you need to keep your hands to yourselves. It's OK to give each other a peck on the cheek or a hug from time to time, but you don't want to practice your tonsil hockey with guests around.

Now what if your guests are acting less discreet about their feelings of affection? Well, you really can't go up to them and say, "Get a room." But you can pull one of them aside (after they've finished necking) and say something like, "It really makes me uncomfortable when people show affection in public like you guys were. Would you mind toning it down a bit?" They might react with an embarrassed apology or they might get really angry with you and leave. Either way, you'll have achieved your goal of stopping the PDA on your couch. And maybe next time you're planning a party, you'll think twice about inviting the couple that can't keep their hands off each other.

Appropriateness of Certain PDAs

Embarrassing guests aside, here's a good primer to keep in mind when dealing with or considering participating in PDAs:

Hugging. Women and men may briefly hug each other when greeting or parting.

Two-cheek kissing. Customarily a European tradition it's fine to give a man or a woman a kiss on both cheeks when saying hello or goodbye.

Casual kissing. A simple quick kiss on the cheek is just fine to do. However, you may want to limit casual kisses on the mouth to relatives only.

Hand holding. Perhaps the most innocuous of PDAs, and always appropriate.

Parents kissing children in front of other children. It's always OK for a parent to kiss a child but starting at around age ten, your child may shun this practice or dodge your kisses, due to sheer embarrassment.

Are people always saying to the two of you, "Hey, get a room"? Well, then you know that your PDAs have gone too far and you need to work hard to keep your public affections in check.

Breaking Up Is Hard to Do

Sometimes, despite your best intentions, you need to end a relationship with someone. Breaking up is never easy to do, but if your heart is no longer into being with this person, good manners should guide you into not stringing him or her along when all you want is to be single again.

What are some of the signs that it's time to say goodbye—or that you're about to be dumped?

You no longer get butterflies when that person calls you.

You're avoiding each other's phone calls.

You're tempted to cancel standing dates—or someone does this to you regularly.

You're not having fun.

You suspect he's dating someone else, or you're interested in dating others.

Like with so many other things related to etiquette, the best way to break up with someone isn't to disappear on them but rather for you to communicate. Tell this person why you're no longer interested in dating him, but don't go into such detail that you end up destroying his self-esteem and hurting his feelings. If you need to stretch the truth a bit, you can do so for feelings' sake. Here's a suggested step-by-step scenario for you to consider:

1. Try to meet the person face to face. Just as you don't want to ask someone out on e-mail, you shouldn't let technology do the breaking up either.
2. Start by saying something positive, such as, "It's been really funny hanging out with you these last few weeks."
3. Get right to the news. What naturally follows the phrase above would be a statement starting with, "But": "But I think it would be best if we didn't see each other anymore."
4. If you feel it's necessary, you can apologize to the person for hurting her feelings.
5. You may want to offer your hand to shake, and then say something like, "I wish you the very best."

That's a very direct way to break up with someone that gets the point across clearly and succinctly. But just because it's efficient doesn't mean it's going to be easy. You may want to practice ahead of time by rehearsing what you're going to say. This may give you the confidence you need to break the bad news to this person in the most polite way possible.

Sometimes the other person doesn't want to hear the truth—that you don't want to date anymore—but you've got to stick firm to your decision. Don't let anyone talk you into to doing something you don't want to do, such as continuing to date.

Don't attempt to let the person down so easily that you send mixed messages. Saying, "I just want to be friends" seems to imply that you still want to hang out. If you do, then that's the perfect thing to say. But if this person is driving you crazy and you want him out of your life, the "just friends" line won't work. You've got to say something more concrete, like, "I think it would be best if we didn't see each other any more."

Nursing Hurt Feelings

If you're the person who just got dumped, the news is bound to sting. No one wants to hear that they're no longer attractive to the person they used to date, and even if secretly you wanted the relationship to end, you still need time to recover. The same goes for a child who's just ended a relationship—you need to give them time to recover, too.

The first thing you need to do is accept that you're upset but don't act on your hurt feelings. Don't take your anger or hurt out on other people, especially those in your family, and don't concoct ways to exact revenge on your former mate.

You have to accept that it may take you some time to get over this break up. Don't use someone as a rebound person whom you can date willy-nilly to make yourself feel better. Eventually, you will move on and find someone else to share your days and nights with.

Chapter 9

(E) **How to Behave While Doing Business**

When you were in school, you probably learned about the appropriate ways to behave in the classroom and on the playground. You knew that it was polite to raise your hand when you wanted to add something to a classroom discussion, that you needed to wait your turn for the water fountain or in line at the cafeteria, and if you wanted to make and keep friends, you needed to be a kind person to others.

Unfortunately, too many people forget these simple rules for succeeding in school once they enter the real world—and they get a job. But there is still a need for certain manners in the office, the conference room or at a business lunch or dinner. Why else would manners classes for employees be such hot commodities these days? Ask any etiquette instructor about good behavior, and she'll tell you that it's the key to succeeding in business, which is why professionals often need a brush-up lesson on how to behave while doing business.

Cubicle Culture

Thanks to the dot-com explosion of the 1990s, office walls came tumbling down. If you work in an office, you probably do your daily business in a giant room, with only temporary walls between you. The idea behind the openness was that employees could enjoy the flow of ideas without any barriers (i.e., walls to block them).

While cubicles (or cubes as they're known colloquially) may enhance the sharing of ideas, they don't do much for manners. Too many people continue to behave at their desk as if they were in a private office.

Everyone Eavesdrops

Unless your employer has installed soundproofing materials in every cube, chances are that when your cube mate or next-door cube neighbor makes or receives a call, you can hear the whole thing. That also means that he or she hears everything that you say when you're on the phone with your boss, your client, or your mother. The same thing applies for any impromptu meetings behind cube walls—there is no door or no ceiling to stop sounds from traveling far and near; anyone sitting close to you or passing by is likely to overhear your conversations.

Just because you can hear what is going on in the next cube doesn't mean you have license to comment on a seemingly private conversation or use any information that you overhear to the detriment of others. If a cube mate of yours doesn't explain the details of a phone call to you, it's best for you to behave as if you didn't hear it. You wouldn't want someone commenting on a difficult call to a client or an emotional phone call to a relative if it were you. Show others the same respect.

Courteous Cubicle Conduct

Because noise does travel so well in open-air offices, you need to work hard at making sure that your everyday way of doing business isn't distracting or bothersome to others. Keep your voice down when talking with others in person or on the phone, and don't play loud music in your cube.

Another consideration to keep in mind is how neat or messy your cube is. Because people can see right into your work space, it would be polite to keep your cube as clean as possible at all times. Having a tidy area will reflect well on you with your bosses and your coworkers, and they'll appreciate that you made the extra effort to keep your space looking neat. Aside from keeping papers, notepads, and folders organized, remember to do the same with food. Don't leave leftover food lying around; it may not only look sloppy but it could potentially smell. Find an out-of-the-way place to store snacks and drinks.

ALERT!

When doing someone a favor and delivering a fax to their desk, don't read it in the process. It's none of your business.

Shared Technology

Unless you're self-employed or have an office all to yourself, chances are you have to share equipment like fax machines, printers, and copiers, with your colleagues.

You don't have to be a messenger for everyone else in the office, but if you happen to be sending a fax and one comes in for your cube mate, be polite and bring it to her. The same thing applies with the communal printer.

Now if there are five or six faxes or print jobs waiting to be picked up, you shouldn't stop your workday and bring them to everyone you know. However, if you happen to pass a fax recipient in the hallway or bump into her soon thereafter in the ladies room, it would be nice to tell her you saw a fax come in for her.

If the printer or copier runs out of paper when you finish using it, spend a few seconds putting a new ream of paper into the machine. It's a common courtesy you'd hope your fellow employees would do for you.

When using any communal equipment, never cut in front of someone in line or stop their job without their knowledge because you need to get something done fast. Either find another printer or fax machine somewhere else in the office, or ask the person in front of you if you could slip in to get your rush job done.

The Communal Kitchen

The best way to be a well-behaved colleague when it comes to shared kitchen equipment is to do what your mother told you and always clean up after yourself. That means wiping down the inside of the microwave if your reheated lunch splattered around when it was cooking. Then, after you're done with your meal, place your used dishes in the dishwasher (if there is one) or wash them by hand so they don't sit around in the sink. Did you happen to take the last cup of coffee from the coffee maker? If so, then you should start a fresh pot. Your colleagues are sure to appreciate your courtesy.

FACT

Take Our Daughters and Sons to Work Day is always the fourth Thursday of April, and if your company participates, then you should feel free to bring a child to work with you. However, if your day care falls through, you would be wise to ask first before bringing your child to work on any other day.

E-mail Issues

Most computers allow you to program a music setting or tone to let you know when you've got mail or when someone is instant messaging you. It's great to get this notification, but if you're working in close quarters with other people, you should keep the volume level to a minimum to not distract others.

Another issue to consider with e-mail is the personal use of it. If you must send e-mail during the day to friends or family members, figure out a way to access your home account or a free, third-party account through the Internet and then save those e-mails for sending during breaks or lunch hours.

You should also keep e-mail forwards to a minimum, especially when they involve jokes that your colleagues might not appreciate (even if you thought they were funny), urban legends, or political statements. Work is not the appropriate setting for sharing these kinds of e-communiqués.

Dealing with Dress Codes

Along with the cubicle phenomenon of the dot-com era came another office first—the notion of business casual dress. Suddenly, suits and ties were out, and polo shirts and khaki pants were in. You may work in a place where business casual is still all the rage, but it's always wise to err on the conservative side, lest you risk making a bad impression on someone.

If you're starting a new job, you should ask well in advance of your first day what the company's dress code is. If it's business casual, have human resources qualify that for you. In some offices business casual is the attire described above. In others it's still dark suits, just without the ties, for men, and conservative pant suits for women.

Even if you work in an environment that's pretty casual all around, here is a list of some articles of clothing you should avoid wearing to work at all costs:

Tank tops (both men and women)
Shorts of any kind
Blue jeans with any signs of wear and tear
Sneakers
Flip-flops or casual sandals

Another dress code consideration has to do with body art—namely tattoos and piercings. If you have any visible ones, you may want to ask if you need to cover them or remove them before going to work.

Appointments and Meetings

Meetings and doing business go hand in hand these days. These meetings could be in person, over the phone, or through the computer. If you're in charge of making appointments for meetings or calling meetings to order, you need to keep some rules of consideration in mind.

Meeting Manners

First, you should always make sure that you don't schedule an appointment with others without first checking their availability. If you need others to be at a meeting, you need to give them plenty of notice, whenever possible.

Next, you should always call or e-mail to confirm a meeting. If you have an agenda for the meeting (always a good idea), you can send it ahead of time so people know how or what they need to prepare for this meeting.

Finally, you need to make sure that you not only keep that appointment as scheduled but also that you show up on time. There's nothing that's worse for business—and a business reputation—than someone who is late to a meeting or cancels an appointment but doesn't call ahead to let you know that he won't be able to make it.

While you're in the meeting, always be on your best behavior. Don't interrupt others while they're talking, and always hear people out. If you don't agree with something someone has said, make a note to yourself but don't roll your eyes or make a disapproving noise.

If you're the person running the meeting, start it on time and keep it moving at a steady pace. It's your job to keep everyone on task and not to let the meeting get off topic. Your colleagues will thank you for being respectful of their time if you can accomplish what needs to get done in this meeting in the shortest time possible.

How to Handle Business Meals

You know that everyone's got to eat at some point during the work day, and it's no surprise that there's often business to be done over a meal. As with dating, the person who has invited others to join him for a meal should be the person who picks up the tab. This is a must when entertaining a client, unless, of course, the client's employer forbids him from receiving "free" meals (as is often the case with the media). In this instance don't argue with him over the bill, and let him pay.

If you're an underling who is out to eat with your boss, don't try to impress anyone by going for the check. Nor should you do this if your lunch meeting has a dual purpose as a job interview. People will see you as pushy and possibly as trying to buy your way to the top if you pick up the tab. If you've invited your boss out for a meal as a thank-you or as a gift, then obviously you should pay. But in all other cases, let those who outrank you pay.

Entertaining After Hours

Many business deals get made in places other than the office. This could be on the golf course, over dinner and drinks, or during a Broadway show. If your line of work requires you to entertain as part of doing business, you should keep the following guidelines in mind:

Keep alcohol consumption to a minimum.
Dress appropriately, meaning nothing too revealing.
Don't walk a client home or let him walk you home.
Never take a client to an inappropriate setting, such as a strip club.

One of the best ways to ensure that your client sees entertaining in a positive light is to make sure you follow up with a thank-you afterward. If you're the one who did the entertaining, you can give a quick call to thank your client for joining you the previous night. If you're the one who was being wooed, then you should send a handwritten note as soon as possible to the person who took you out.

ESSENTIAL

Once you reach a certain level in business, entertaining clients becomes par for the course. However, if you've never learned how to properly hold a fork and a knife or wouldn't know a soup tureen from a salad bowl, now might be a good time to sign up for an entertaining etiquette class.

Solicitations and Gifts

You'll notice that many companies have a "no solicitations" sign outside their door or office building. This is a clear sign that they are not interested in receiving any unsolicited information from businesses that tend to distribute fliers and menus as a way of marketing themselves.

FACT

Instead of risking your employment by soliciting your staff, make a donation to the good cause and then ask that your employer match it. Many companies offer a matching-donation policy for any fundraising efforts you want to support.

Once you walk into the company where you work, however, you may notice a very different culture. That is, despite the "no solicitations" sign outside, plenty of employees do solicit their colleagues for donations inside the office walls.

Fundraising Faux Pas

If you're in a situation where someone is asking you to donate money to a cause or you need to solicit donations, make a pit stop to human resources to find out what the company's policy is on such activity. Many companies encourage their employees to give back to good causes, which may include fundraising activities. However, even though they like their employees to participate in charitable work, your employer may not want you to do so on company time or on the premises.

For example, many corporations support organizations like the United Way through employee giving programs. If your boss asks you to head up this program or another employee approaches you about this kind of employer-sponsored program, then you won't be committing a fundraising faux pas by participating.

While company-sponsored fundraising may be acceptable, solicitations for personal charities or good causes not related to your employer may set off etiquette alarms as far as proper behavior goes. You may be one of those parents who always help your child sell Girl Scout cookies by bringing them to the office. Unless you know that cookie sales, for example, are an approved activity to pursue during work hours or on the premises, don't risk your job just to help your child reach a higher level of fundraising sales.

Gifts to Colleagues

A good boss always remembers her employees' birthdays, and if you want to make a good impression on your underlings or colleagues, you would be wise to send birthday greetings on the appropriate day. Same thing goes for holidays—it's always a good idea to celebrate the year's gift giving holidays (Christmas and Chanukah, for example) by giving a little something to those who work for you, who have had a positive impact on your work experience in the past year, or clients that you hope to continue working with in the near future.

Some companies have rules on how much you can spend on gifts to each other, and you should check first to see if you are subject to any price constraints. Beyond spending too much, the other issue you need to keep in mind is the appropriateness of gifts. Don't give a bottle of wine if having alcohol on the premises is forbidden, and never give a gift that could be misconstrued. This might be a gift that seems overtly personal, such as underwear, or perhaps risqué, like a DVD of a movie with strong sexual content.

In-Office Celebrations

If your employer holds an annual holiday party, then by all means use that celebration as the time when you share gifts with your colleagues. Beyond an employer-sanctioned celebration, you need to be careful about having other kinds of in-office celebrations.

Sharing cake in the conference room for someone's birthday is fine, but booking the conference room for a baby shower, complete with gifts, or a bridal shower, complete with a male stripper, will likely cross the lines of courteous behavior. If you're so set on celebrating someone's special occasion, have it off premises and not during work hours. Should you try to squeeze the celebration into a lunch hour and it runs long or people imbibe too much, all that is going to cast a pall on your work reputation. Besides, that kind of behavior during business hours simply is unacceptable.

Politely Going for Promotions

Anyone who has ever climbed the corporate ladder has had to go up for a promotion at some time. There's nothing wrong with wanting to advance your career, just as long as you do so without harming others in the process.

E ALERT! Never go for a promotion to spite your boss or another employee. You may just end up getting the job and being miserable in the end, which won't be very gracious of you.

One of the most important things to remember when vying for a promotion is that someone, somewhere is going to have her feelings hurt. Whether it is you, because you didn't get the promotion, or a colleague, because you got the job, you can't avoid hurt feelings.

If you know someone is upset because you got the job he wanted, you can take the high road and write that person a note. You can say something like, "You were good competition to go up against for this manager's position, and you should be proud of the work you've done. I hope we'll continue to be able to work on projects together in the near future."

Just because you've reached out to this person doesn't mean that he's going to like hearing from you. You may find that he avoids you in the hall, doesn't answer your e-mails or phone calls, or partakes of some other rude, avoidance behavior. This is definitely not the way to behave in a professional situation, and if you ever find yourself on the losing end of a promotion, do not stoop to this level.

Sexual Harassment

When you work in an office, you've got to tread lightly when it comes to sexual harassment. In this day and age of politically correct conduct, sometimes even harmless flirting (which years ago wouldn't raise an eyebrow) now raises red flags.

It is never polite to make unwanted advances on another person. The United States Equal Employment Opportunity Commission (EEOC) defines sexual harassment as more than just unwanted advances. It could be a request for sexual favors, threatening to fire or demote you if you don't do as the harasser asks, or speaking in an overtly sexual way.

You could be the victim of sexual harassment just by overhearing one employee speaking sexually to another. That person doesn't have to direct his action directly toward you for it to affect you. If you overhear disturbing behavior and it upsets you, then you've been sexually harassed.

The best way to deal with someone harassing you is to first tell him or her that you don't appreciate his or her conduct and that you don't welcome his or her advances. If a verbal warning doesn't do the trick, go to a supervisor (unless, of course, your supervisor is the guilty party). Human resources should be your next step. Since most employers have plans of action in place for sexual harassment, which is considered a form of sexual discrimination, human resources should be able to help you put a stop to this behavior and, if necessary, punish the harasser.

FACT

Both men and women can be the victims of sexual harassment. Women don't have carte blanche to speak to men at work however they feel. Not only would doing so be in bad taste but it could land you in legal trouble, too.

Culture Class

One of the realities of today's business world is the fact that not everyone in a single office shares the same culture. You may work with people from ten different countries, each of them having a different religion or set of customs. Even American-born folks can vary greatly in their customs and beliefs, just based on where in the country they were raised or in which religion.

You need to keep these cultural differences in mind as you make your way through the business world. This is especially important if you're dealing with colleagues who don't speak English as their native language and may not understand all the nuances that English-speakers take for granted, such as the use of "um" and "you know," or making jokes to get a point across.

When it comes to cultural clashes at the office, it's best to err on the side of caution. Do some research to better understand a colleague's culture.

Dealing with Different Holidays

Other people's holidays and religious observances are another issue to consider. For example, observant Jews are likely to leave the office early on Friday nights (the start of the Sabbath) when they're required to be at worship by sundown. If someone you work with fits this bill, you'd be impolite to schedule an important team meeting late on a Friday afternoon.

Similarly, Muslims celebrate Ramadan, which involves a month of daytime fasting. (They eat small meals after dark.) If someone in your office celebrates Ramadan, don't invite him to a lunch meeting or eat in front of him without first checking to see that he's OK with being exposed to food when he's fasting.

Assistants

Talk to anyone who has ever worked in an office, and they'll tell you this: while the boss may be in power, it's often the assistant who runs the show. That's why when you have to deal with someone's secretary (even your own), you need to know how to proceed. Here are some suggestions:

- If you're mad at your boss, never take it out on his or her assistant. Not only is this rude and unfair but it could get you blacklisted from ever getting a timely appointment with your boss again in the future.
- Always refer to someone's assistant by his or her last name. It's Mrs. Smith unless she tells you that it's OK to call her by her first name.
- Assistants should always refer to their own bosses, especially when answering the telephone, by last name, too.
- Never refer to someone's assistant as "the girl" or "the boy." This is demeaning all around.

Chapter 10

The E-tiquette of Technology

Technology has probably taken over your life in one way or another. Chances are you don't leave the house without your cell phone or electronic date book (called a PDA, for personal digital assistant), and you probably log onto your e-mail or the Internet at least once a day.

With the advent of the Internet and other related twenty-first-century technology came a new set of rules, called "Netiquette." Even though technology is now a way of life, it's no excuse for behaving badly.

Whether you're an e-mail junkie, make your living trolling the Internet, or have more gadgets attached to your belt than a futuristic star traveler, you've got to keep certain rules of decorum in mind when dealing with technology.

ALERT!

The Internet has helped to fuel the spread of urban legends. If you receive an e-mail about a story that leaves you skeptical, dump it in the trash. Don't help to perpetuate any urban legends by forwarding them along.

E-mail Etiquette

If you're like most people, you probably stay in touch with your friends and family through e-mail more often than the old-fashioned phone call. Because e-mail has become such a mainstream way of communication, too many people use it without keeping manners in mind.

E-mail Rights and Wrongs

There are some unique idiosyncrasies that you need to keep in mind when typing an e-mail. These include:

- Do not type in ALL CAPS. People construe that as you're shouting at them—definitely not polite behavior.
- Do not type all lowercase, either. This is too casual, especially if you're sending a business e-mail.
- Avoid using emoticons in a business e-mail. Again, too casual.
- Do not neglect to address someone as Mr. or Ms. the first time you contact him or her by e-mail.
- Keep good spelling and grammar in mind when typing.

In Place of Personal Communication

With so many people logged onto the Internet both day and night, it would seem logical that you could replace nearly all your personal communication with e-mails. In a pinch that's fine, but if your way of communicating has become e-mails only, then you need to take a step back and examine how you're using e-mail to deal with others—and how that use may have affected your personal relationships.

One of the problems with only communicating through e-mail, besides the lack of the personal touch, is that things can easily become misconstrued. What may sound funny or joking in a one-on-one voice conversation can come across as snotty and standoffish in an e-mail. If you've noticed that people haven't been responding to your communications in a positive light, it might be time to log off and start meeting folks face to face again. E-mail should help you maintain relationships with others, not destroy them.

Next time you're tempted to send a "What's up?" e-mail to your grandmother or girlfriend, pick up the phone instead. Sometimes all you need in this modern world is a small dose of good old-fashioned communication.

ESSENTIAL

If you're doing most of your communicating via e-mail or instant message—including with business colleagues—you should be careful about how you're coming across. Literally. When choosing your e-mail or instant message moniker, you don't want to use a name that others will find offensive or that will reflect poorly on you.

Proofing and Grammar Police

Like any document you write on your computer, you should always proofread, spell check and make sure your grammar is up to snuff before sending an e-mail. This is especially critical if you use e-mail as a way of doing business at school or at work.

Sending a poorly crafted e-mail to someone says, "I don't care enough about you to make sure I've written something sensible to you." That's not exactly the message you want to send to people.

If you don't have the time to run a spell check, then you really don't have the time to be sending an e-mail. Log off and deal with those messages later, when you have the appropriate amount of time to give them the attention they need and deserve.

ALERT!

Computer spell check programs aren't always 100 percent perfect. Proofreading an e-mail after you've spell checked it is always a must and will allow you to pick up on any mistakes that the spell check program may have missed.

Thinking About Forwards

When you receive an e-mail that you think is interesting, it's so easy to simply forward it along to others. With the click of a mouse key and your well-stocked e-mail address book, soon enough that interesting message will be making its way along to other people's mailboxes.

Before the spirit moves you to share messages in this way, think about what you're forwarding and to whom. First, it could be considered a breach of copyright law (if not civil behavior) to forward someone's message without his permission, especially if there is a disclaimer at the bottom of the e-mail that prohibits you from forwarding it. Also, if you've received a message in secrecy and you end up sending that confidential message to the wrong person, what kind of bind have you put that person and yourself in?

Second, think about all of the forwarded messages that you receive. Do you always enjoy and appreciate them? Or do you roll your eyes and go for "delete" whenever you see an e-mail with "FW:" in the subject line? Think about how you feel when others overwhelm your e-mail box with unsolicited forwarded messages before you pass the next e-mail along.

The Long and Short of Long Lists

One of the neatest inventions on e-mail is the notion of the "bcc" or the blind carbon copy. This nifty little tool lets you send an e-mail to a large number of people without them seeing exactly whom you're sending the message to, and without having hundreds of other e-mail addresses pop up on the top of the e-mail. The latter requires a lot of scrolling down, which can be annoying to the time-starved recipient of your e-mail.

Whenever you have to send an e-mail to a long list of people, use "bcc" for the aforementioned reasons, along with this one: if one of the recipients decides to respond to your e-mail by hitting "reply to all" instead of just "reply," that seemingly personal message won't get bounced back to all the other people you'd originally e-mailed. There's nothing like a mistakenly sent "reply to all" message to get on people's nerves.

Acting Appropriately at Work

Many companies these days have some kind of spy ware on their company computers to track their employees' use of the Internet, including e-mail. If you know that your employer frowns on the personal use of e-mail at work, don't do it. It's that simple. If you think to yourself, "Oh, this one time won't hurt anyone," then you're being disrespectful of your company's policy, and you could be risking your job.

If personal e-mails are allowed at work, don't overwhelm your colleagues with forwards of cutesy jokes or urban legends. You're at your job to work, not to share funny messages. Even though it's really easy just to forward an e-mail to a friend, you should save such cavalier use of your e-mail for your personal use at home.

Instant Message Manners

Instant messaging (IM) is the utmost definition of instant communication, even more so than e-mails. They're just like being on the phone with someone, except that you're typing all your messages to one another.

While IMs may seem to be the exclusive domain of teenagers, plenty of adults use IMs to keep in touch with family and friends and also to conduct business. You may have even noticed that people include their IM ID on their business cards.

When using IMs in business, you should remember that even though you're communicating with someone in a very casual medium—the instant message—you should keep your message professional. That means:

- No use of emoticons. They have no place in business.
- Make sure the caps lock key isn't on, otherwise you'll be shouting at this person.
- Do your best to type as accurately as possible.

The most important thing to keep in mind when sending someone an IM or a text message is whether it is a good time for him or her to receive your IM. That's why the very first thing you should ask after typing, "Hi," is just that—"Is this a good time for you to chat?" If the person messages back that it's not, respect her answer and log off.

Another way to politely handle unsolicited IMs when you're too busy to deal with them is to simply turn off that software on your computer.

Well-Behaved Web Surfing

The World Wide Web is a great and varied communication tool that seeps into your everyday existence is many ways. You'll notice that advertisements nearly always include a company's URL these days, and you can seemingly find the answer to nearly any question you have by searching the Internet. But just because the Internet is everywhere doesn't mean that you can deal with it without considerations in mind.

Courteous Cookie and Bookmark Use

Cookies are devices that allow Web sites to "remember" your computer and you each time you visit. They make shopping online and anything else Internet-related easier by storing information.

A computer's cache is where it stores cookies. Never clean out someone else's cache without checking first. You could cause them to lose valuable information that they wanted saved.

Bookmarking Web sites also makes Internet use easier. When you visit a site that you think you'd like to return to in the near future, you can "save" it as a bookmark in your Internet browser. This will let you return to it with just a click of the mouse.

Despite the ingenuity of cookies and bookmarks, not every Internet user sees them in a positive light. Some people set their computer so that it doesn't accept cookies and others don't like to clutter their browser with bookmarks.

If you're sitting at someone else's PC and surfing the Web, do not change their settings so that it accepts cookies. And do not bookmark any Web sites, without asking first if it would be OK. If you mess up and either accept cookies or create a bookmark by mistake, make sure that you return the settings to their previous state before you log off.

Inappropriate Sites

There are surely a lot of Web sites worth visiting out there, but there are also many sites that you'd be wise to stay away from, especially if you're Web browsing with children nearby or if you're at work. It's never a good idea to surf on over to a Web site that you're not familiar with, especially if someone is with you who may find the content offensive. Always do your homework and check out sites first before logging onto them if you're going to be doing so with children or those with a sensitive nature sitting nearby.

ALERT!

Web site blocking software is a good idea if you want to ensure that your kids never surf over to any inappropriate Web sites. It's your right as a parent to install this on your child's or your family's computer, and you needn't tell your children ahead of time that you're doing this.

You should be vigilant of your Web site use at work as well. There are certain sites that your employer might deem unsuitable for visiting during work hours or on a work computer. If you're concerned that your employer may put such restrictions on your Internet use, clarify things with your human resources department before you log on.

Respectable Research

If you've spent any time on the Internet, you know that you can find a Web site devoted to just about any topic somewhere on the World Wide Web. But just because you find a site related to something you're researching, it doesn't mean that the information there is trustworthy or correct.

If you're looking to do reputable research on the Web, you should stick with searching sites that are affiliated with known entities. For example, if you need to find official information on anything the Federal government might keep track of, look for Web sites that end with .gov. These usually mean that they are a part of an official governing body.

Regardless of what kind of suffix a Web site has, though, you should always approach Internet-based information with a grain of salt. There are plenty of savvy Web designers who know how to make a site look official, even when it has bogus information. That's why it's always a good idea to have a healthy dose of skepticism when you decide to quote any information you've uncovered on the Internet.

If you find your e-mail overrun with spam, you can set up a filter that automatically dumps those kinds of messages in your trash. Deleting spam for sanity's sake is never rude.

Considering Spam

Spam isn't just a congealed lunchmeat anymore! In the Internet age, spam is defined as unsolicited messages of any nature, whether it's for a get-rich quick scheme or an advertisement for a product that promises to enhance your love life or certain body parts. Spam has invaded many people's fax machines as well.

Unfortunately, plenty of discourteous businesspeople have figured out how to make a living spamming folks. You can't send the manners police after them to make them stop. However, there are some things that you can do to cut down on the amount of spam you receive—and to make sure that you, in turn, do not become a spammer by proxy.

Ignoring Is Ideal

Spam is the only time in your courteous life when you can get away with ignoring someone or something as a way of dealing with it. The worst thing you can do when you receive spam is to e-mail or fax back, "Remove me from this list."

Spammers take a machine-gun approach to sending out their message (sending to as many addresses as possible, hoping they'll hit a live target). If you reply, they know they've got you. Suddenly, your e-mail or fax number becomes a "marked" address where spammers know that they can reach a real-live person. Since spam can be a lot like breeding bunnies—out of control, once it gets started—if you get marked, you'll receive more spam in the long run. That's why it's best (and perfectly polite) to ignore spam messages.

Making Spam

One of the ways that Internet marketers grow their customer list is to ask their existing customers to refer a friend. While it's your right to shop on the Web, you shouldn't share friends' or family members' information with any Web sites without asking them first. You may welcome a message from your favorite e-tailer, but someone else may not.

Another way you can spawn Spam without even realizing it is by being a serial forwarder of messages. Not only can across-the-board forwarding appear rude to the recipient, but also that's how viruses get spread. If you get anything with an attachment and you can't verify where it came from, don't spam others with this message. Spam should stop with you, if you want to be a gracious Web surfer.

Polite Listserv Participation

One of the great ways that the Internet has enhanced communication between people is through listservs, online forums, and chat rooms. These are all virtual places where folks can gather for the exchange of ideas.

If you disagree with someone on a listserv or in a chat room, it's OK to have a polite back and forth about where your differences lie. But you've got to be careful that your disagreement doesn't escalate into a flame war—flaming is when you irrationally criticize someone else's post. It's never polite to flame, and if you find yourself disagreeing with someone online, you've got to take the high road, ignore how obnoxious the other person is being, and move on.

As is the case with e-mail, it's easy to misconstrue someone's intentions in a written message, without body language or voice inflections to help with communication. That's why you should always take a deep breath and keep your manners in mind on a listserv before responding to something seemingly inflammatory with a flamed message.

Civil Use of Cell Phones and Pagers

Like e-mail and instant messages, the technology of cell phones and pagers means that people can reach you any time of the day and in any place in the world—as long as that place has a cell phone or satellite service. Despite this technology's pervasiveness, you need to think each time your cell phone rings or your pager goes off whether this is truly a convenient or considerate time to answer it.

The Right Way to Use Ringer Tones

Many people choose to assign a ringer tone to certain people's phone numbers that they've stored in their cell phone. That way when they hear a certain song, they know who is calling or text messaging them.

While this may be convenient for you, it isn't always polite for the people near you—especially if you've got your ringer tone on a loud volume or set to a potentially obnoxious song. If you must use anything but standard ringer tones on your cell phone, do others a favor and at least keep the volume down.

Taking Calls with Others Around

You should never answer a cell phone that rings in the middle of dinner or a business meeting—unless you've told the people you're with ahead of time that you're expecting a call. It's always courteous to give your full attention to the people you're with in the here and now—not to a ringing cell phone. You may want to turn your cell phone off or to vibrate when you're going to be busy.

If you know you're going to be tied up in a business meeting or meal for a long time and don't want to miss any calls, take comfort in knowing that your voice mail can take messages for you. You could even record a message that tells callers exactly when you will be available later. Then you won't seem rude if you can't get to an important call. Later on, when you need to use the ladies room at some point, you can quickly check your messages and, if it's an emergency, make a quick call back to let the caller know that you'll be back in touch as soon as you can.

Calls in Public

With the advent of the cell phone came the demise of the old-fashioned phone booth. This nifty contraption was fully enclosed and ensured that everyone making a phone call in public could do so in relative privacy. Not anymore. Today, you'll find people taking calls on their cell phones at the most inopportune times or in the most inconvenient locations. You've probably experienced the commuter who's having a loud conversation en route to his office or someone walking down the street while screaming into his phone.

There's nothing wrong with taking a cell phone call in public. In fact, being outside may be the ideal place to talk on your cell phone, because you won't be bothering those in close quarters. Here are some places where it's fine to take a call on your cell phone:

In the park
At the beach
At the playground
While walking your dog
On the platform of a train station
At the airport

Here are some places where you might want to think twice about talking on your cell phone:

In any store, restaurant, or service establishment.
At a sporting event, including intramural or your kids' Little League.
In the line at the bank, movies, or anywhere else where others are nearby.
At a cultural event, including plays, movies, or museums.

Go ahead and have that nonchalant conversation with your best friend on your cell, but if you're going to get into anything personal or emotional, you would be best to find a private place to have that conversation.

ALERT!

The only time it's OK to check up on someone else's call log or chat room use is when you suspect that this person may be getting herself into trouble, such as a child chatting with a potential abductor.

Call Logs Are Private

If you've ever forgotten someone's phone number, you know you could scroll back into your "calls received" log on your cell phone to find that person's phone number.

Despite the ease with which you could snoop on your significant other or a family member through her cell phone, you shouldn't do it. You should feel confident that you're making any cell phone calls in private and that people won't be checking up on you.

Privacy, PDAs, and Blackberries

You need to respect another's privacy when it comes to technology. Just like the cell phone with the call log, you can easily figure out whom someone has been talking to or meeting with by looking in his PDA or Blackberry.

Unless you have a bona fide reason to think that this person is in danger, it's not your place to check up on whom they've been contacting. Someone else's digital assistant is none of your business, and besides, how would you feel if you knew a friend or family member was looking through your Palm Pilot? It's a violation of your privacy, and it's a violation of theirs, too.

Chapter 11

The Genteel Traveler

Whether you're traveling for personal pleasure or for business, there's no reason you can't take your manners with you when you go away. This is a definite must from the minute you get into the taxi that takes you to the airport until you get back home again—and it applies to every single mode of transportation you might take when traveling. Travel is much more pleasant for all those involved when everyone is on his best behavior and keeps common courtesies in mind.

Cruise Ship Protocol

In the last decade you've probably noticed how pervasive cruise vacations have become. Now you can sail out of practically any city in America, such as Boston and Baltimore, along with popular ports like New York and Miami. This makes cruising much more approachable for the average person who doesn't want to tack an airfare onto his vacation expenses.

With more competition in each of these markets, cruise vacations have become more approachable financially for families. That means that more people are cruising each year. However, if you're new to cruising, you may be unfamiliar with onboard etiquette.

Etiquette of Embarkation

Embarkation is the fancy word for when you get on the ship. Given that most cruise ships hold thousands of passengers, this is a time when you're really going to have to be patient as you'll surely be waiting in one line or another. Here's how you should prepare for embarkation and what you should expect to occur in the process:

1. Always arrive at least a few hours before the ship's scheduled cruise time, lest you hold up your fellow passengers with your late arrival or miss the boat altogether. It's best if you can plan to get to the cruise ship terminal four or so hours before departure, if you'd like to avoid long lines.
2. Make sure that you have all your paperwork in order before you check your bags (as you would do at the airport) and get in line. Each of the people you're traveling with will need proper identification.
3. Make sure you bring a few pens with you, as you'll be spending your time in line filling out paperwork. Everyone standing in line is going to be rushing to fill out customs' declaration forms and boarding passes, so don't waste their time asking, "Do you have a pen I can use?"
4. Remember, waiting in line is a reality in embarkation, so be patient. The line will move, and you will eventually get on the ship. It just may take some time to do so.

Behavior at the Buffet

If there's one thing that cruise ships are known for, it's their buffet dining. It's gluttons galore on most cruise ships, where the buffet is open from dawn to midnight, and you discover the true definition of all you can eat.

Despite food being available all the time, don't let yourself get into a mob mentality at the buffet. Again, you'll need to wait in line for all the serve-yourself food, and if you see someone taking the last piece of chocolate cake, don't panic. The kitchen staff is sure to bring out more very soon.

The Protocol of Onboard Entertainment

Cruise ship lines like to keep their passengers well fed and entertained at all hours of the day and night. That's why wherever you go on the ship, you're bound to find something to do. However, some of the onboard entertainment isn't always appropriate for everyone on the ship, specifically the youngest sailors.

You'll notice that when you walk into a ship's casino, there are signs all around that ask underage people to leave the premises. Do not take children into this area.

Also, some of the Las Vegas–style shows or comedy acts will have a mature audiences–only warning on them. This warning is for your children's well being, and it's likely that this kind of entertainment may contain something that you might find offensive. Don't expose your child to a show like this, just because you want to see it and you don't want to use the onboard daycare.

Respectful Smoking

A cruise ship would seem to be the perfect place for smokers to congregate. There are lots of places where you can go outdoors to smoke and seemingly not bother anyone. While that may be true, plenty of cruise ships have designated certain areas as being smoke free. These areas might include the restaurant, one side of the ship near the pools, or on certain decks.

If you don't see ashtrays or others nearby smoking, don't light up. Always ask a cruise ship employee where it is OK to have a cigarette and make sure that you only smoke in these areas.

Also, most cruise ships are working hard to protect the oceans where they sail, and they request that passengers do not throw any waste into the water, including cigarette butts. If you must smoke, dispose of your cigarette in a proper receptacle—never flick it overboard.

FACT

The one place on a cruise ship where most smokers can freely light up is in the casino. Even if you don't gamble, you should head to the casino to have a cigarette if you're a smoker.

Keeping Children Civil

With more families turning to cruising as the perfect family vacation, more cruise ships have responded by creating children's programs for kids of all ages. These programs are in place not only to make your vacation more pleasurable (and your children's, too), but also to prevent kids from running amuck on the decks or up and down the cabin hallways when others might be trying to sleep.

Whenever you can't keep an eye on your kids or you want to go do something that isn't child-friendly, put your children in the childcare center or arrange to have them participate in an organized activity.

At mealtimes you should make sure that your children aren't turning the buffet into a free for all, and as far as assigned dining goes, try to request the earlier seating time on the ship. This is usually the seating time with the most kids—and the most understanding and tolerant waitstaff and diners.

Tips on Tipping

Get used to the idea of tipping on the cruise ship, because it's the norm. Thankfully, most ships have "sail and sign" cards onto which they automatically add standard gratuities for the folks you'll deal with on a regular basis. These include your dining room staff and your cabin steward. However, if one of these people seems to go above and beyond the call of duty, you can always add more of a tip at the journey's end. If you think about how hard these folks work during your vacation, you'll understand why tipping is so important. Here is a list of people you'll likely come into contact with on your cruise and how much you should tip each:

> Stevedore is the person who carries your bag to your cabin. Give him at least $2 per bag.
>
> The cabin steward is responsible for cleaning your room daily and turning down your bed nightly. You may want to add $25 or $30 onto the tip the ship will automatically assign to him.
>
> You will see the dining room staff nightly during your assigned dinner seating. Again, she will be getting an automatic tip but you should feel free to add $25 or more if she does an outstanding job.
>
> The room service staff is self-explanatory and should receive $1 to $2 per meal they bring to your room.
>
> Childcare center workers are sure to appreciate a $30 to $50 per child tip for watching your children during a week's cruise.
>
> If you partake of the onboard spas and get a haircut, manicure, massage, or other service there, you should tip the person the same amount you would for someone providing a similar service at your usual salon or spa, which is 15 to 20 percent of the bill's total.

The Polite Airplane Passenger

Everyone has a story about a horrific flight they had, not due to bad weather or airport delay, but due to a fellow passenger's horrible behavior. Don't become one of those anecdotes that people will tell for years to come because you just couldn't keep it together during your flight. It doesn't take much for you to behave like a polite airplane passenger, even if you've got children in tow.

Boarding Behavior

There is a reason that airlines choose to use a certain system to board their passengers—they load and unload airplanes multiple times each day, and they know better than anyone else the most efficient way to get passengers to their seats and airplanes off the ground. You may not like the idea that you have to wait until everyone else is on board to take your seat, based on where you're sitting, but it isn't your business to go against airline rules simply because they annoy you.

When lining up to board the airplane, do not stand up and crowd the door before the crew calls your row. If you see a family with children, step out of their way. They're juggling enough baggage (both live and carried) that they don't need you and your impatience getting in their way.

The only exception to the lining-up rule is if you're flying a low-cost carrier that seats people on a first-come first-served basis. Then it's up to you to arrive in plenty of time so you'll get a spot in line that makes you happy.

Airlines are notorious for recycling air throughout a flight. Do your fellow passengers a favor and avoid wearing any strongly scented perfumes or colognes, which could easily overwhelm others in such close quarters.

Once you're on the plane, stow your bags as quickly as possible. Try to step into your row as you put your bags overhead or under the seat. If you continue to stand in the aisle, you'll just hold everyone else up. However, if someone ahead of you is standing in the aisle and having trouble with his or her bag, don't sigh impatiently—lend a hand instead. Not only is this a polite thing to do, but also it will help everyone else (yourself included) get seated faster.

Consideration At Your Seat

Flight attendants always encourage passengers to stow their carry-on luggage under the seat in front of them, and you should follow their suggestion. Never take up more than one seat's worth of space for your bags, especially if there's someone sitting next to you. However, if you've asked first whether it's OK with him—and he doesn't have any luggage to put there— then go ahead and stow it under the seat in front of him.

If the flight attendant asks you to put your seats straight up and your tray-tables away for take off or landing, she isn't speaking to everyone except you. Get your seat out of the reclined position, and put your tray-table away. The same goes for stowing portable electronic devices before take off. Following these simple directions will help ensure that your flight takes off on time.

Speaking of reclining seats, if you happen to be flying in a plane with very little room between the rows, try to avoid reclining your seat altogether. Sure, you may want to catch up on a couple of winks during the flight, but how do you think the person sitting behind you is going to feel when suddenly your seat goes back and your head is practically in her lap? By the same token, how would you feel if you wanted to get work done on your laptop and the seat in front of you came crashing down? Reclined seats may be fine for sleeping on transatlantic flights but when it comes to most daytime flights, you should keep your chairs in their upright and locked position.

Don't Diss the Flight Attendants

You may think that a flight attendant's primary purpose is to be your waiter or waitress during your flight. While that is partially right—they do serve you food and drink—flight attendants are there to keep passengers safe, if something goes awry with the flight.

That's why you should always show flight attendants respect, courtesy, and cooperation during a flight. Argumentative behavior is likely to get you removed. With strict rules in effect to ensure everyone's safety and security, it's wise to do what you're told, even though you may not agree with it.

Travel by Bus and Taxi

When you're traveling, you may have to get from point A to point B by bus or taxi. There are certain etiquette rules to keep in mind when using either mode of transportation.

Bus Behavior

For starters, if a bus is your primary mode of transportation, it's a good idea to have your ticket in hand before you board. It's usually only on mass transit buses where you can get away with paying onboard. Not so with long-distance bus travel. If you want to avoid holding up your fellow passengers, allow plenty of time to get to the ticket window before the bus departs.

If you're stowing any luggage in the bus's belly, you should tip any redcap or driver who helps you $1 per bag, just as you would a skycap at the airport.

When you take your seat on the bus, keep this unwritten rule in mind: those who want to sleep on the bus should sit toward the front. Those who intend to be a bit more rowdy—even if it's just chatting—should sit toward the back of the bus.

Tips on Taxi Use

One of the most important etiquette lessons for riding in a taxi cab is this: always tip the driver, especially if you're coming from an airport, train station or cruise ship terminal and have bags in tow. Give him $1 per bag that he puts into the cab, plus 15 to 20 percent on top of the fare.

How To's on Hotel and Resort Stays

You need to plan ahead when you stay at a hotel or resort. While some hotels may be able to accommodate walk-in customers, the polite thing to do is to always have a reservation before showing up with your bags in tow. Here are other ideas to keep in mind when dealing with hotel and resort stays.

Common Courtesy with Check-Ins

If you're staying at a tourist hotel during tourist season—or you're a tourist yourself at a resort—prepare yourself for the reality of long lines at check-in time. You can be patient and wait your turn, or if you feel yourself losing your patience, why not check your bags with the bellman and come back later? There's nothing wrong with waiting for the crowds to disperse before getting checked into your room.

When a bellman brings your bags to your room, you should tip him. A good rule of thumb is $1 to $2 per bag that he carries. It's the polite thing to do.

Hotels and resorts always post their check-in and check-out times. Please respect these times as they allow for the hotel to clean and prepare rooms in between guest stays. Don't get in a huff if you show up at noon and your hotel won't have a room for you until 2:00, their official check-in time. It's your problem that you arrived so early, not the hotel's.

The Gracious Hotel and Resort Guest

Even though you're away from home when you stay in a hotel, you should keep your manners in mind. If you're staying on a hotel's upper floors, you should be considerate of the guests below you. Don't stomp, jump, or make noise on the floor at a time when people might be sleeping—usually after 10:00 P.M. and before 8:00 A.M.

Check to see if your hotel or resort has quiet hours that seem to go beyond the norm, which might begin early in the evening and end in the morning, or vice versa. If the hotel does, respect those quiet hours at all times.

The same noise rule applies for the guests staying on either side of you. Keep your television volume and your voices to a minimum whenever possible, and don't let your kids run up and down the halls whenever they please.

Use common courtesy as far as smoking goes as well. If you're staying in a nonsmoking room, don't smoke in it. If you must smoke, make sure you request a smoking room when you make your reservation.

If someone in a room near you isn't following these rules of courtesy, don't be shy about calling in a complaint to the front desk. You don't know anything about your fellow guests, and while you may want to handle the situation yourself, it may not be safe to do so. Let the hotel deal with things and, if the situation doesn't improve, insist that the hotel move you to another room and/or offer you a discount on your room rate for the inconvenience. It's well within your rights (and not rude at all) to make both requests.

Laws of the Lobby

Many hotels and resorts ask that their guests dress a certain way when they're in the lobby. At some upscale metropolitan hotels, this may mean no conference nametags in the lobby (it makes the place look like a convention center, not the fine establishment that it is). At tropical resorts, it could be a rule that you must wear something over your bathing suit after coming inside from the pool or the beach. Whatever the policies are, you must respect them if you want to be a polite guest in that hotel or resort.

It's good manners to tip the housekeeping staff by leaving money on the last day of your hotel stay. Depending on the size of your room and how many people are staying in it, you should leave $2 to $3 per person, per day as a tip.

Behave at the Beach

The most important thing to keep in mind when you're at a beach, beyond your safety, is the well being of your fellow sunbathers. That means no loud radios at the beach, no kicking sand when walking along or shaking out blankets near others. If you must play games on the beach, keep them away from other people who might find them distracting.

Don't let your children run unattended on the beach—they're likely to be the ones who inadvertently kick sand on someone else. Also, you can't possibly keep an eye on your youngsters if they're running every which way, and having out-of-control kids is not the way to win a "polite parent of the year" award on your vacation.

Most hotels and resorts supply towels specifically for pool or beach use. Don't break the rules and bring your room towels down to the beach or pool. Make the effort to use the correct towels.

Tubes, floats, and other water toys can be a lot of fun to play with at the beach, but if you're dealing with crowded conditions, you might want to put them away. There's nothing like having someone on a boogie board bash into you to ruin your day at the beach.

Politeness at the Pool

Most of the rules you need to follow at the beach apply to the pool as well. Keep your radios to a decent level and don't let any games you play get so out of hand that you start crashing into other people at the pool. The same goes for water toys—if the pool is crowded, you probably want to hold off tossing a ball around. Otherwise, someone could get hurt.

Don't let your children run around the edge of the pool, where they could fall in, hurt themselves, or annoy others. If a pool has been designated as adults-only, as some lap swimming pools are, respect those rules and swim elsewhere with your family. And when you take young children to a pool, don't forget to put them in a swim diaper.

Topless or nude sunbathing is the norm in some tropical and foreign destinations, but many resorts that cater to Americans ask that guests sunbathe this way in certain designated areas only. Respect the resort's rules and only take your top or bottom off where you know it's OK to do so.

Civil Camping

For some folks camping in the great outdoors is a rite of passage. One of the reasons that people are still allowed to camp in parks is because campers before you have done a good job being respectful of their surroundings. That is, they've been respectful of the nature around them and of their fellow campers.

One of the best ways to be a civil camper is to always keep your campsite neat and tidy. You don't want to do anything that might attract wild animals, such as leaving food out unattended, and you should always clean up after yourself each day or when you leave. Nature can't stay pristine if you litter it with garbage.

Another way to show courtesy to your fellow campers is to be considerate of them while you're camping there. Don't get too loud and rowdy after dark or early in the morning, and don't do anything that others might consider to be a nuisance, such as blasting music all night and day.

ALERT!

Even though camping and hiking seem like easy things for people to do, you must always be equipped for weather changes or unexpected emergencies. Don't head out unprepared or you risk your safety and the safety of others.

If you suspect other campers need help, don't ignore them. See what you can do to assist them. Of course, you should never wander off into the woods by yourself to help someone else, because this is too dangerous. When in doubt, phone or radio a park ranger to provide assistance.

Civil Behavior on Boats and Personal Watercrafts

One of the joys of vacationing in a waterfront locale is getting to ride on a boat or a personal watercraft, such as a Jet Ski. But you must remember to follow the rules of the water as you would the rules of the road.

ESSENTIAL

Make sure that at least two people on the boat know how to operate the craft. This will help avoid inconveniencing your passengers if something goes wrong or you are suddenly unable to drive the boat.

First and foremost, make sure you understand any port rules you may need to know when sailing out of a harbor. If you don't know your "port" from your "stern" or aren't sure exactly what the placement of buoys means, find out before you start your boat's engine.

Second, make safety your top priority for polite boat behavior. Always wear a life jacket on any watercraft, and never drive your boat or Jet Ski so close to others that you could risk hurting someone.

Third, driving a boat or personal watercraft is just like driving a car. Not only do you need to follow the rules mentioned above, but also you simply cannot drink and drive. If you know you're going to be drinking during your day or night on the water, find a designated driver and make sure he's the one who gets you safely back to port after your day is over.

Besides causing accidents, alcohol use can also lead to rude behavior, such as playing loud music or indulging in inappropriate displays. Whatever you do, don't leave your morals on shore when you take to the water, and if you must drink, do so responsibly.

Keep in Mind Customs Abroad

The best way for you to be a genteel traveler in a foreign land is to do what that old saying says: "When in Rome, do as the Romans do." That means that as best as you can, you should adopt the local way of doing things over your regular habits. (See Chapter 13 on Etiquette from Around the World on specific behavior to avoid.) When in doubt, ask your hotel or resort's concierge for help in adapting to the local culture.

QUESTION?

How do I know who and how much to tip when I'm traveling in a foreign country?
You can always turn to your travel agent or the hotel concierge to find out what the local customs on tipping are. Don't be afraid to ask when you're not sure about the appropriate tip.

One of the best ways not to insult local sensibilities is to dress like locals you see around you. That may mean covering your legs and arms in a conservative country or saving sneakers for your morning runs only if no one else is wearing them. Ask most Europeans how they spot Americans, and they'll tell you that they look for folks in t-shirts, shorts, and dark socks with sneakers or sandals. If you'd like to respect some of the dress codes in the country you're visiting, you'd be best to leave your at-home fashion sense, well, at home.

Chapter 12

E Manners and Transportation

Regardless of where you're going or how you're getting there, you've got to remember that transportation etiquette starts behind the wheel. If you don't know how to behave when you're in transit, you can't possibly be a well-behaved driver (or passenger, if someone else is doing the driving).

Most people travel every day—whether it's skipping up to the corner store for a gallon of milk or commuting clear across the county to your job. There would be a lot less road rage if everyone understood how to be polite when they're in the car, on the bus, or in a taxi. If just one person tries to pay politeness forward, starting with you, the roads would be a much nicer place for everyone to be on a daily basis.

The Decorum of Driving Your Car

Most kids grow up believing that driving a car is a right. But once you are old enough to get behind the wheel, you realize that operating a motor vehicle is more of a privilege than a right, and it's a privilege that you can't abuse.

One of the easiest ways to abuse this privilege is to break laws, such as when you speed, drive without a seat belt, or drive without a license. If you want to be a polite driving member of society, you've got to do more than simply follow the laws, though. You really need to follow the rules of the road, which require each driver to be as gracious as the next.

Show Respect with Signals

Before you even pulled away from the curb during your driving test, you probably turned on your signal to let other people know that you were about to hit the road—and to impress the person who was testing you that you knew how to use your signals. If only every driver would remember the role signals play in driving, then you would never be cut off.

Using turn signals is a sign of polite driving, and turn signals also a safety necessity. When you turn your signal on, you're probably going to be slowing down to make a turn. The guy behind you knows this. He's either going to change lanes to get around you or slow down so he doesn't ram into you. This is how the chain of events should go on the road, not a chain reaction collision because someone forgot to put on his signal.

Some state laws say that you must signal five seconds or about fifty yards before you exit or change lanes. However, just because your signal is on, that doesn't mean that you can move into another lane without checking first that you're clear to go. A turn signal is designed to warn other drivers of your intentions. It is not to be used to say, "Hey, get out of my way! Here I come."

Everyone knows what flipping the bird means, and there are probably times that you're tempted to do this to other drivers. Don't—it's bad manners, and, if the other driver is armed, it could be dangerous.

Most cars these days are designed so that the turn signal automatically turns off after you turn the wheel. However, there are times when this mechanism doesn't work. That's why you should always double check that your signal has gone off after making a turn. Otherwise, you're going to end up tricking the drivers behind you into thinking that you're turning now, no, wait, you're turning now, no wait, you're turning now, and so on for miles down the road. There's nothing more annoying to other drivers on the road than a car with its turn signal perpetually on.

Merging Mania

No matter where you drive on the road, chances are that at some point you're going to have to merge. The general rule with merging is to let one car on the road pass for every one car that merges. This rule applies both to the driver already on the highway and to the driver who is trying to merge in. Impatient drivers resist letting anyone get in ahead of them, but to help make merges go smoothly, you should really follow the one-for-one car rule at all times.

It's always a good idea to give someone a "thank-you wave" when he lets you cut in front of him in traffic or when merging onto a roadway. You may even want to wave twice—once when he signals for you to cut in and then again once you start driving away.

If you're approaching an exit merge and traffic is going down to one lane, don't race up to the exit in an adjacent lane and then cut in at the last minute. Also, don't hop onto the shoulder and zoom up to the exit on the shoulder. Both are perfect examples of bad manners and great ways to cause an accident.

Righteous Radio Use

The first warm days of the year always seem to inspire people to get into their cars, roll down their windows, and crank up their radios. It's fine to listen to music as you're driving along, but make sure that the music isn't so loud that you can't hear other cars around you. That doesn't promote safe driving.

On the manners side of things, if everyone outside your car can hear your radio—and your windows aren't even down—then your radio is simply too loud. That is definitely rude.

The same goes for souped up vehicles with extra bass speakers in the trunk that allow cars to "thump-thump-thump" down the road. Most people don't find those appealing, and if you're driving one of those cars, you probably can't hear what's going on around you anyway. Again, this is an unsafe driving practice.

E ALERT! Never wear headphones when driving your car, even if this keeps others from hearing your music. It may seem like a polite option but it's actually a very unsafe practice—and against the law in some places.

Talking on the Phone

You may think that you can multitask behind the wheel, but studies have shown that the more things you've got going on behind the wheel, the less likely you are to be paying attention to the road. One of these culprits is talking on a cell phone while driving, which is why many states have banned cell phone use in the car—that is, unless you're wearing a hands-free headset.

If you're concentrating on taking a call, you can't be concentrating on being a polite driver on the road, and you can't concentrate on safety. You'll notice that drivers in front of you who are talking on the phone tend to drive at erratic speeds or in an erratic manner. Chances are you're no different when you're talking on the phone while driving.

If you get a call and you think it will take a lot of your mental energy to talk to this person, put on your flashers, pull over to the side of the road and take the call. Otherwise, let the person leave a message and call them back later.

Problems with Car Alarms

Car alarms are an ingenious idea. They emit an ear-piercing noise if someone is trying to steal or damage your car. But with the beauty comes the beast: car alarms tend to go off for all sorts of unexpected reasons, including when a truck drives past or another car taps your car's bumper. The result is just another everyday nuisance that people expect and tend to ignore.

If your car has an alarm and you suspect that it's gone off, go outside and check things out. Don't just let your alarm run its course because you think that eventually it will shut off. It may, but in the process you'll have annoyed anyone and everyone within a couple block radius of your car.

Headlight Customs

Your state may have a law that requires you to have headlights on when your wipers are on, but you may also have noticed some unofficial headlight laws on the road, as well. Not every headlight custom is seen as being universally considerate, such as flashing your high beams to pass a slow-moving car. (In this instance, just be patient or figure out a safe way to pass the car. But don't flash your brights to make your point.)

There are some common headlight customs that you should familiarize yourself with that go a long way toward civility on the road. Keep in mind, however, that these are neither legal nor recognized by the law but are, nonetheless, good to know. They are:

- Flashing your high beams to let another car know he can cut in.
- Having more than one car flash its lights to let you know of a hidden police car.
- Calling out "Lights!" to let a driver know he doesn't have his on.

- Having another driver flash his high beams at you to let you know your highs are on.
- Flashing your lights to warn of an accident or trouble ahead.

The next time someone flashes his high beams at you, pay attention—he's probably doing you a favor.

Being Pulled Over

Being pulled over for a traffic violation, such as speeding or a faulty headlight, is no one's idea of fun. Being pulled over is no excuse to forget your manners. It's good etiquette to defer to the officer and to do the following:

1. Pull off the road as soon as it's safe to do so.
2. Turn the car's engine off.
3. Roll down your window.
4. Keep your hands where the officer can see them as he approaches.
5. Let the officer speak first. He'll likely tell you why he pulled you over, and then will ask for your driver's license and registration.
6. If you have to reach for either or need to rummage in a bag for them, tell the officer that you're going to do so. Otherwise, he might think you're reaching for a weapon.
7. Hand over your information.
8. If the officer returns with a ticket (sometimes you just get a warning), thank him.
9. Don't argue with the officer, even if you think you're right. Save your argument for court.
10. Once the officer returns to his car, you can start your car and drive away.

If you are a passenger in a car whose driver has just been pulled over, you need to be on your best behavior. Sit quietly, with your hands in sight, and don't engage in any conversation unless you're asked to.

Parking Lot Protocol

There are people in the world who simply don't know how to behave in parking lots. Whether it's stealing spaces from their rightful owners or parking their cars in inconsiderate ways, chances are you've dealt with these kinds of parking lot problems from time to time.

Here's what you need to keep in mind to stay well behaved in a parking lot. If you see someone signaling for a spot, keep driving. Don't try to sneak in when the other driver isn't looking and take his spot.

Make sure that your car can fit in the spot you've selected. If it takes more than two tries to get your car parked, move to another space. By squeezing your car in, you risk boxing in another car or denting the cars next to you when you open the door.

Finally, don't take up more than one space. If you're driving a huge SUV, don't park it in a lot reserved for compact cars. It may take you a little longer to find the appropriate place to put your car or truck, but you need to make that extra effort if you want to keep parking lot courtesy in mind.

The Courteous Commuter

When you've got to be in close quarters with others on your drive to the office or your train or bus trip to work, you need to keep your manners in mind. If everyone on the road or on the train and bus would do the same, commuting wouldn't be such a bad thing to have to endure on a daily basis.

Train Etiquette

Making your train ride more pleasant for your fellow passengers and yourself isn't difficult to do. Just think back to when you were a young child at school and how you were supposed to behave on the school bus. This will give you the clues you need to be a courteous commuter.

1. When the train approaches, line up in an orderly fashion on the platform.
2. When the doors open let those exiting the train get off first.
3. Once the door is clear, enter the train on a first-come, first-served basis.
4. Find your seat as quickly as you can.

5. Don't let your stuff take up more than one seat.
6. If someone asks if she can sit down, make room for her.
7. During the ride, keep noise to a minimum.
8. If you must take a cell phone call, do it in a soft voice.

ALERT!

Many people use their commute as a time to catch up on extra sleep. If you happen to know what stop your seatmate is getting off at and he falls asleep, give him a little nudge when you approach his station.

Driving in Traffic

There is nothing more frustrating to a commuter than sitting in bumper-to-bumper traffic when you really need to be somewhere now. Unfortunately, in many cities, rush hour traffic means no one is going anywhere fast.

If sitting in traffic is part of your morning commute, try to make the best of it. Don't lose your patience with your fellow drivers if things aren't moving very fast. If someone needs to merge onto the road, don't speed up and then laugh into the rearview mirror. Instead, keep the one-for-one car-merging rule in mind so you can do your part to act polite and keep traffic moving at the same time. Eventually you will get to where you're going, and you'll arrive in a much better mood if you keep courtesy in mind.

Often each bus will develop its own unwritten rules of etiquette, and you would do best to follow along as your fellow passengers are doing, so you don't step on anyone's toes—literally and figuratively.

Bus Behavior

The manners you need to be a well-behaved bus rider are very similar to those that folks who ride the train need. When you line up at the bus stop, do so in an orderly fashion. Don't push, shove, or try to cut someone in line when the bus arrives. You should always get on a bus in a first-come, first-served basis.

Board the bus and find your seat quickly. Stow your briefcase or backpack, and get out of the aisle so others can find their seats as well. Whether you sit at the front of the bus or the back, keep things moving quickly and smoothly.

Taxicab Technicalities

In cities where you need to cover a lot of ground but you can't always drive yourself, taxicabs are a great solution. For many urbanites, taxis are the only way to get to and from work each day. The best way to make your taxi ride as pleasurable as possible is to know the ins and outs of hailing, riding in, and paying for a taxi.

How to Hail a Cab

Depending on the city you're in, there may be different ways or locations where you need to go to hail a cab. In big cities like New York City, all you need to do is stand on the curb and stick your arm out in an informal wave. This is sure to get the attention of a couple of taxi drivers. You should get into the first cab that pulls up in front of you.

In other cities, you may have to stand in a queue at a designated spot or corner where rules say that taxis are allowed to pick up and discharge passengers only. If this is the situation, then you'll just have to wait in line like everyone else.

Never try to steal a cab from another person, no matter how late you're running to an appointment. It is acceptable, however, to approach someone near you who is also trying to hail a cab and suggest that the two of you share a cab.

Your Cab Ride

As soon as you get into the cab, you should say, "Hello" and "Thank you" to the driver. Then you should give him the information about where you're going.

Most cabs come equipped with seatbelts these days, and you should always buckle up. If you forget and your cab driver reminds you, don't scold him. Thank him for the reminder and then put your seatbelt on.

Tipping the Driver

It is customary to add on a tip to a cab fare, no matter how long or short your ride was. Tipping cabbies is a bit more complicated than tipping other service people. Instead of just adding 15 percent or 20 percent to the fare, many people round up the fare to form the tip.

Let's say that your cab ride cost you $4.25. Why not round the fare up to $5.00? This gives the driver almost a 20 percent tip and it gets you out of the cab in a jiffy. Of course, if your cabbie went the extra mile and not only loaded your bags into the trunk but also opened your door for you, you might want to be a bit more generous with your tip on a $4.25 fare and give him $6.00. On the other hand, if your cab driver was rude, drove erratically and never even acknowledged your presence, you could give him $4.50 (in exact change) and call it a day.

Courteous Ways to Complain

Many American cities have rules regarding exactly how they expect drivers to treat their taxi passengers. Some of these expectations might include:

- An English-speaking driver who knows his way around the city.
- A driver who drives safely with traffic laws in mind.
- A comfortable cab with heat in the winter and air-conditioning in the summer.
- A cab that is quiet or a driver who will put on the radio upon a passenger's request.
- A driver who picks up any and all passengers who hail his cab.

If you ride in a taxi and don't feel like you've been treated courteously, it's fine to file a complaint with that city's taxi commission. Just make sure you get all the information you'll need to identify the driver before you leave the cab. This includes the driver's name and taxi license number, the medallion number of the cab, and your location when the problem occurred.

Gas Station Guffaws

You might not think that your local gas station is a place where you have to keep manners in mind but you would be wrong. There are plenty of ways that drivers exhibit rude behavior when filling up their cars.

For starters, whenever you pull up to the filling tank, pull in as far as you can so that if any other cars need to fill up after you, they can fit in, too. You've never seen people so outraged as when a single car stops at the very first filling station he comes to, preventing everyone else from pulling in and filling up.

Once you're done fueling your car, move on. If you need to run inside the mini mart or you want to wash your windshield, don't keep your car in front of the filling tank, just because it's convenient. Move it somewhere else. If you leave your car where it is, you prevent others from filling their cars up in a timely manner.

Most gas stations have directions on where to enter and exit, and they understand that not every car has a tank on the same side of the car. That's why you can fill up on either side of the filling tank. You should do your best to follow these directions, even if it means waiting in line. However, if you've entered a self-service station and you can back your car into an empty spot at the filling tank, that's OK to do. Just make sure that you park your car in a way that doesn't prevent anyone else from filling up at the gas pump next to you.

Chapter 13

E Etiquette from Around the World

Remember that saying, "When in Rome, do as the Romans do"? Well, the same logic applies when you travel to Canada, Central America, or China.

You should familiarize yourself with local customs before you arrive in a foreign land, and if you can, brush up on some idioms ahead of time. It's always a good idea to learn how to say "please," "thank you," and "hello" before your plane touches down on foreign soil. Then, while you're there you can pick up on other common phrases or words you'll need to use to get around like a quasi-native. Most hotels employ a multilingual staff, which will allow you to get any last-minute language tips once you arrive.

Acting Graciously All Around the World

Beyond language, there are certain customs that you need to keep in mind to avoid offending your host or others you might meet during your travels. No one expects you to act like a native your first day on foreign soil, but you should assume that not everyone will accept your American ways as cute or novel. In fact, they may find them downright offensive.

Hand Jive

For starters, there are certain gestures or hand signals that you wouldn't give a second thought but might give someone in a foreign land pause. Here's a rundown on the most common foreign faux pas to avoid:

1. Using your thumb and pointer finger to make the OK sign is insulting to people in Brazil, Portugal, Central America, and Russia.
2. In the United Kingdom, the V-shaped peace sign is a way to say, "Up yours," and is definitely not a way to keep the peace.
3. Buddhists consider the head to be a sacred part of the body, meaning you should never give someone's hair a playful tussle in a Buddhist country.
4. Muslims see the left hand as being unclean, so you should always use your right hand to greet someone or to hand someone something.
5. The middle finger is universally seen as rude so don't point with it, especially in African or Asian countries, where it is highly offensive to do so.
6. You'll offend your host in a Muslim country if you sit cross-legged, with your ankle resting on your knee.
7. You are threatening someone in an Arab country if you are pointing directly at him.

Body Language

Beyond rude hand gestures, a good way to get off on the right foot with the folks you meet in your travels around the world is always to err on the side of formality. For example, when you meet someone, address that person as Mr. or Ms. Only after someone has given you permission to call him or her by a first name can you feel free to put formality aside. Also, when in doubt, dress on the conservative side, especially in countries where covering the body is a must.

Tipping service people is a universally accepted custom. You should tip in restaurants, hotels, and taxicabs abroad as you would back in the States. Just keep the currency differences in mind. It may take denominations in the hundreds or thousands to equal a single U.S. dollar, and you wouldn't want to undertip anyone.

Now that you know some universal ways not to offend anyone overseas, here are geographic-specific etiquette rules to keep in mind.

Etiquette and Protocol in Canada

America's neighbors to the north are probably most like Americans in their everyday lives. They drive on the right side of the road, export plenty of entertainers to the United States, and, most importantly, speak the same language (except for the Quebec province, where French is the first language).

Despite the similarities, it's a different country, and the last thing that Canadians want to hear is how they're just like Americans. They may embrace a portion of American culture, simply due to proximity, but Canadians are proud of their heritage. In another sense, Canadians are a bit more formal in their everyday interactions, simply based on the fact that their motherland isn't traced back to the United States, but to England, where propriety is par for the course.

United Kingdom

One of the great things about traveling to the United Kingdom is the fact that folks speak the same language as Americans. However, even though they share many of the same customs with their English-speaking compatriots across the pond (Americans), you always have to remember that you are in fact in a foreign country. That means that customs and sayings don't always translate once you cross the Atlantic. If you want to avoid insulting people you visit in the countries of the United Kingdom, you need to be on your best British behavior at all times.

Not every country in the United Kingdom sees England in the best light. This is especially true of the Scots. Never refer to these folks as being British or English, or you just might find yourself in a brawl.

British Sayings

You know everyone in England, Scotland, and Wales speaks English, but once you get there you may find that words you think of meaning one thing mean something entirely different there. Here are some common words that Americans use but which have other meanings in the United Kingdom.

ALERT!

Scotch is a drink, not a proper way to refer to someone from Scotland. He is a Scot, and his customs are Scottish. Make this mistake with the wrong Scot and you'll end up with a Glasgow kiss (a head butt).

- In the United States, "fag" is a derogatory word for a gay person; in England it's a cigarette.
- In England, bum is someone's backside.

- In England, the boot isn't footwear; it's the trunk of the car.
- In the United States, a full stop is something you do at a stop sign; in the United Kingdom, it's the period you place at the end of a sentence.
- You may store things in bins in America but it's where you put the trash in the United Kingdom.

British Customs

Around 4:00 in the afternoon in the United States, most people are getting ready to end their workday and start thinking about going home and having dinner. In the United Kingdom, it's teatime, a refresher, if you will, during the day for people to refuel between lunch and dinner, the latter of which occurs hours later.

Don't expect to see American tea bags or any frou-frou flavored teas at a British tea. The United Kingdom's version of tea (the drink) is much stronger and, in their mind, a better choice to accompany scones and finger sandwiches. When taking tea in England, you can drink it anyway you like, including with lemon and sugar. However, if you're hoping to impress people with your knowledge of "proper British tea," then you should add milk to your teacup only.

Doing Business in Britain

Most business meetings in England occur in the morning, so you must plan accordingly for any jet lag you may experience. If you're flying in on the day of a meeting and arriving in England the morning of the meeting, you should sleep on the flight over. Not only will this make you more alert for your meeting but also it will give you the stamina for any activities that you may participate in that night. Many British businessmen continue meetings over drinks at pubs in the evenings and will often close deals there.

Also, unlike other foreign countries, where you hand out business cards like candy, in the United Kingdom you should hold off giving someone your business card at first. It's only after you've established that you're interested in doing business together that it's OK to go ahead and exchange business cards.

European Countries

One big difference between American and Europeans is their dining practices. While breakfast and lunch tend to occur at roughly the times that Americans are used to, dinner can really throw you for a loop.

You've got to prepare your stomach for the fact that most Europeans don't sit down to dinner before 8:00 at night and may not finish their meal until well after 10:00 P.M. This is one of the reasons that the British practice of afternoon tea (a form of which you may find in other European countries) is such a good idea. If you don't have a late afternoon snack, you'll be pretty hungry by the time dinner rolls around.

Another difference is the temperature at which drinks are served. Americans are used to cold beverages all around but Europeans are not. Don't expect ice with your soda or your beer served in a chilled mug. Nearly every drink that comes across the bar in Europe does so at room temperature.

Keep in mind that Europe is a continent, not a country. If you know that someone hails from a specific country, don't refer to him as being European only. You owe him the courtesy to call him by what he is, such as French or Swiss.

Faring in France

For starters, unless you're fluent in French, don't try to speak it when you're in France. Unlike other countries where merchants and citizens welcome your attempt to speak their native tongue, the French (especially Parisians) aren't so tolerant. Don't go into a cafe or other establishment and assume that the proprietor speaks English. Even French folks who know English well will not go out of their way to respond in English if you come in speaking English.

Of course, the contradictory nature of the French may leave you in a language quandary of not knowing what to say or what language to speak in French establishments. You could always try to make the best of both worlds by asking, "*Parlez vous Anglais?*" (or "Do you speak English?").

Acting Graciously in Germany

Keep in mind that while Germans may be gracious and eager hosts to travelers, they are also a bit formal in how they prefer to be addressed. Never assume that you can call a German by his or her first name, unless you hear otherwise. This is definitely verboten, or forbidden. Instead, use *Herr* (for Mister) and *Frau* (for Mrs.) with the person's last name. (These are pronounced "hair" and "frow.")

Eastern Europe and Former Soviet Union

In the 1990s, when the Berlin Wall came down, everything changed in Eastern Europe and the former Soviet Union. Countries that once were communist became democratic, and the Soviet Union itself dissolved into many individual nations. Despite the change in the country's name or its government's approach to governing, many of the manners and customs of old remain. Don't be offended if in certain countries, like Russia or the Czech Republic, people seem a bit standoffish at first. On the other hand, in countries like Poland and Hungary, you shouldn't be taken aback if someone you've just met greets you with a hug and a kiss on both cheeks. To remain in your host's good graces, follow his lead. You can't go wrong with this approach.

Raising a Glass

Drinking alcohol and toasting one another is a big part of being social in Eastern European countries and the nations that used to be the Soviet Union. Again, follow your host's lead. You should only take a taste of your drink after the host has offered his toast and never before.

Keep in mind that while Russians will raise a glass of anything alcoholic for a toast, in countries like Poland, you only toast when holding a glass of vodka, and in Hungary, you never clink your glasses together for a toast.

Religions to Consider

Most of the countries in this region of the world have a Christian-based religion. The one exception to the rule are the Muslims who live in the former Yugoslavia. Their holiest holiday is the month-long celebration of Ramadan, which requires fasting during the day. (People eat and drink at night.) If you're visiting this region or any other Muslim country during Ramadan, you will show the locals great respect by abstaining from eating, drinking, and smoking in public during daylight hours.

The Native Tongue

Folks in these countries appreciate that their collective languages are hard to understand and even harder to speak. But unlike some Western European countries, residents here will get a real kick out of it if you attempt to speak their language, even if it's only to say "Hello" or "Thank you." Graciousness and courtesy go a long way, and trying to speak a foreign language, albeit not well, shows people you are interested in their culture and customs.

India

Protocol is a top priority in India. Just look at the country's caste system. It predetermines a person's social class and what is expected of him or her during a lifetime, based on his family's history. The caste system is still a big deal in India. The same holds true for how men and women interact with one another.

When you greet someone of the same sex in India, it's fine to shake that person's hand. But men should never shake a woman's hand as a greeting as it is insulting. A good fallback greeting is to clasp your hands, as if in prayer, place them under your chin and nod your head.

If you're invited in to someone's home, always take off your shoes. When you get there, your host invariably will offer you something to eat or drink. Even if you just finished a meal, accept her offer for tea and snacks. It's possible that while visiting someone's home, you could find men and women separated for a meal, dancing, or other social interaction. This is simply a part of Indian culture, and to be a polite visitor, you should respect the culture you're visiting. Another important thing to remember is that Hinduism is the predominant religion in India, where cows are considered sacred animals. Anything that derives from cows (milk excluded) is forbidden to eat and things made from leather or other cow byproducts are considered disrespectful.

Other Asian Countries

Unlike Western countries people in Asia do not like to be singled out for praise or shame. If you always think of the group first when traveling in Asia, you'll do a great job of being a gracious guest.

Another constant to keep in mind: red is the color of good luck. That's why you always see Asian brides dressed in red, not white. (White is the color of mourning and death.) If you need to bring someone in Asia a gift, it's a good idea to find something crimson-colored.

Dining Customs in China

When you eat in a Chinese restaurant in the United States, you may notice that the servers always bring food for everyone at your table to share. You may not always pass around certain dishes to your dining companions because you may be the only one who likes that dish or you may have ordered something with the intention of being the only person to eat it. In China, this kind of behavior is unacceptable and viewed as selfish.

Chinese eating is communal in nature, and everyone at the table with you will dig into the same large serving dish with chopsticks when it appears on the table, whether or not you personally ordered it. A germaphobic person may weary of this custom, but if you want to avoid insulting your Chinese hosts, you're going to have to take a deep breath and dive into the communal serving bowl as well. And you're going to have to get used to using chopsticks. You might want to take a crash course in chopstick use before you leave for your China trip, because you will be expected to use them at every meal.

When faced with eating rice, though, don't worry: no one expects you to eat rice one grain at a time with your chopsticks. Instead, when you sit down at a Chinese table, you're supposed to lift your rice bowl to your mouth and use your chopsticks to move the rice into your mouth. You do the same when eating a bowl of soup or noodles. However, don't try to eat a long noodle in one mouthful. Bite off the noodle at convenient lengths so it doesn't hang out of your mouth while you attempt to eat it.

Dining Customs in Japan

The first thing you need to do when you arrive for a meal at someone's home or a restaurant in Japan is take off your shoes. Japanese rarely wear outdoor shoes inside (a great way to keep the floors clean), and your host will offer you slippers to put on.

Cleanliness is key before meals in Japan. Your host will give you a warm, moist cloth to clean up with. Use it on your hands only. Then when you're done, place it neatly aside.

Like its Asian neighbors, the Japanese see meals as a shared event, except that instead of everyone digging in when the food arrives, you should pass it around. Serve yourself by using the "clean" end of your chopsticks—that is, the end you won't be using to eat off of. This is usually the thicker end of the chopstick.

Where should the chopsticks go when you're not using them?
Once you get the hang of eating with chopsticks, you need to know what to do with them when you're not eating. In between courses, you should put them down. Make sure you rest them on the appropriately named chopstick rest, which looks like a little indented table, or place them parallel to the edge of the table, in front of your seat.

When it comes time to eat, you should pick up any large pieces of meat, fish, or sushi with your chopsticks. Try to bite off a delicate bit at a time, but if that seems impossible, plop the whole thing in your mouth. You should bite off pieces of noodles instead of slurping the whole thing into your mouth. And as with Chinese meals, bring a bowl of soup to your mouth and drink right from the bowl. If there are any large pieces of food in your soup, you can drink them down with the broth, or you can use your chopsticks to pick up those pieces of food and eat them.

Greetings

Your first inclination when you meet or greet someone may be to shake his or her hand. In Japan, this is actually something that is never done. Instead, the polite way to greet someone is to bow. Since bowing isn't second nature to you, you might want to wait until the other person bows, and then you can bow in return. Some people bow just their heads; others bow while bending at the waist. Some people keep their hands at their side when bowing; others might hold them together in a prayer pose. Since you can't be sure exactly how someone in Japan is going to bow to you, it's wise to let the other person bow first. However, if waiting for the other person to bow feels awkward, simply nodding your head as your greeting should suffice.

Business Meetings

If you're in a business setting in Japan, not only should you bow but also you give the person your business card as a way of saying, "Pleased to meet you."

Once the business meeting gets underway, you should never interrupt someone else to make a point. In Japan people wait until one person is completely done talking before they add their contribution to the conversation.

When doing business abroad, don't take someone's business card and put it in your pocket. This is a sign of disrespect. Keep it out on the table or in front of you for the duration of the meeting.

If you hear people saying "*hay*" (which is Japanese for "yes"), that doesn't mean that everyone is in agreement. Instead, these folks are saying, "I hear what you're saying, and I'll take it under advisement."

Central and South American Countries

The one commonality you'll find in Central American countries is the Spanish language. While many of the more developed countries have many people speaking English—these include Costa Rica and Panama—you would do best to brush up on your Spanish before you plan to travel to this area of the world. You'll be seen as a much more polite American if you do so. The same is true for South America, where Spanish is the official language except for Brazil, where Portuguese is the language of choice.

Sense of Time

Another courteous consideration is not to have any rigid ideas of time. Time is a fluid thing in Central and South America, meaning meals and service in restaurants will likely take a lot longer than you're used to back in the United States. Having people show up on time is another loose restriction in this part of the world, and being late to a social function or other gathering isn't rude—it's expected. Work hard not to lose your patience if things don't go according to your American concept of time, and you'll have a great visit in Central and South America.

Polite Picture Taking

One of the most important things to remember when traveling here is how differently they view cameras. Think first before taking pictures of anyone or anything, especially if that person or building is official in nature. Most Central and South American countries prohibit people from photographing any government buildings or structures, bridges included. They see this as a security threat. If you ignore this protocol, not only do you risk having your camera taken away from you, but you could end up in jail.

Another constant with cameras, especially in countries with a large Indian population (as in Mayan or other Native American cultures), is the fact that they see cameras in a negative light. To take someone's picture is to steal someone's soul. Hold off on picture taking unless you receive permission ahead of time.

Middle Eastern Countries

With the exception of Israel, a Jewish state, all the countries that you'd consider to be the Middle East or Arab countries, are Muslim nations. You need to think about proper protocol during the fasting holiday of Ramadan (no eating, drinking, or smoking in public during the day), and you've got to be careful not to use your left hand. Because Muslims see it as being unclean, you need to do everything, from greeting people to passing food at the dinner table, with your right hand. Also, remember that alcohol is not considered appropriate to Muslims, no matter what.

FACT

In Hebrew, the word Shalom has three meanings: hello, good-bye, and peace. When you're in Israel, you can never go wrong in greeting people or saying good-bye to them in any situation by saying, "Shalom."

In certain Arab nations, there are strict restrictions on women, such as they must cover their head in public, and they are not allowed to drive themselves or be alone in a car. Not only do you need to be careful not to offend anyone if you're a female visitor there, but also you need to make sure that you don't break any laws. Foreign women are expected to abide by these rules when visiting Arab nations, including the rule about not driving themselves anywhere. Israel has its own set of rules that can have visitors wondering at every turn if they've just offended someone. For example, in Jerusalem, you may want to visit such historical places as the Wailing Wall. However, very conservative Jewish men may prohibit you from doing so, especially if you're female. They may also judge you by your dress and tell you to cover up. As far as food goes, many Israeli restaurants are kosher, meaning that you can't have meat products and milk products at the same time (forget about ordering a cheeseburger). Be careful what you order to avoid insulting your waiter or the restaurant's owner. Also, for the Sabbath, expect businesses to close down Friday afternoons and not to open again until Sunday.

African Countries

Many African nations are Muslim, meaning that all the protocol rules that you would use in other Muslim countries apply here. You want to avoid alcohol and pork, and try not to use your left hand for anything. Remember: that left hand is considered to be unclean. Also, Africans are fond of their titles—even if they're only Mr. and Mrs.—so always use them when addressing people.

There are exceptions to the African rule. One of them is South Africa, which is more European than most African countries. The other is Egypt, which is more like its Arab neighbors than its African ones.

The Caribbean

When talking about the island nations of the Caribbean, most people include Bermuda and the Bahamas, even though they are technically in the Atlantic Ocean, not the Caribbean Sea. The most important thing to remember when visiting these tropical countries is that their etiquette usually harkens back to their mother countries.

What that means is that places like Bermuda and the Bahamas, which the English once owned, take many of their customs from England. This includes driving on the left side of the road and English tea. In French derived countries, such as St. Martin, you'll discover more of a French feel. Since all these countries are tourist-centric, you should check with your travel agent or hotel's concierge to get a good idea of what's considered acceptable behavior and what's considered insulting.

Something else to consider is island time. Life moves at a slower pace in the Caribbean, and no amount of prodding or complaining can change this. If you want to have good manners when visiting here, you'll simply have to be patient. Your meal will eventually arrive, and your taxi will eventually get to its destination—it's just going to take a little longer than it would back home.

Chapter 14

Being a Good Neighbor

The poet Robert Frost wrote the following: "Good fences make good neighbors." While fences do go a long way toward sustaining civil relationships, the saying that goes a longer way toward getting along with those living near to you is this one: "Do unto others as you would have them do unto you." That is, treat your neighbors with the same amount of respect, kindness, and courtesy that you hope they would treat you with, and you'll end up having a more pleasant experience living in your neighborhood.

Welcoming New Neighbors

One of the best ways to get off on the right foot with your neighbors is to reach out and welcome any new families that move onto your street, block, or apartment complex. Think about how you would feel if you moved somewhere new and no one came over to introduce himself or herself. You would feel awfully isolated and not very welcome. That's how your new neighbors probably feel, which is why you've got to make the first move.

One of the best ways to make a new person feel welcome is the old-fashioned way: going up to her door, knocking or ringing the bell, and introducing yourself. This will give you the chance to meet the neighbors and to find out if you share any commonalities, such as children the same age.

Beyond introducing yourself, if you have the time and you're so inclined, you should offer to help your new neighbor get acclimated to the area. You can say something like, "If you have any questions about good nearby supermarkets or need the phone number for a dog groomer, stop by or give me a call."

The next time that you entertain, invite this new neighbor to your event, especially if other people living nearby will be there. This provides an excellent opportunity for the neighbor to feel welcome in your home and to meet the rest of the neighborhood, and you'll have done a good deed by being the conduit through which the new neighbor can meet others in the community.

Housewarmings

One of the best ways to welcome someone to the neighborhood—or celebrate a friend or family's move to a new home—is to throw a housewarming party. These kinds of get-togethers are a wonderful opportunity for folks to meet their new neighbors and to make people feel more at home in their new surroundings.

Since it's likely that people moving into a new home might need new kitchenware or other household products, it's a good idea to gear any housewarming gifts you give to either of those themes. Here are some good housewarming gifts to keep in mind the next time you're invited to such a celebration:

- Coffee or tea

- Doormat
- Kitchen gadgets (peeler, grater, etc.)
- Dishtowels, placemats, and cloth napkins
- Any kind of green plant or other greenery
- Bottle of wine, corkscrew and everyday wine glasses
- Subscription to the local paper

Living in Close Quarters

People living in close quarters, such as in an apartment or condominium, have a unique need to be considerate of one another. When there's only a wall between you and the guy next door, it's easy to feel like you're always on top of each other. That's why you need to be especially sensitive to how your lifestyle may negatively affect your neighbors.

Common Ground

Most organized communities have something called common ground, which is an area where everyone living in that place can access. In apartments and condominiums, this could be a paved or grassy area that abuts your building.

FACT

The shared space between adjacent buildings is called an easement, and you should always make sure that it remains clear, not only as a courtesy to your neighbors but also in case any fire engines need to access it.

This land is common ground, and you should treat it as such. Don't let your kids leave their toys outside on common ground, and always clean up after yourself if you have a barbecue or party on common ground. If you choose to walk your dog on common ground, you must pick up after him. By applying common courtesy to the use and care of your common ground, you'll have a better chance of staying on good terms with those living nearby.

Home Exterior

When you live in a neighborhood, you have to remember that your home is not only a reflection of you but also it's something that your neighbors have to look at every day. Do your best to keep your home's exterior as neat and tidy as possible, including cleaning up your garbage cans immediately after trash pickup or discarding newspapers that may collect on your front step. You should also avoid decorating the outside of your home in a way that others might not enjoy as much as you do. This could be an abundance of Christmas lights at the holidays or painting your shutters an offbeat color, like bright purple.

Your community association may have restrictions on outdoor embellishments, including seasonal items like holiday decorations. Make sure you check with your association first before repainting or redecorating the exterior of your home, lest you risk breaking its rules.

Noise in the Interior

When you live in an attached home setting, whether it's a townhouse, condominium, or apartment, you're going to be sharing at least one wall with your neighbor on one side or the other. You may also share a floor/ceiling with a neighbor upstairs or downstairs.

For an apartment with hardwood floors, you may want to consider putting down area rugs all around. This will help cut down on noise that travels downstairs through your floor and your neighbor's ceiling. Your downstairs neighbors are sure to appreciate your effort to keep the noise down.

Each of you needs to be considerate of the other by keeping tabs on how much noise you make. If you live above someone and have hardwood floors, you should always take your shoes off in the house. There's nothing more annoying to listen to than the "click-clack" of high heels on a hardwood floor above you. You should also avoid any loud thumps from running and jumping, and make sure you're vigilant about having your kids do all of their rough housing outside, where they won't bother the neighbors downstairs as much.

Noise not only travels up and down but side to side. If you have folks living on either side of you, keep the volume on your computer, TV, or radio at a reasonable level so you don't bother the neighbors. You should also keep your voices down, especially if you decide to chat late into the night. And if you have dogs, make sure that they don't bark incessantly. Most apartment complexes have quiet hours that every resident needs to respect, and the notion of quiet applies to all noises—manmade and otherwise.

Parking Lot Protocol

When parking your car in your complex's lot, always keep the rules in mind. If you park according to permits and numbered lots, always put your car in its designated space, even if that spot isn't convenient for you.

Be conscious of how you park your car every time you come home—you wouldn't want to take up two spaces or prevent someone else from parking in their designated spot because of your carelessness. Remind friends who visit that they need to park in guest parking and that putting their car in your neighbor's space this one time isn't OK.

Keeping Your Exterior Neat and Tidy

Regardless of where you call home, chances are you've got neighbors somewhere near you, and it's your job always to be a pleasure for them to live near. That's why you need to keep certain common neighborhood courtesies in mind as you go through your daily life, such as keeping the exterior of your home neat and tidy. If you don't, no one is going to want to have you as a neighbor.

Maintaining Your Yard

Most homeowners take pride in their yards, and a great way that you and your neighbors can work together to keep your street looking great is always to make maintaining your respective yards a priority. Here are some yard maintenance must-do's to keep in mind:

- Mowing your grass on a regular basis.
- Keeping weeds from overtaking your gardens.
- Putting away toys, tools and other nonessentials from your yard.

If you can plant colorful flowers from time to time, such as mums in the fall or tulips in the spring, this will go a long way toward making your yard a pleasure for everyone in the neighborhood to look at. It will also give you a great sense of pride in your home's appearance.

Trash Removal

Most neighborhoods have trash pickup one or two days a week. Do your neighbors a favor, and don't put your trash cans out days in advance. Not only is this unsightly, but also having trash outside on the street for a long period of time increases the chances that a wild animal (or your neighbor's cat) will get into your garbage and make a mess.

ALERT!

No one expects you to run out and put away your trash cans as soon as the garbage gets picked up. But do try to put the cans away by the end of that day. Everyone will agree that a neighborhood looks nicer when everyone puts away trash bins in a timely manner.

Also, don't leave your trash cans out for days on end after pickup has come, or keep them perpetually by the curb, where you just dump your garbage as you go along. You should find a convenient place to store the garbage cans, and try to keep them out of sight. This could be on the side of the house, behind a fence, or in your garage.

If you choose to store your garbage cans outside, make sure that you have a secure top on them that prevents animals from having an all-night buffet in the can. This should also help stop any noxious odors from leaking out.

Sidewalks and Walkways

It's wonderful when a neighborhood has sidewalks for its residents to use. Unfortunately, there's always at least one inconsiderate person in the neighborhood who doesn't seem to understand that a sidewalk is for everyone's use, and it's not just a slab of concrete that happens to run in front of his house.

When you shovel your snowy sidewalk, do something neighborly. Instead of only shoveling up to your property line, take a few extra minutes and shovel from your driveway to your neighbor's driveway. This is one of those small good deeds that go a long way toward developing good relationships with neighbors.

One of the ways you can avoid joining the ranks of inconsiderate neighbors is to check that your section of sidewalk is clear at all times. That means when it snows, you need to get out there and shovel it. (Shovel your walkways in your yard at the same time.)

When people come to visit and park in your driveway, make sure that their car doesn't stick out into the sidewalk. And if you've planted any shrubbery on the perimeter of your yard near the sidewalk, make sure it stays neat and trim and doesn't grow onto the sidewalk.

Everyday Nuisances

Even though you may love your neighbors and enjoy their company, they are likely to annoy you from time to time. It's possible that they may find you a nuisance at times as well, but not if you watch your behavior—and the behavior of any of your pets—to make sure that it is as courteous as possible at all times.

Walking Dogs

The best way to stay in your neighbor's good graces when you own a dog is to make sure that you pick up after your dog when you take him for a walk. In addition, you shouldn't let your dog walk up onto someone's lawn and pee on a bush near the house. Of course, it's best to have your dog lift his leg on inanimate objects only, such as fire hydrants and telephone poles. However, anyone living in a neighborhood should understand that any flora near the curb really is fair game to a canine.

Most towns have leash laws as well, and you need to keep your four-legged friend on one at all times. You may consider your dog a well-behaved animal, but your neighbors probably won't appreciate it when your off-the-leash dog suddenly runs up and startles them. The only place in your neighborhood where you should let your dog run free is in your fenced-in yard or an enclosed community dog run.

Everyone knows that barking is a dog's way of communicating, but if your dog is trying to tell you something for fifteen minutes or more, he's probably annoying your neighbors in the process. To be a good neighbor, you should never let your dog bark for an extended period of time. If you can't keep an eye on your dog, don't leave him outside.

E ALERT!

While it's a good idea to keep quiet hours in mind, always check with your town to see if its definition of quiet hours is much more conservative than your own. That way you can always be sure that you're not disturbing your neighbors and you're not breaking any laws.

Quiet Hours

If you've ever received a phone call late at night or in the early morning hours your first reaction was probably to wonder who died. To avoid scaring your neighbors, you should avoid calling them during your neighborhood's quiet hours, which are likely to be at times when they might be sleeping.

A good rule of thumb is only to call on weekdays after 8:00 A.M. and before 10:00 P.M.—earlier if you know they have young children who may be sleeping by 10:00 P.M. On weekends, only pick up the phone after 10:00 A.M. and never after 10:00 P.M. These quiet hours apply to these situations as well:

- Animals being outside and making noise.
- Children playing in your yard or on the street.
- Construction work being done to your home.
- Yard work, such as mowing the lawn or using a leaf blower.

Loud Parties

If you live in a crowded residential area and you're planning a large party, it's your responsibility not to let the celebration get out of hand and to make sure that it doesn't inconvenience your neighbors too much. One of the best ways to ensure you don't annoy your neighbors is to invite them. If they're a part of the party, they're less likely to find it a nuisance. There are other ways you can help to make any celebrations you have at home less of a problem for those living nearby. These include:

- Keeping the party indoors.
- Limiting the amount of alcohol you serve.
- Setting a clear time that the party will end—and sticking to it.
- Inviting no more people to the party than your home can handle.

If any of these suggestions seem too restrictive, then perhaps you should find some other, nonresidential place to hold your celebration.

Neighborhood Pools, Playgrounds, and Associations

In many neighborhoods, you'll find more than just single-family homes. Some neighborhoods also include a community pool and playground and a governing body that oversees everything that goes on in the neighborhood. This is usually the neighborhood association, which is also responsible for general upkeep. Residents pay dues to this association to cover its assigned duties, which may or may not include the upkeep of the pool and playground.

At the Pool and Playground

Two of the extras your community dues or neighborhood association fees may cover are the pool and playground. To make both of these extras enjoyable for everyone, you and your neighbors should act considerately whenever you take your children to the playground or swimming pool.

Never let your children swim or run around unattended at the pool. You may want to sit and soak up the sun, but it's too dangerous around water to let your manners go lax. Besides, it's rude to the other pool goers if they have to deal with your unattended children. Another no-no at the pool is disagreeing with the lifeguards. Their job is to protect swimmers, and it's just not right to argue with them.

When you take your kids to the playground, you should also keep an eye on them. Make sure that they're sharing toys and not bullying any other children into giving up playground equipment.

Trouble in the Neighborhood

Just because everyone living in the neighborhood has a financial investment in the common properties, thanks to the dues they pay, that doesn't mean that all the residents know how to exercise common courtesies on those common grounds. Nor does everyone know how to get along with their neighbors.

If your neck of the woods has a neighborhood association, you may be tempted to run to the association whenever you have a problem with a neighbor. Really the best way to solve person-to-person problems is on a person-to-person basis. Give your neighbor the benefit of the doubt and have a friendly conversation about what's bugging you. Perhaps your neighbor is unaware of his seemingly discourteous behavior and your chitchat is all he needs to shape up and fix the problem. Of course, if the problem is something ongoing and no amount of pleading with your neighbor seems to be working, then it may be time to bring in the neighborhood association to address the problem.

Chapter 15

Entertaining Etiquette

One of the joys of owning your own home is having people over. With more and more Americans continuing the nesting trend, you've probably noticed how often people entertain at home rather than going out somewhere to celebrate a special occasion—even if that special occasion is just getting together with good friends.

Invitation Etiquette

It's your choice whether or not to send a formal invitation to friends and family when you're planning to entertain at home. However, a written invitation is a great idea if you're celebrating a specific occasion, such as a promotion, birthday, or anniversary, where people might want to bring gifts, or your party has a specific theme. Written invitations are also a good choice when you're planning a pot luck dinner or a bring-your-own affair. The invitation will give your guests plenty of notice that they need to plan ahead for what they're going to bring to your home that day.

If you do go the written invitation route, definitely send it out two to four weeks in advance. You've got a little more leeway with verbal invitations, which are usually for much more casual events anyway—a week's notice is fine in this case.

ALERT!

Whether you issue a written or verbal invitation, don't forget to include an R.S.V.P.-by date, along with your contact information. Otherwise you won't know who or how many are coming, and your guests won't know by which date they need to respond to your invitation.

Beyond invitations, there are many other elements of entertaining that you need to keep in mind as your plan for your event.

Menu Considerations

When planning the menu for your at-home entertainment, you should think of the foods that are easy to prepare and serve. You never want to try something new for the first time at a party, such as making lobsters or baking a soufflé, when you've never done either before. You're setting yourself up for too many unknowns with an untested dish, and this will only increase your stress level.

Another option is to have your dinner party catered or to repackage precooked foods. If you choose the latter, presenting these prepared foods in your serving pieces will lend an air of sophistication to your event that you'd never be able to achieve if you served everything from their original containers.

Dietary Needs

Whether you choose to cook or cater your event, you would be a polite host if you kept your guests' dietary needs in mind. These may include having a pasta dish for your vegetarian friends to enjoy or not serving something that goes against a person's cultural or religious background, such as beef to a Hindu (cows are considered sacred).

That's not to say that you should plan an entire meal around your vegetarian friends when all you really want to serve is a nice juicy steak. Nor should you bring in a rabbi to turn your Christian kitchen kosher before you invite a few Jewish friends over. However, taking your guest's likes and dislikes into consideration is always good manners.

Taking Children into Consideration

If children will be coming to your party, you should take their tastes into consideration as well. Every parent wants their child to expand his or her palette and try new things, but when you take your children to other people's home, you shouldn't force them to eat anything they don't like. Sure it would be nice if they took just a taste, and maybe they will. But the good mannered host will always have something kid-friendly on hand to serve so that the little tykes don't go through the evening hungry.

You are under no obligation to invite your guest's children to your home, especially if you're having a nighttime affair. At the same time, it would be rude for an invited guest to show up unexpectedly with children in tow. However, if this happens, you should welcome all graciously into your home.

Again, don't go overboard by ordering in pizzas just for the kids. However, if you're making something that could easily be adapted for your young guests, such as pasta, then do so. Your guests who are parents will really appreciate your effort, and so will the youngsters.

Civil Seating Arrangements

It is your prerogative as the host to decide if you're going to have assigned seating and, if so, where you'll seat each of your guests. It's a good idea to create seating cards for each guest when you do have assigned seating, although offering verbal direction as people take their seats is fine to do as well.

However, if you know you're going to be crazed in the kitchen as people start to sit down, it's a good idea to put the seating cards out ahead of time, before your guests arrive. Assigned seating makes the most sense when you've planned a sit-down meal that will include a number of courses.

As a guest you should never try to switch around assigned seating, just because you don't like where the host has placed you. Your host has likely spent a lot of time working on these seating arrangements, and you must respect his wishes.

Behaving at the Buffet

As social rules have relaxed, more and more people are choosing to have a buffet meal for their dinner parties. The buffet might be set up on the sideboard or serving table in the dining room where you will be eating, or there could be food stations throughout the home, and you take whatever open seat you happen to find to eat your meal.

When hosting a buffet dinner party, there are two important issues to keep in mind. First, if you're going to have open seating, make sure that you have not only enough chairs, couches, or other surfaces for people to sit on but also tables nearby where they can put down their plates, glasses and silverware. Second, always have at least 20 percent more plates, cups, and flatware than the number of people who will be joining you for a meal. Buffets lend themselves well to seconds, and it isn't polite to take an already used plate back up to the buffet. Your guests will need plenty of clean plates to use if they decide to go back for seconds.

As the guest at a buffet, you shouldn't fill your plate to overflowing proportions. Since it's OK to take seconds at the buffet, work hard to pace yourself and take conservative amounts of food at each round.

QUESTION?

Is it OK to serve children on paper goods?
Children aren't always as delicate with glassware and plates as you'd like them to be. For this reason, you should never feel shy about using paper goods for their place settings when inviting young guests to your home for a meal.

While standing at the buffet, don't mix up serving utensils. Also, if you feel a sneeze or cough coming on, turn away. In a situation like this, it's pretty obvious why restaurants have Plexiglas sneeze guards over their buffets that you usually have to reach under to serve yourself. Since homes aren't going to have these kinds of protective devices, you need to turn away and, of course, say, "Excuse me" after you sneeze or cough.

The Children's Table

When you invite children to a celebration at your home, it's a good idea to plan ahead to serve kid-friendly food, as mentioned above. It's also a good idea to set aside a place for them to eat. This could be the proverbial children's table, which is separate from where the grown-ups are eating. Or you could arrange to have the children eat in an entirely different room, such as in your finished basement while the parents enjoy a meal upstairs. If you'd like your meal to go as smoothly as possible—and to give your adult guests a bit of a break from their offspring—definitely go with some kind of separate children's seating situation.

Proper Place Settings

Those who have eaten in a formal restaurant or at a formal affair know that there is a certain way of setting a table that's very proper. There's no reason that you can't recreate formal place settings at your home when you entertain there. Here's what you need to keep in mind.

Silverware

When setting your table, always keep European convention in mind—you use your fork in your left hand and your knife in your right. A multi-course meal is going to need multiple pieces of silverware or flatware. It's not polite to borrow a fork from one course to another. As each course gets cleared away, so does the flatware.

A meal that will have soup, then a salad course followed by pasta and then a meat dish will have the following flatware set out, from left to right:

1. Salad fork
2. Pasta fork*
3. Meat fork
4. Meat knife
5. Salad knife
6. Soupspoon

* Some diehard pasta eaters believe in twirling their fork on a spoon. Therefore, you might want to put out a pasta spoon, which you could bring with the course since it doesn't fit naturally on the place setting described above.

FACT

A bread-and-butter knife and plate are both part of formal table settings. When setting your table, you would situate them between 10 and 12 o'clock or in the upper left corner of the setting to follow proper etiquette.

Plates, Bowls, and More

When you set a formal table, you should always start the plate setting with a charger dish. This oversized plate remains on the table until you serve the main course. If you're serving soup, salad, and pasta, you would always place each dish onto the charger plate. It's only when you bring out the main course that you should take the charger plate away. Not only does the charger plate add an air of elegance to your table but also it keeps your tablecloth from getting dirty as your guests enjoy their first few courses.

If you're serving anything that needs its shell peeled or removed, like shrimp or lobster, always put an extra plate on the side of the place setting. This is where your guests can place their peelings. Otherwise, they may be tempted to spit them out into their napkins.

Gracious Use of Glasses

The upper right-hand corner of your place setting is where you should put all of the glassware you'll need for your dinner. Unlike silverware, you don't line glasses up in reverse order, based on when your guests will need them. Instead, glasses are like kids in a class picture—you put them out in size order, with the smallest glass on the right and the largest on the left.

If you're running low on matching glassware, you don't have to run out and buy more for your party. You should feel free to mix and match your stemware. Not only will this give your table an interesting look but you can take comfort in knowing that you won't be breaking any protocol rules in doing so.

If you're going to be serving a variety of wines with dinner, you should have glasses out for each kind of wine or spirit. Keep in mind that red wine and white wine glasses vary quite a bit in size and shape, and there are two kinds of champagne glasses—the flat and round kind and the flute. It's up to you which kind you use; just don't mix the two at the same table.

Host's Behavior

The gracious host is always ready to greet her guests with a welcoming smile and a gesture to come in. You don't want your guests to be ringing your doorbell while you've still got curlers in your hair or when your husband is just putting away the vacuum cleaner.

The best way to ensure that you're a happy and calm host is to plan ahead. Don't leave anything to the last minute, whether it's your shower or cleaning the bathrooms. Do all your chores well in advance, including setting the table. Many savvy hosts will have their tables ready to go the day before they're entertaining at home.

The ideal as a host is this: About an hour before your guests arrive, you should be able to sit down and relax with a glass of wine, if you so choose, so that you're in a positive state of mind when the first guests gets there.

It's OK to Get Help

One of the best ways to make sure that you're not running around crazy is to get help in the kitchen. By bringing someone in to cook or serve your meal, you can focus all your attention on your guests, as you should. Also, when you've got serving help, you can instruct these folks to take away any dirty dishes that may accumulate around the house, to keep the ice bucket filled and make sure that the coffee goes on in time for dessert.

Hiring help doesn't have to be an expensive or elaborate ordeal. Plenty of college students have restaurant experience and would be perfect to bring in for your dinner party.

Thoughtful Introductions

One of the best ways to have people feel welcome in your home is to make sure that as your guests arrive, you introduce them to one another. You don't need trumpets to sound or an announcer to yell, "Hear ye, hear ye . . . "

Rather, as a guest arrives, take him by the arm and introduce him to the people standing nearby.

When making an introduction, always do more than just say a person's name. Try to think ahead of time about any interesting descriptive information that you can add with an introduction. By offering this extra bit of background on each of your guests, you'll help people to spark conversations, even if they've never met before.

It's possible that in the middle of your introductions, you may space out on someone's name—even someone whom you've known for years. Instead of trying to cover yourself, tell the truth: "The excitement of the night has gotten to me, and I'm embarrassed to admit this, but I've forgotten your name." Usually people react to this kind of forthright confession with good humor.

Dealing Graciously with Snafus

No matter how well you plan for your dinner party or any entertaining that you do at home, Murphy's Law will probably kick in at some point or another and something will go wrong. It could be a glass of red wine spilling on your white carpet or the fact that you forgot to check the oven, only to have the smoke alarms go off as your reminder.

The best way to graciously deal with any dinner party snafus is to do so calmly and with a sense of humor. Don't lose your cool and start running around like crazy. It's OK to enlist your guests' help in cleaning things up: "John, would you be a dear and get me some club soda and a towel to clean up this red wine? They're in the kitchen." Your guests will feel a lot better if they can assist you in some way, as opposed to standing around, watching you go bonkers, so don't feel bashful about asking them for help.

Being a Good Guest

It's wonderful when friends invite you over for dinner or to celebrate a special occasion. A great way to ensure that folks will continue to include you in their entertaining events is knowing what it takes to be a good guest—the kind that people will always want to invite into their home.

Timeliness Is Top-Notch

An invitation that asks that you arrive at 8:30 P.M. means just that—show up at the door at 8:30. Never arrive a few minutes early, as you may be barging in on the host as she makes any last-minute preparations. If you hate the idea of being the first person to the party, then you would still be safe arriving five to fifteen minutes after the stated time. But any time after that, you should call and let the host know you're going to be late. It would be terrible if you arrived for dinner at 9:30 P.M. when the host wanted to start the meal at 9:00.

Arriving Empty-Handed Is Impolite

Whenever someone invites you to be a guest in his or her home, you should always bring a hostess gift. A bottle of wine, box of chocolates, or some kind of greenery is always a good fallback hostess gift.

Just keep in mind that you can never force the host to serve that bottle of wine or put out that box of chocolates that you just brought. It could conflict with the meal he's planned, and besides, it's a gift for him—he should be able to enjoy it when he wants to and on his own terms.

QUESTION?

I told a friend that I could come for dinner, and now I can't make it. What should I do?
Always call if your plans have to change, even if it's at the last minute. Your host will appreciate the call. Also, make sure that you're canceling for a bona fide reason, not just because you changed your mind. You don't want to tell the host that you have to go out of town and then run into her at the store the day of the dinner party.

Bring a Friend

Direct-selling parties always implore people to bring a friend, because that way the party's host can get more business. But you should never assume that an invitation for dinner is a bring-a-friend situation.

Your host may not realize that you've recently begun dating someone, and there's no reason for you to have to go to dinner alone. However, you can't just show up that night with your boyfriend on your arm.

When you call to R.S.V.P. say something like, "I've been spending a lot of time lately with this really great guy who I'd love for you to meet," at which point the host should say, "Oh, why don't you bring him along for dinner?" Never invite someone or suggest that a host change her guest list based on your dating needs, but it's fine to politely hint at your desire to bring someone with you. And if the host agrees, then you're set. If not, then you've got to respect the "no unexpected guests" rule and either R.S.V.P. that you can't come or show up alone.

Judging Others

It's really easy to automatically judge people when you go to their homes. You may disagree with their decorating taste or find that their house isn't as clean or tidy as you keep yours. Maybe you don't like the food they're serving or the people they've invited. Regardless of what you're thinking, keep your thoughts to yourself.

It would be in the utmost worst taste to let your feelings be known. Not only will you be rude but also you could hurt the host's feelings, and she was nice enough to invite you to her home.

Chapter 16

Holiday Demeanor

Holidays are a time to embrace the people you love and care about, not the time to be distant or shun them. That's why people feel all warm and fuzzy when they think back to the holidays they spent during their childhood. There were always lots of people around and, ideally, lots of people having fun.

As an adult you may not think of the holidays this way—often there's more stress than there is fun, especially when you're hosting a holiday celebration. However, if you keep the idea of including others and good manners in mind, then your heart and your holiday demeanor are sure to both be in the right place.

A Nice New Year's Eve

New Year's Eve is the night that most adults look forward to all year. It symbolizes the start of a new year, with many resolutions to be made, and it's always an excuse to stay up late and party with your friends.

Drinking champagne is a given on New Year's Eve, but don't let anyone leave your party if they've had too much to drink. You won't be seen as a good host if you let your guests ring in the New Year with a DWI charge.

If you're planning a New Year's Eve celebration at your home this year, make sure you include all your neighbors. While most cities require that people be quiet by 10:00 P.M. during the weekdays and 11:00 P.M. on the weekends, New Year's Eve is an exception. The best way not to annoy your neighbors is to invite them to celebrate with you. Then when everyone steps outside to welcome the New Year with pot banging, horn blowing and singing, you won't have to worry that you're bothering your neighbors—they'll all be there with you!

Bring the Kids

Including children in your New Year's party is a good idea since babysitters are often in short supply that night. And you should make plans for how you'll entertain the children as the night wears on.

Older children will surely want to stay awake to ring in the New Year and may not need as many organized activities to keep them occupied. But the novelty of the night will wear off fast for your youngest guests, who will likely fall asleep before the ball drops in Times Square. Don't get annoyed if they do—instead, plan ahead for it.

When you send out your invitations, ask parents to bring their children's pajamas and sleeping bags. Then you can set aside one room in the house with kids' movies and where the kids can settle down to have a quasi-slumber party. Parents will really appreciate that you've made this extra effort to include their children, and you've given them a place to go to celebrate the New Year.

Midnight Kisses

If you happen to be at a New Year's celebration without a date, you may want to plan ahead about what you're going to do about your midnight kiss to ring in the New Year. It's a tradition most men and women look forward to, but if you're dateless that night, you really don't want to go up to a stranger and plant one on his lips at the strike of twelve. Although some people may enjoy being kissed by strangers, you always run the risk of insulting that person with your forward behavior.

ALERT!

Couples who are at a New Year's Eve party together should keep their midnight kiss short and simple. You don't know how embarrassed or uncomfortable other people will feel if the two of you start kissing at midnight and keep it going for minutes on end.

Valentine's Day

Beyond New Year's Eve, Valentine's Day is when most women hope they'll have a date. No one wants to be a member of the lonely-hearts club on this love-filled day of the year. Even so, you should never throw yourself at someone you're not genuinely interested in having a relationship with, just so you don't end up alone on Valentine's Day. This will only lead someone on and lead him or her to have hurt feelings, come February 15th.

Be careful about what kinds of gifts you give to someone on Valentine's Day, again so you don't give someone the wrong impression. Just because every guy you know is getting a girl a dozen red roses, you shouldn't give them to the person you've just started dating. You really want to reserve red roses for when you're truly serious about someone. However, if you are dating someone and don't want to go as far as getting her flowers, at least make a date with her for Valentine's Day, even if it's just to go bowling. She'll appreciate your efforts to be a real gentleman by taking her out on Valentine's Day.

Easter Etiquette

Despite the prevalence of baby chicks and cute bunnies on Easter decorations, the most important thing to remember when dealing with this holiday is its importance. Some may think that Christmas is the biggest Christian holiday of the year but in fact it is Easter that takes the cake—it's when Christians remember Jesus' death. That means that unless you're hosting an Easter egg hunt for young children, you need to show respect for the holiday's solemnity and people's observation of it.

Attending Church

One of the best ways to observe the holiday is for Christians to go to church. Those who aren't religious need to respect other people's decision to celebrate this holiday by going to church and make their Easter plans accordingly. That is, don't decide to have people over for an Easter luncheon at a time when most Christians would be in church. This would be very rude.

Easter Egg Hunts

There's nothing wrong with adding a little fun to a serious holiday by planning activities for the youngest members of your family. Most people have fond memories of the Easter egg hunts they went on as children, and unless someone strictly forbids their children from participating in such good-natured fun, you should include all your children's friends in any kid-oriented Easter parties you decide to hold. You may even want to splurge on an Easter Bunny costume to give the littlest kids the biggest thrill when the Easter Bunny shows up.

Easter Bunny Legend

Speaking of which, the Easter Bunny is up there with Santa Claus as far as legends go. You'd be wise to continue believing in these legends (at least outwardly for children's sake) until you hear otherwise. Every child grows up believing in mythical creatures and characters, and you'd better not be the one to shatter one kid's fantasy, simply because of your cynical views of such holidays. You need to impart the importance of this message to any of your older children, too.

One of the joys of childhood is being able to believe in the unbelievable. Let children hold onto those fantasies for as long as possible. It's only after you've heard directly from their parents that they now believe otherwise can you talk about the Easter Bunny in matter-of-fact terms.

Passover Protocol

Passover is the spring Jewish holiday that commemorates the Jews' escape from Egypt where they were slaves. It is an eight-day-long event during which you can't eat leavened bread (bread with yeast in it). This is supposed to symbolize the rushed exit people made from their homes, in that the bread they were baking did not have the chance to rise. Without yeast, it became flatbread and that flatbread is matzoh, a staple of the Passover diet.

ESSENTIAL

Make sure to allow time for discussion about the meaning of the holiday when you invite non-Jewish friends over for Passover Seder. This will help your guest understand your traditions and fell more comfortable in an unfamiliar situation.

One of the ways that orthodox and conservative Jewish families prepare for Passover is by cleaning out their homes of all leavened products and anything that isn't kosher for Passover. It's a long and arduous process that also requires you to switch your dishes for the week of Passover to make sure that they're "clean" for the holiday.

The Passover Seder

The way that Jewish families welcome the start of Passover is by holding a Seder, during which they retell the story of the long-ago escape from slavery. This ceremony usually occurs around a dinner table and culminates in a great feast. If you happen to be including non-Jewish friends in your Seder, make sure that you adapt your plans to include lots of explanations about what's going on or the relevance of certain traditions. This will help those in attendance better understand what's going on.

If you happen to be invited to a friend's home for a Passover celebration and you're looking to bring a hostess gift, make sure that any food you choose says "Kosher for Passover" on it. Otherwise, your Jewish friend won't be able to bring it into her home or enjoy it until after Passover is over.

Mother's and Father's Days

Both of these springtime celebrations are designed to make mothers and fathers feel special for at least one day out of the year. Mother's Day and Father's Day are especially eventful for new parents who've never had the pleasure of being remembered on these days. If you know someone who has just had a baby, definitely do something special for his or her first Father's Day or Mother's Day.

To a parent, Mother's Day and Father's Day have a similar importance to a wedding anniversary—it's a day that you don't want to let slip by without remembering in one way or another. For starters you should always send your mother or father a card and then call your parent on this special day. If you live nearby, you should make plans to see your parent, especially if you have children. It's a big deal for a grandmother to be with her family on Mother's Day and a grandfather to be with his family on Father's Day. It would also be nice if you could take your parent out for a meal and/or buy them a gift.

Polite Thanksgiving

Thanksgiving is the only holiday that every American celebrates, regardless of race or religion. No wonder the days leading up to and after the holiday are the busiest travel days of the year. Everyone is on his or her way to someone's house for Thanksgiving.

If you have to travel to get to a Thanksgiving dinner, you're going to have to be patient. Unless you leave in the middle of the night or only have to go down the street, chances are you're going to be dealing with crowds and traffic. There's no reason to lose your cool if you find yourself stuck—everyone else is in the same boat. If you keep your wits about you, everyone will arrive at their Thanksgiving dinner in good spirits.

Hosting Thanksgiving

Most families follow an unwritten rule when it comes to Thanksgiving. That is, the oldest living relative who is capable of hosting Thanksgiving dinner is the person whose home everyone plans to go to at Thanksgiving. The responsibility may fall to the grandparents of the family, who may or may not relish the thought of hosting this annual gathering.

Unwritten family rules aside, if you suspect that an older relative has become burdened with preparing, cooking, and hosting Thanksgiving, you should definitely offer to help or to host Thanksgiving in your own home. You may also want to suggest that this year your family goes out for Thanksgiving, which will leave the cooking and cleaning up to someone else. Either way, you may discover that the family member who normally hosts Thanksgiving may welcome this change of venue.

Houseguests

Besides traffic you're likely going to have to deal with houseguests at Thanksgiving. Either you'll have people staying with you or you're going to be someone's houseguest somewhere else.

As the host it's up to you to make your guests' stay as comfortable as possible. Make sure that you give your guest room a thorough cleaning ahead of time, including washing the linens, vacuuming the carpet, and dusting the furniture. Don't forget to go over the guest bathroom, if you have one, to make sure it's clean. If your towels and face cloths have seen better days, now would be a good time to go out and invest in new ones that your guests can use.

It would also be nice if you could ask whoever is going to be staying with you if they have any food preferences. That way you can food shop in advance and are sure to have their favorites on hand.

Hopefully, if you're staying with someone for Thanksgiving, they've shown the same courtesy to you as you would to your houseguests by having you stay in a clean room and asking ahead of time what food they should shop for.

While you can't demand that your host food shop for you in advance, if anyone in your family has any food allergies, you can request ahead of time that your host keep the home clear of suspected allergens, such as peanuts or seafood. You're talking health here, not just manners.

If you get to someone's home and find nothing appetizing or that you're used to, such as your all-important morning coffee, you could always ask to run to the store for the person, under the guise of picking up any milk or bread that they need. Then while you're out, you can buy the staples you'd like to have during your stay.

Helping in the Kitchen

Whether you're staying at someone's house for Thanksgiving or only visiting for the day, you should always offer to help in the kitchen. This is good manners that span the gender spectrum, meaning each person sitting at the table should ask at least once, "Is there anything I can do to help?" The Thanksgiving cook can always use a few extra hands. Even if the cook tells you that she's OK, at the very least clear your dishes after the meal as a way of pitching in, albeit in a small way.

Helping Others at Thanksgiving

Sometimes with all the cooking and traveling for Thanksgiving, you may forget the true meaning of the holiday—which is that you should be thankful for all you have. A great way to have the holiday take on new meaning is to help others give thanks, such as those that are less fortunate than you are.

Instead of just cooking a big meal for your family this year, for Thanksgiving you could also:

- Donate food to a food pantry.
- Work in a soup kitchen.
- Deliver meals to homebound seniors.
- Invite a widow or widower you know to join you for Thanksgiving.

Dealing with Football

Along with turkey and traffic, one of the constants of Thanksgiving is football. If your home is like most, all the men end up sitting down to watch a football game while the women are left to clean up after the meal. It's fine to give the men in your life a free pass to take in a football game on this holiday, but men take note: at least offer to help do something before settling onto the couch. The women in your family will feel a lot more appreciated if you do.

With the advent of services like Tivo there's no reason to rush from the Thanksgiving table to the couch to catch a football game. Have Tivo tape the football game so you can think of your manners and finish your meal first. Then you can start the game later.

Civil Chanukah

Unlike Christian kids who only get one batch of presents on Christmas (two if their family opens gifts on Christmas Eve and Christmas Day), Jewish children may feel like they've hit the gift goldmine with Chanukah. During this eight-day holiday many children receive a present each night, which means the gift giving just keeps going and going.

There's no reason for you to rub this fact in your friend's faces, if they don't celebrate Chanukah. In the end, you may end up with as many gifts as your Christian friends, and besides, gift-giving holidays aren't supposed to be a competition. Just be thankful for any gifts you've received and don't brag about your gifts.

FACT

Even if you're the only Jewish home on the block, no one should make you feel as if you can't put your Menorah in your window as your contribution to holiday decorations. It's rude for neighbors to push their views on others, and you should feel free to celebrate your holidays as you see fit.

Courteous Christmas

Christmas may be one of the happiest times of the year but it's also a time when many people feel overwhelmed with work, family, and religious obligations. Then there's all the shopping for gifts that you have to do, and if you've got kids, they're probably driving you crazy with excitement. Yes, it's a happy time of the year but one that you're likely wishing away almost as soon as it starts. Even though everything may be trying your patience, do your best to keep courtesy in mind as you go about your day-to-day dealings during Christmas.

Dealing with Decorations

The most important thing for neighbors to remember is that decorating for Christmas isn't a competition. You should put up lights and other items in front of your home that you enjoy and find pleasant. Never use an overabundance of tacky Christmas decorations as a way of making a point or getting back at a neighbor you dislike. Not only will you annoy him, but in the end you'll probably annoy everyone else living near you as well.

Legend of Santa

No matter how cynical you feel come Christmas, don't let your cynicism ruin Christmas for any children you know. You must keep the legend of Santa Claus alive for as long as possible. It's only after a child's parents have told you that their children believe otherwise can you speak about Santa in different terms. In the meantime you must play along.

Finding and Guessing Gifts

A surefire way for a kid to drive his mother crazy is to find the Christmas gifts that she's hidden and then to figure out what's inside each box. If you're old enough to understand manners, then you're old enough to understand this: don't put your mother and father through the grief of your guessing your gifts. They spent a lot of time picking out the right present for you, and they look forward to surprising you with this great gift. If you take away the surprise, then you'll have ruined things for them.

Try to remember that you want to make your parents happy on Christmas—not disappoint them. Even if you manage to guess what's in the box, act surprised when you open the wrapping. You'll make them very happy if you do.

Holidays That Are Foreign to You

While companies like Hallmark may feel as if they have cornered the market on holidays throughout the year, there are plenty of other holidays that occur that you may not be familiar with—but for which it might be appropriate to send a Hallmark card. These include the Jewish New Year, called Rosh Hashanah, which occurs during fall, and Kwanzaa, the African harvest festival that falls around Christmas time.

What's important to keep in mind when dealing with holidays that are foreign to you is this: to be polite you need to respect each other's right to celebrate their own holidays. You don't want to do anything they could find offensive, such as eating in front of a Muslim who might be fasting for Ramadan or a Jew who is fasting for Yom Kippur (also part of the Jewish New Year).

When in doubt, ask your friend who celebrates these holidays to educate you on his traditions. By learning more about his celebrations, not only will you have a better understanding of his beliefs, but also you'll have become a better friend for approaching your differences with an open mind.

Chapter 17

Genteel Gift Giving

There are probably times when you feel like you're always in the market to buy a gift. This is especially true around the holidays or if your friends' and family members' birthdays all tend to fall at the same time.

It's always a good idea to remember someone's special occasion with a gift, especially if that person is a child or a close family member. You should always try to deliver a birthday or anniversary gift before the actual date occurs or, if you've been invited to a party, make sure that you come to the celebration bearing a gift. If you need to get someone a gift a little later than you'd hope, such as for a birthday, always call on their birthday to send your good wishes and then let that person know that a gift is forthcoming.

Choices for Children

Perhaps the most fun you'll have when shopping for gifts is when you have to buy something for a child. There's nothing like visiting a toy store to take you back down memory lane, which is why so many adults find joy in getting gifts for the youngest folks they know. This is especially true of grandmothers who love to spoil their grandchildren with treats.

Savvy Shopping

If you're in the market for a child's gift because your own son or daughter is going to a friend's birthday party, then by all means bring your child along on your shopping expedition. While a grown-up may find herself frozen in a toy aisle, not quite sure what to get for another child, your son or daughter should be able to hone right in on the perfect gift.

A good rule of thumb is to spend about $3 per year of a child's age, although this amount may not seem sufficient for very young children. In this instance, you should feel comfortable spending about $20 on a gift.

You may want to check with a child's parents first before hitting the stores. By doing so, you'll get a good sense of what the child already has or any themed gifts the parents might be going for this year.

Don't shop too early for a child's gift, or your gift may seem passé by the time you give it to him. A good rule of thumb is to shop about two weeks or less before a child's birthday.

Toys are always a good gift for children. Try to get a toy that's somewhat educational, such as a board game that requires counting or solving a mystery. This way you can kill two birds with one stone—you'll appease the parents with something that helps their kid learn and grow, and you'll make the child happy by getting him a toy.

FACT

Books are always an appropriate gift to give to a child. They are an especially good choice if you know that the gift recipient is a reader. If you can get an autographed book, that's even better and will make a book gift more meaningful.

The Gift of Clothing

While most grown-ups get a kick out of getting children cute clothing, the child will surely groan when he opens the package and sees clothing inside. Sure, groaning isn't polite but sometimes kids can't help themselves.

The only time clothing is a good gift to give is when you've been invited to a very young child's birthday or other special occasion for a new baby. New parents can never have enough clothing, and the child is too young to react negatively to your present.

Gifts for Teens and Young Adults

As children grow into tweens, then teens, and young adults, gift giving tends to get dicey. Kids this age tend to be very finicky about their likes and dislikes, including their need to follow trends and to fit in. Unless you happen to be a teen yourself, don't even try to get inside a teenager's head and figure out what you should give him or her for a gift.

You'll make a better impression on the kid if you go with something simple and safe—a gift card. Try to get this gift card at a store where you've seen teens hanging out, such as a music, video, or department store.

If you're not comfortable with the impersonal nature of gift cards, then you can try your luck at buying a book, videogame, or CD that you think he might like. But do him a favor, just in case your teen radar was off by a long shot: include a gift receipt so he can exchange the gift for something more appropriate.

Just because someone gave you the gift of cash, as opposed to a tangible "thing," that doesn't mean that you're off the thank-you note writing hook. You will still need to send the gift giver a formal thank you for his thoughtfulness.

When you need to get a teen a gift fast and you don't have time to get a gift card, cold hard cash is always a good idea. But, don't just hand him a $20 bill. At least make the effort to buy a card and write a note inside. Then you can put the money in the card, and you'll have the perfect gift that's sure to make any teen happy.

Birthdays Through the Years

One of the highlights of everyone's childhood is when your birthday would roll around, and you would get to have a party and open lots of presents. As you got older the novelty of birthdays probably wore off, especially as you approached your late teens and twenties.

When you're stumped for a gift to give an adult, it's always a good idea to consider whatever hobby the person enjoys. Then you can buy a gift that is somehow affiliated with that hobby.

When it comes to giving people gifts for their birthdays, you should keep the following in mind:

1. Until a child is eighteen, you should buy him a gift every year.
2. After eighteen you can probably get away with only giving a tangible gift on milestone birthdays, such as twenty-one, thirty, forty, and so on.
3. Parents, children and siblings should give each other gifts each year, regardless of the person's age.
4. If you're invited to a birthday party for an adult, you should always bring a gift.

Remembering Birthdays

You may not always remember your anniversary, but if you're a mother, chances are you'll never forget a child's birthday. Not everyone is blessed with a mother's intuition or memory, though, and you may need help remembering important people's birthdays throughout the year.

One of the best ways to always remember a birthday (or anniversary, for that matter) is to spend the week before New Year's updating your calendar for the next year. Spend an afternoon filling in everyone's birthdays and other important days on the respective dates of the upcoming year's calendar. This will ensure that throughout the year, as you turn pages on the calendar, you'll always see what special days are coming up. Then you can shop accordingly and make sure that you always have a present to give or to mail in time for someone's birthday.

FACT

It's acceptable for older adults to ask that their guests bring no gifts to a party. However, that doesn't mean that everyone will heed the request, and they should always accept any gifts graciously.

Parents of adult children shouldn't take it upon themselves to badger their kids into remembering others' birthdays. If you've done your job right and raised your kids to be well-mannered adults, then they will send birthday cards and gifts when necessary. If they don't, you have to remember that they're adults, and they're old enough to make their own decisions, including to be badly behaved about birthdays.

Receipts and Returns

There is never anything wrong with returning a gift that you've received for your birthday. It may seem like you're being polite in keeping a gift you don't really like or don't want, simply because someone took the time to give it to you, but that's not true. If you know where the gift came from, and it's easy for you to return or exchange it for something else that you'll enjoy and use, then do it. Of course, you don't have to wave this fact in the gift-giver's face.

If someone happens to ask about a gift that you ended up returning (which is rude to begin with), you can always tell a little white lie to protect that person's feelings. You could say something like, "Your gift was so perfect for me that, believe it or not, I got two of those birdfeeders for my birthday. I ended up exchanging one for a garden ornament instead, which I'll have to show you the next time you come to my home."

Speaking of returns you will always be seen as a gracious gift giver if you include a gift receipt with someone's gift. This tells the person that while you're happy to be giving them this gift, you understand that sometimes gift givers get things wrong. Therefore, you're giving them your implicit permission to use the enclosed gift receipt to return or exchange the gift, if they so choose. In a perfect world every gift giver would include a gift receipt with a present.

Gracious Gift Receiving

People spend so much time worrying about the right gift to give someone that they often neglect learning the art of receiving gifts graciously. It's a skill that takes time to develop and one that you can let slide a bit with young children, who tend to tear into their packages like forbidden candy.

Helping Children

The first thing to keep in mind—and to teach your children—is that when you're opening gifts in front of others, you've got to put other people's feelings first. No matter what you find inside a box or how much you like (or hate) the gift, you've got to be gracious. Some people call this putting on a poker face, and the idea behind it is simple: You can't let your face reveal what's going on inside your head, if you're having negative thoughts about the gift. Even though you're thinking, "What was this person thinking when she bought this for me?" your expression should be grateful while you are saying, "Wow, this is a great gift!"

Thanking the Gift Giver

The other thing that's important to remember about getting gifts is that, again, no matter how little you think of the present you've just received, you must send the person a thank-you note. It may be a bit of a challenge to think of something original or genuine to say in a thank-you note for something you intend to throw out, give away, or take back to the store. But you must send a note anyway. You can always get away with a generic thank you for the gift, along with a thank you for remembering your birthday.

Anniversaries

If you want to stay on good graces with your husband or wife, you would be wise never to forget your wedding anniversary. If you tend to forget these kinds of important dates, use the calendar trick mentioned earlier to make a note of the dates. This will help spark your memory and help you avoid spending your wedding anniversary sleeping on the couch.

Anniversary Themes

When it comes to anniversaries, it's a good idea to give a gift that somehow relates to the anniversary you're celebrating. Here are the common themes for wedding anniversaries, some of which you'll notice repeat. That's because the following is a combination of traditional and modern anniversary themes:

1st anniversary: paper or clocks
2nd anniversary: cotton or china
3rd anniversary: leather, crystal, or glass

4th anniversary: fabric, fruit, flowers, or electrical appliances
5th anniversary: wood or silverware
6th anniversary: candy, iron, or wood
7th anniversary: wood, copper, or home office equipment/desk sets
8th anniversary: electrical appliances, linen, lace, bronze, or pottery
9th anniversary: pottery, willow, or leather
10th anniversary: tin, aluminum, or diamonds
11th anniversary: steel or jewelry
12th anniversary: table linens, silk, or pearls
13th anniversary: lace or furs
14th anniversary: ivory or gold jewelry
15th anniversary: crystal, glassware, or watches
20th anniversary: china or platinum
25th anniversary: silver
30th anniversary: pearls or diamond jewelry
35th anniversary: coral or jade
40th anniversary: ruby or garnet
45th anniversary: sapphire
50th anniversary: gold
55th anniversary: emerald
60th anniversary: diamond
75th anniversary: diamond

You can use these anniversary themes to help you find a gift when you're stumped about what to buy. Think of them as a guide that gets you out of the doghouse, because you'll always have some idea of what to buy your significant other for her anniversary.

Gifts for Religious Celebrations

There are a number of religious rites of passage that involve inviting guests to celebrate with a family. During these times, you will probably be expected to bring a gift for the young lady or man who is the center of attention. However, if this religious celebration is foreign to you—or if this is your first child celebrating such a rite of passage—you may not know what's appropriate to give. Here are some ideas to consider.

QUESTION?

What's an appropriate monetary amount to give for a bar mitzvah, bat mitzvah, or first communion gift?

For bar and bat mitzvahs, $50 is a good starting point, though close friends and family may want to start their gifts at $100. For a first holy communion, friends may want to give a smaller amount ($25 to $50) while family members may want to give a more significant amount (starting at $100).

Bar Mitzvah

In the Jewish faith, a boy is considered to be a man at age thirteen, when he celebrates his bar mitzvah. Part of the ritual of the bar mitzvah is an elaborate temple service, during which this boy, now a man, is called to read from the Torah (the collection of laws, written in Hebrew, that define Judaism). It is the first time he is allowed to do this, and it's a big deal.

Traditionally, parents give the bar mitzvah boy a prayer shawl, called a tallis, as a gift. He is expected to wear that tallis when he reads from the Torah.

Part of a bar mitzvah is a celebration afterward, which usually involves a lot of dining and dancing. It is customary for guests at a bar mitzvah to bring gifts for the bar mitzvah boy of honor, and these gifts are traditionally the gift of money. These gifts of money could be in the form of cash or a savings bond.

Bat Mitzvah

A bat mitzvah is similar to a bar mitzvah, except it's what you call the rite of passage that Jewish girls go through when they turn thirteen. It is their first time being called to read the Torah and, like for boys, it's a big deal.

Jewish women don't wear prayer shawls when attending synagogue, so a typical gift from the parents may be an ornate prayer book. It usually features her name engraved inside.

Like the bar mitzvah boy, a bat mitzvah girl can expect to have a large celebration after her temple service. Gift guidelines for guests are the same as when attending a bar mitzvah.

First Holy Communion

In most archdioceses in North America, Catholic boys and girls receive their first holy communion in second grade. This is the first time that they are allowed to participate in the Eucharist, which is a part of a Catholic Church service where parishioners accept a wafer and wine that represents or is considered the actual body and blood of Jesus Christ.

Girls usually wear white dresses and veils to their first holy communion. Boys wear dark or white suits. Friends and family members are invited to witness this first communion, including the child's godparents. Then there is usually a celebration afterward.

Traditionally, parents and godparents give the child a gift that is religious in nature—a bible, rosary beads, or a prayer book. However, it's acceptable to give the child the gift of money as well.

Confirmation

This is the third of three religious rituals that Catholic children are expected to go through to fully embrace their faith. It starts with a baby's baptism after birth (see Chapter 2 for more on baptism gifts). Then there is first holy communion. Finally, around age twelve, a child is confirmed and is accepted as a full member of his church congregation.

Nearly every Christian religion has some form of confirmation for its youngest members, and this process usually involves attending confirmation classes that culminate in a church service, called the confirmation.

Families usually celebrate a child's confirmation with a party, where it's traditional to give the newly confirmed child a gift. Again, anything that's religious in nature is an appropriate gift to give, as is the gift of money.

Gifts in a Business Setting

It's always appropriate for a boss to remember her employees' birthdays—and for the employee to remember his boss's birthday, too. The same thing goes for holidays when you would normally exchange gifts with others, such as Christmas and Chanukah.

ALERT!

If you buy your secretary a gift, you have every right to write that purchase off on your expenses. But do your secretary a favor and file your expenses yourself that month. Otherwise, you risk her seeing that write-off and feeling that you didn't give her that gift genuinely.

You need to handle gift giving carefully in a business setting, since you don't want to send the wrong signal or go against company policy in the gift you choose. One way to avoid both is to avoid giving the gift of alcohol, which some companies may prohibit on the premises. You'll also stay away from any euphemisms of sexual harassment if you stay away from gifts of clothing or other personal items. The exceptions to the clothing rule are a tie or scarf, which are benign gifts and are always appropriate to give.

Food is always a good gift to give colleagues, because it's easy to share food with others in the office. This helps to spread the wealth. Another safe gift to give an officemate is a gift certificate or gift card for a local retailer or restaurant.

Tips as Gifts

Come the holidays, not only do you have to buy gifts for your family, friends, and business colleagues, but also you need to set aside cash to tip the service people you deal with on a regular basis. There are always folks you want to recognize at this time of the year.

What to tip these people depends on your relationship with them. For example, you may want to give your babysitter an extra week's salary as a gift or holiday bonus but you wouldn't be this extravagant with your mailman. For starters, the United States Postal Service prohibits mail carriers from accepting gifts over $20, and other government and private organizations may have similar rules. That's why you always want to check first for any employer prohibitions before slipping anyone $20 as their holiday tip.

Tip Guidelines

Here are some of the people you'll likely want to add to your holiday tip list each year and how much you may want to consider tipping them:

- Person who delivers your newspaper ($10).
- Hairstylist or barber (additional 20 percent tip given during a visit near the holidays).
- Day care staff, nanny, or babysitter (at least $20).
- Housekeeper or cleaning person ($25).
- Letter carrier and UPS/FedEx driver ($10 to $20, unless you know that the person's employer has a limit on the value of gifts this person can receive).
- Garage attendants where you park your car ($20).
- Doormen ($25 to $50, depending on your relationship or how much the doorman has done for you in the past year).
- Trash collectors ($20 per collector on the truck).
- Personal trainer ($25).
- Any other person who provides at-home or door-to-door service, such as a driver or dry cleaner delivery service ($20).

It's good manners to tip the people mentioned above who make your day-to-day life easier; that's why you don't want to forget them at the holidays.

Chapter 18

The Protocol with Pets

There's nothing quite as wonderful as owning a pet, especially the domestic kind. You get unconditional love from another living being and a lifelong buddy to boot.

Americans are quite fond of their pets, as evidenced by the number of pets in this country. According to the American Veterinary Medical Association, there are approximately 60 million dogs and 70 million cats as pets in American homes. Next in popularity are birds—there are 10 million birds as pets in this country—and then there are horses, with five million of them considered to be pets.

If you're a pet owner you know how easy it is to think of your furry, feathered, or fishy friends as an extended member of the family. But just because you're so madly in love with your pet, doesn't mean that others will feel the same when they visit your home, meet you on the street, or come into contact with your dog, cat, or other pet in one way or another. To be a polite pet owner, you've got to be considerate of others at all times.

Dogs and Cats

As the statistics state, dogs and cats are the most popular pets in America. Probably a day doesn't go by that you don't see someone in your neighborhood walking a dog or notice a cat sitting in someone's window. When it comes right down to it, there are dogs and cats everywhere.

Home Care

One of the ways that pet owners forget their manners is with the upkeep of their home. If you're going to have a dog or cat living with you, then you've got to make the effort to keep your home clean. You should vacuum and mop the floors on a regular basis so that your home isn't overrun with fur tumbleweeds.

FACT

Bathing a pet on a regular basis is a great way to keep shedding and allergens to a minimum and odors at bay. However, it is an owner's prerogative to bathe or not to bathe his animal on a regular basis. If you find a friend's pet to be especially odorous, keep your opinions to yourself.

If your pets sit on the furniture, you should clean those surfaces as well. No one wants to sit down in a dining room chair or on a living room couch with a dark pair of pants on, only to discover when she stands up that she's covered in fur. If you haven't yet familiarized yourself with a lint brush or similar kind of fur-trapping cleaning tool, you need to do so. Otherwise, for as long as you have a furry friend around, no one is going to want to come over to your house.

At the same time that you're learning to become vigilant about fur balls around your home, you should be aware of any animal odors that might be emanating from your cat's litter box or from your dog's bed, which is really overdue for a washing. You don't want your house to smell like dog or cat, even if you have one living under your roof.

Protocol of Dog Walking

Unless you've got a fenced-in backyard, you're going to have to walk your dog on a regular basis so he can do his business. Here are some protocol tips to keep in mind when you leash up your dog and lace up your walking shoes:

1. Always walk your dog on a leash.
2. Never let your dog walk up onto a neighbor's lawn to do his business.
3. Limit peeing to inanimate objects only, such as fire hydrants and telephone poles, or to the grassy median between the sidewalk and the street.
4. Always bring plastic bags that you can use to clean up after your dog.
5. Always dispose of poop bags in your garbage, not your neighbor's garbage (unless it's trash day and pick-up hasn't occurred yet).
6. If you see another dog approaching, always ask first if the other animal is friendly before letting the dogs get nose to nose.
7. If your dog starts barking at another animal nearby, quiet him down immediately.

Walking your dog can be a pleasurable and social way to spend your time. As long as you behave like the responsible dog owner that you are, you and your dog will always be welcome in the neighborhood.

Noises

When your dog is upset, excited, or sees another animal, he may start to bark. While it's perfectly normal for a dog to communicate this way, it isn't considerate to let your dog bark all the time—especially if he's doing this barking outside where he can bother the neighbors.

Dogs aren't the only animals that can cause a ruckus outside, though. Outdoor cats have been known to do their own version of serenading at night, especially when a female is in heat, or two tomcats decide to fight over their territory. If your cat is a howler and you suspect he's been doing some after hours "entertaining" for your neighbors, try to keep him indoors at night and during the early morning hours so he doesn't bother others.

ALERT!

If your dog spends a lot of time outside, you may want to invest in a bark collar. By putting a bark collar on your dog, you can feel confident that your dog can spend ample time ambling about your backyard without bothering your neighbors with his barking.

Other Animals as Pets

Not every pet owner finds himself in the dog and cat contingent. Birds and horses are also popular pets. Some folks favor fish, rabbits, rodents like hamsters or guinea pigs, and ferrets for their pets. People also keep turtles, snakes, and reptiles as pets, but no matter what genus your pet falls into, there are common courtesies that you, as a pet owner, must always keep in mind. Many of these are the same courtesies as cat and dog owners must deal with. Despite treading in the same territory, they do bear repeating.

Keep Your Home Clean

No one should be able to use their nose to figure out what kind of pet you own the minute they walk in the door. Nor should they have disgusting sights assault their eyes upon walking into a room. That means that you've got to be judicious about keeping your animal's tank or cage clean at all times. Remember—this is your home, not a barn or a pet store. You need to work hard so that it doesn't look or smell like either of these.

FACT

Some reptiles carry illness-causing bacteria on their skin, and you don't want to have any guests getting sick from petting your pet. Always keep hand sanitizer near your animal's cage and encourage anyone who touches your pet to clean his hands afterward.

Quiet Your Pet

A house full of exotic birds may be interesting to look at, but you probably wouldn't want to live next door to one. There's likely to be a lot of squawking going on.

If you can't quiet down your pets indoors, then at least do something to soundproof your home. This might mean hiring someone to install extra insulation in your walls or replacing your old windows with more sound-resistant ones.

Don't Force Your Pet on Anyone

You've got to remember that not everyone who comes over to your home is going to share your enthusiasm for your pet. This is especially true if your pet is of the exotic kind or is a creature that most people associate with scary things, such as mice and spiders. It's fine to introduce people to your pet, but don't be offended if they aren't interested in ogling over your Gila monster or cuddling up with your ferret.

Visitors to Your Home

As a pet owner, especially with dogs, you know the joy you get when you walk through your front door and your four-legged buddy is there to meet you. There's nothing like a happy animal greeting to lift your mood.

Unfortunately, not everyone who walks through your front door will feel the same way about your dog or cat. As hard as it is for pet lovers to believe, not everyone welcomes an animal with open arms, and when someone visits your home, you've got to keep this in mind.

If you're the person doing the visiting in a home with pets and you have allergies, you need to take any precautions against having an allergy attack, such as taking medication ahead of time. It's not the host's responsibility to make his home allergen free before your visit.

Greeting Your Pet

When someone new comes to visit, don't assume that it will be OK for your dog to jump up and give him a "Hello" lick or for your cat to encircle his ankles with a purr-filled greeting. Always find out ahead of time how that person feels about animals and then act accordingly. You may need to put your dog on her leash or hold your cat when you answer the door, and then maybe the person will warm up enough to the animal that you can eventually let the animal roam freely. But as the host, you should never do anything that makes a guest feel uncomfortable. Don't force your animal on that person, saying something like, "Oh, it'll take just a few minutes for the dog to get used to you," when really your priority should be with your guest, not your animal.

There are plenty of animal lovers who may be taken aback by your dog's enthusiasm at greeting them as well and, again, you should keep the dog on her leash until she calms down. However, if the person lets you know that it's OK to let the dog go, you can let her off her leash. Keep an eye on her at all times, though, and if she seems to be getting unruly, put her back on her leash.

There's no reason to leash or lock up your animal every time repeat visitors come over. The only time you should do this is when you know that this visitor is still afraid of your animal or that there have been problems with the animal in the past.

Putting Your Animal in Another Place

Sometimes despite your best intentions your visitor doesn't feel comfortable with your animal around. Or maybe your guest doesn't seem to be mixing well with the animal, not a stretch if that person came with children, and your animal isn't used to children. In that case, don't say as an excuse, "Oh, he's not used to children" and then ignore the animal.

If your dog or cat truly isn't used to children being around, there's no telling how he may react to a child pulling his tail or getting in his face. You never want to risk having an animal attacking a child, even if it seems to be in a playful fashion. Put the dog in another room when uncertain visitors are in your home.

Don't put your dog outside to get away from your visitors, if all he's going to do is bark. You may be doing your visitors a favor but you aren't doing any favors for your neighbors who have to listen to your dog barking for long stretches of time.

You should always plan ahead of time where you will put the animal, in case you need to put him somewhere else. And even though it might seem like a burden to you to have to lock your dog in the laundry room or put your cat upstairs in the bedroom, it really is the polite thing to do when folks are over to visit.

Going Visiting

When you think of your pet as a member of your family, it seems natural to want to bring him with you wherever you go. You've probably seen dog lovers who take their canines in the car with them when they run errands, with the dog sitting in the front seat like just another passenger. If this is how you think of your dog or cat, you have to remember that not everyone appreciates a pet like a pet owner does, and you've got to be respectful of others when you go out and about with your animal.

Asking First

When pet owners get together with other pet owners for a dinner party or other kind of celebration, they may not want to leave their animals home alone. The same thing goes for when they go on vacation. If this describes you, then your first inclination probably is to bring your pet along with you to the other person's house. This is fine to do, as long as you ask first. You should never show up on someone's doorstep with your dog on a leash and expect that you'll both be invited in.

If your dog or cat does go visiting with you and the animal seems to be having a hard time getting along with the other pets in the home, you've got to change your plans. Even though the homeowner welcomed you to bring your dog, if your dog spends the entire evening terrorizing that person's cat or bird, that's not fair to the animal that lives there. You need to bring your dog home immediately or figure out a way to keep him under control for the duration of your visit.

When Nature Calls

One thing you definitely don't want your pet to do at someone else's home is to have an accident. If you come visiting with your cat, you should always bring an extra litter pan and a bag of litter. Putting the litter pan in a similar place to where you have it at your home will help ensure that your cat has a direct hit when it has to go to the bathroom. (Of course, if you usually keep your cat's litter pan in the master bathroom, you might want to ask the homeowners first if it's OK to put it there.) You shouldn't assume that your cat could use the other cat's litter pan, because then you're basically asking your friend to clean up after your pet.

E ALERT!

If you bring your dog to a friend's house, be prepared to walk him on a regular basis. Sometimes dogs react weirdly to new environments, and if you can take him out frequently, you lessen the likelihood of his lifting his leg inside.

Also, do your host a favor and offer to walk her dog when you take yours out. She was nice enough to let you bring your dog along, and you should do something nice in return, such as letting her off the dog-walking hook for the evening.

Feeding the Beast

Just as you should feel responsible for your animal when nature calls, you should do the same about food during your visit. Do not rely on your host to provide dog or cat kibble for your pet—you should always bring your own along. Or, if you're only going to be at the house for a little while, don't worry about food at all.

If you catch your dog eating from another's bowl, don't just stand there and say, "Oh, that's so cute." It's not good for your dog to eat another's food (different brand foods have different effects on animals' digestive systems), and besides, it's rude to have the dog eat another pet's food. Scold the dog and move him away. You may even want to politely ask your host to take the food up from the floor.

Dealing with Damage

Sometimes despite your best efforts to keep your visiting animal under control, it manages to do some damage to a friend's home. This is unequivocally your responsibility. Not only should you apologize for what your pet did, but also you should offer to clean things up immediately or, if the damage is more serious, to pay to have fixed whatever it was that your pet ruined.

Pet Sitters

There are times in your life when you simply cannot take your pet with you when you travel. That's when you'll need to find someone to pet sit for you, either by boarding your pet at a kennel or veterinarian's office, or asking someone to come over on a regular basis to watch your animal.

When you're in the market for someone to watch your pet, it's always best to ask other pet owners you know for a recommendation. Understand that some people may not want to "share" their service people with you and may balk at your request. It's their right to do so, although it is rude. At the same time you should never steal a pet sitter away from someone else, simply because they didn't want to give you the sitter's phone number. It's one thing to find a pet sitter that comes highly recommended from other pet owners you know but it's another (and entirely rude) thing to let revenge be your hiring guide.

Don't let price be your only judge in deciding which pet sitting option is best for you. You've got to think of your pet first.

Most independently minded animals (read: cats) are fine if you leave them alone and have someone come by to feed them only. However, more dependent animals (read: dogs) might not fare as well if you left them alone, and you've got to keep that in mind. You don't want to take the cheap pet-sitting route, only to discover that your dog barks for hours at a time during your absence. Not only will this be a nuisance for your neighbors who had to contend with the nonstop barking, but think about your dog—he may be traumatized by the experience.

Saying Goodbye to a Pet

There are times as a pet owner when you need to bid your pet farewell. This may be because you need to give your animal away or because your animal has died.

If you can't make politeness a priority in keeping your pet, then maybe it's time to admit that you simply don't have the time or willingness to be a respectful pet owner. And that means that you're going to have to give the pet up.

It's never easy to give a pet away but sometimes doing so is for the best—especially if your pet has become a nuisance to your neighbors and has affected your quality of life.

When a pet dies—either because of natural causes or because you had to put him to sleep—you'll need to grieve for that pet. For many people, a pet is just as important as a family member, and death is just as difficult to deal with, whether the loved one who died had four legs or two. If someone you know or care about has lost a pet, it is always appropriate to write a note of condolence to that person.

Chapter 19

Being Polite on Paper

There's no doubt that e-mail has inspired many more people to keep in touch. Unfortunately, with e-mail has come the decline of written correspondence and traditional card sending. But if you want to act properly in business and life, you'd be wise to continue sending handwritten notes and cards to the important people you deal with on a regular basis. There is no substitute for a handwritten and heartfelt sympathy card or timely thank-you note.

Ins and Outs of Invitations

With Web sites like *www.ersvp.com*, it's easy to invite people to celebrate with you, whether it's a holiday party or your child's birthday. But there's something to be said for sending a formal invitation for any celebration you may be planning. Your invitation will tell your guests the who, what, where, and when for your party, and it will also alert them to any theme or formality for your get together. For example, a Memorial Day weekend afternoon party sent on gingham-bordered cardstock tells folks that you're planning a casual affair, whereas a Friday night wine tasting with a hint of glitter and glamour imparts a more formal feel for your dress-up affair.

The Particulars

The most important thing to remember in writing and sending an invitation is making sure you include everything your guests will need to know about the celebration. Be sure to tell them:

- The date, time, and duration of the party.
- The address where you're having the party.
- Whom to R.S.V.P. to and by what date.
- If they need to bring anything, such as to a potluck dinner.
- Any dress particulars, such as if you're having a costume party.

ALERT!

While it's proper to invite your guests via a written and mailed invitation, you can be flexible about how they R.S.V.P. You can give them the choice to phone you or to send you an e-mail.

When to Send the Invitation

It's always best to give your invited guests as much advance notice as possible for your upcoming soiree, and an invitation sent three to six weeks before your party is ideal. This gives enough time for the postal service to deliver your invitation and for your guests to R.S.V.P.

Including Others

The worst thing that a polite host could do is to exclude others from her celebration, especially those who are bound to find out about your party. So when in doubt, invite your next-door neighbor or the women from your play group—that is, if you're inviting people they socialize with and are likely to talk about your event. Just think about how you would feel if everyone on your block or from your apartment complex was invited to a celebration and you weren't. Don't do the same to others by excluding them.

Sharing Sympathy

If there's ever a time in your life when you need the comfort and support of others, it's when somebody dies. Your condolence card won't make the hurt go away for the grieving person but it might make him feel a bit better.

Sending a Sympathy Card

There is no official timeline that tells you when you should send someone condolences. Rather, as soon as you hear that someone has died, you should send a sympathy card. You can mail a handwritten card on your own stationery or you can send a store-bought card. With the latter option be sure to add more than just your signature, though. Include something like, "I was devastated to learn of Joe's death, and I hope your fond memories of him will help you get through this tough time."

You may send one sympathy card for an entire family or, if adult children are living elsewhere, send a sympathy card to each person in the family that lives at a separate address. So if the father of your best friend from high school dies, you should send a card to your friend's mother, and, if your friend lives in her own home, send one to her as well.

If life gets in the way and you can't send a sympathy card immediately, don't assume you shouldn't send one at all. Often there is a great outpouring of sympathy wishes right after someone dies. But that show of support dwindles over time, and the people who lost a friend, family member, or other loved one may feel more alone in the world. A belated condolence card may be just what they need to know that, yes, people are still thinking of them.

Religious Messages

If the person who has died was Roman Catholic, you may give the family great comfort in sending a Mass card, along with your handwritten sympathy card. You can purchase a Mass card from your local Roman Catholic rectory for a nominal fee, and in exchange the church will say a Mass in the near future for the deceased.

QUESTION?

What if I can't find an appropriate faith-based card at my local store?
If you can't find something appropriate, you can always call your local church, synagogue, or mosque to see if they stock faith-based sympathy cards, and then make your purchase accordingly.

You can also send a religious-themed, store-bought card, if you feel that this will be well received by the grieving parties. Most well stocked card stores have sympathy cards for all denominations.

Charitable Donations

Sometimes the best way to show you're thinking about a person dealing with the death of a loved one is to make a donation to that person's favorite charity. The family of people who have had extended illnesses often request that in lieu of flowers you send a donation to a designated charity, such as one related to the illness that the person suffered from. When you chose to honor the person this way, be sure to send a handwritten card letting the family know of your gesture. You can write something like, "In order to remember Joe, we've made a donation in his name to the American Cancer Society."

The Thoughtfulness of Thank-You Notes

In a perfect world, every child would grow up learning the importance of writing thank-you notes. That way every adult would be in the habit of thanking people, in written form, for good deeds done on their behalf or gifts received.

It really is a simple concept: When someone takes the time to do something nice for you, you really owe thanks to that person for his kindness. You may think that a verbal "thanks" suffices, but it doesn't. To be truly polite, you should always send a handwritten thank-you note when a thank you is due.

When to Send the Thank-You Note

So when should you send a thank-you note? Obviously, when someone gives you a gift, such as for your birthday, anniversary, or a holiday. You should also get in the habit of writing a thank-you note if someone walks your dog or takes in your mail while you're on vacation, when you have a business meeting with someone you hope to do business with in the future or want to make a good impression on, or if you just feel that someone has gone out of her way to do something nice for you.

How to Write a Thank-You Note

Writing a thank-you note is probably easier than you realize. All you have to do is this:

1. Start your note by greeting the person by name.
2. Thank him for the gift or good deed.
3. Tell briefly why this meant so much to you.
4. Thank him again.
5. Sign your name.

When in doubt send a thank-you note. Sure, the recipient may reply by saying that it wasn't really necessary but deep down he does appreciate your taking the time to thank him for whatever it was that he did for you.

Birthday Wishes

Can you remember back to the thrill of being a child and receiving a birthday card in the mail? No matter how old someone is, the person always appreciates it when someone remembers his or her birthday. So make it a point to list friends and family members' birthdays in your calendar or day planner so that each week, when you check your calendar, you can stay on top of any birthday wishes you may have to get into the mail.

Kids always seem to enjoy a birthday card that commemorates their age. If you want to ensure that you always know how old a child is going to be, when writing down his or her birthday in your calendar, put the year the child was born next to his or her name. (Jane, 1995, for example.) You can do the same with adult friends or people's anniversaries, so you won't let something like a fortieth birthday or silver anniversary pass you by.

When sending a card to commemorate a child's birthday, you should try to find a kid-friendly card to send. When you can go with a card that features a popular icon—it's sure to be a hit with the recipient. When you're unsure of exactly which icon the child might favor, choose a generic card with balloons or something else festive on it.

A card for an adult can be a bit trickier. So many cards these days have an edge of risqué humor or less-than-tasteful messages on them. You may do best to stick with a more middle-of-the-road birthday card. However, if you know the recipient will get a kick out of such a card, go for it.

Always include a short personal note on any birthday card you send. For a child that might be, "I can't believe what a big boy you're becoming." For an adult, you might want to try a stab at humor, such as, "So you're turning twenty-nine . . . again?"

Offering Congratulations

There are a number of times in your life when people may have told you "Congratulations" and when you should offer those you know the same sentiment. These include graduations, births, job promotions, or other professional achievements. As soon as you hear about a job well done or a new addition to a friend's family, send your heartfelt message her way.

If you want to go far in business or at work, you should send handwritten congratulations notes whenever possible. For example, if you see an article about a colleague in the local paper or mention of her promotion, send her your good wishes. Better yet along with your card of congratulations, enclose the newspaper clipping for her benefit. You'll definitely make an impression on someone and stay top of mind by offering such a simple yet memorable salutation.

You have two choices when sending someone your congratulations. You can send them a store-bought card that matches the occasion or you can send them a note on your personal stationery conveying the same wishes. If you choose the former option, definitely include one or two lines of your personal thoughts on the occasion you're commemorating.

There's no reason to fret over what to write. Just tell the person that you heard the good news of her promotion or graduation (or whatever the occasion may be) and then tell her how proud you are of her or happy for her. Then just sign your name. It's that easy.

Now what if you're on the receiving end of a note of congratulations? Well, you should definitely send the person a thank-you note for taking the time to notice that congratulations were in order. Just as you would when thanking someone for a gift, keep your thank-you short and simple, and send it as soon as you can after receiving his or her note of good wishes.

Choosing the Right Card

The notion of sending someone a handwritten card to commemorate a special occasion is simple—you want the person to know that you are thinking of him, so you send him a card that lets him know that. These days many people think they can get away with e-cards sent from Web sites or phone calls made on the run, but deep down what touches most people is when you take the time to send a traditional card.

There's no reason to stress out over which kind of card you send—store bought or your own stationery. Just choose whatever works best for you. Of course, there are pros and cons to each.

Using Your Own Stationery

Sometimes those of a cynical nature feel they must turn up their noses at the idea of store-bought cards. If you think this way and would never be caught dead in the card aisle at your favorite store, then by all means you should send all your good wishes written on your own stationery.

Definitely stock up on blank note cards, and you should make sure that you always have an ample supply on hand. That way if suddenly you realize that it's your mother's birthday, your sister's anniversary, and your best friend got promoted at work, you'll be able to whip off a note to each in no time.

Store-Bought Cards

If you don't fancy yourself a wordsmith, you may want to stick with store-bought cards for recognizing someone's birthday, anniversary, or other occasion. You may just feel more comfortable having a card provide most of the flowery language that conveys your thoughts.

You can always stop into your local card store during a lunch hour or the card aisle at the supermarket to find an appropriate card to send. Just make sure you personalize the card by doing more than just signing your name to it—add a line or two that lets the recipient know you put a little thought into the card, even if it was at the last minute. Saying something like this should suffice: "I hope you find time to do something special on your birthday, and let's try to get together soon. Have a great day."

ESSENTIAL

A wonderful way to ensure that you're never left without a card to send for someone's special occasion is to stock up on them and then store them by occasion. Just keep them in a tickler file from an office supply store or in file folders, each labeled by the appropriate theme of the card.

Pen Pals

One of the best ways to hone your writing skills is to have a pen pal. Most people think of pen pals as something that's strictly for children, and you're right—it's a hobby that many children have and benefit from. If your children are interested in having a pen pal, definitely encourage them to do so.

However, there are plenty of opportunities for adult friends to keep in touch by writing to each other. You may not label a faraway friend a pen pal, per se, but if you write back and forth, then, in fact, you are pen pals. Regardless of your age, keeping your writing skills up to snuff is something everyone should try to achieve, and pen pals are a great way to do this.

Unearthing Your Potential Pen Pals

Often the most natural way for a child to find a pen pal is when someone moves away. Did a girl in your daughter's class move out of state? And did this girl leave behind an address for people to write to her? Then encourage your daughter to send her former classmate a letter, and see if a pen pal relationship develops naturally.

Your child may also want to keep in touch with friends from camp, children she met on vacation, or cousins who live far away. All these are great ways for you to help her develop her writing skills. Is your son in a Boy Scout troop? Might he have met another boy with similar interests at a recent Jamboree? See if he can track down that boy's address and have them become pen pals.

If your family moves around a lot because of one of your jobs, then you would all be naturals for having pen pals—the kids writing to the kids from their old neighborhood, and you writing to your former neighbors or the ladies from your book club.

What and When to Write

What makes a great pen pal letter? Lots of colorful information and lots of questions. When writing someone a letter, you should include details of cool things that have happened to you or your family since the last time you wrote. Did your son have an amazing Little League game? Encourage him to share some of the play-by-plays with his pen pal. Did your daughter just read a great book? Have her give her pen pal a synopsis, because maybe her friend would like to read that book as well.

Another way to inspire great conversation in a letter is to ask questions. So after your son talks about his Little League game, he could write, "What sports are you playing right now?" Or after your daughter tells her pen pal about the book, she could write, "Do you like these kinds of books? If not, what's your favorite book? Why do you like it so much?"

As far as when to write, it would be nice if you responded to a pen pal's letter within a week. Some children are so excited to get mail that they want to sit down right away and write back. When your child is this enthusiastic about having a pen pal, that's great.

ALERT!

While most correspondence is best done the old-fashioned way, you have some etiquette wiggle room when it comes to pen pals. If you or your children are computer savvy and the only way you'll stay in touch with folks is via e-mail, then by all means encourage e-mail pen pals. But to mix things up from time to time, send that person a traditional note, too, such as a postcard from vacation.

With adults and pen pals, you may not write as often as children do and your letters may be limited to once-a-year holiday letters. However, whenever possible, you should drop your pen pal a quick note. If you see a movie that reminds you of your friend or you're just dying to tell her about this great recipe you've recently discovered, jot a note to your buddy. She's sure to appreciate the unexpected greeting.

Ending a Pen Pal Relationship

If you're on the receiving end of a potential pen pal relationship that you're not interested in cultivating, let that person know right away about your feelings. You don't have to go into any long and drawn-out explanation. Rather, jot a quick note—even a postcard if it's easier—to say something like this, "Thanks for writing to me and asking to be pen pals. Unfortunately, I don't have the time to have a pen pal. Thanks again and best of luck to you." Yes, it's a bit blunt, but it's better to be upfront and honest than to be rude and ignore this person by not responding.

Chapter 20

What You Need to Know About Weddings

Weddings are supposed to be one of the happiest times in a person's life. But however rosy or romantic you think a wedding should be, there are certain sticky situations that can crop up when you're planning a wedding or when you've been invited to a wedding as a guest. Do you know how to be a polite host or the perfect guest? With a little bit of forethought, it's easy to make a wedding a pleasant experience for all involved.

Engagements

Did the man you love just get on bended knee and ask you to marry him? Or did someone you know just get engaged? Either way, congratulations are in order. But good wishes aside, do you know how to share the good news of your engagement with the people you care about—or how to react if you've just found out a loved one plans to tie the knot? Read on to find out about the etiquette of getting engaged.

Announcements

There's no reason for you and your parents to stress out over your engagement announcements. That's because sending them out isn't a necessity in this day and age. Sure you can, but keep it simple.

You can write your announcement on your parents' behalf, desktop publish it on your computer, and send it out to the local paper and to friends and family. If your parents are a stickler for tradition, they may suggest that you have your engagement announcement engraved at a stationer. Hey, if you've got the time and the money for such an extravagance, go for it.

ALERT!

If you are getting married for a second or subsequent time, you may feel silly having your parents announce the engagement. It's OK if they do, or you can do it yourself. Or, you can decide not to do engagement announcements at all.

Even though we live in a modern world, it's still the rule that the bride-to-be's parents announce the engagement. If your parents are divorced, then your mother should be the person making the announcement but always with a mention of your father. If both of your parents are deceased, then a close relative can be the one to make the announcement.

The other elements to keep in mind when writing your announcement are the dramatis personae—that is, you and your fiancé's name, along with your parents—the city and state where everyone mentioned in the announcement lives, you and your fiancé's educational background and your current employment status, and then the piece de resistance, your wedding date, if you've set it already.

When you're on the receiving end of an announcement, what do you do? Sending a card to congratulate the couple is always a nice gesture, as would be a phone call to share your good wishes. Should you buy an engagement gift? It depends on how close you are to this person. A great engagement gift you can give the bride-to-be would be books on wedding planning—she's definitely going to need them in the days, weeks, and months to come.

Engagement Parties

If your son or daughter just got engaged, keep in mind that it's the bride-to-be's parents who are supposed to throw an engagement party. But if you can't put together the party you want for your daughter or future son-in-law, then take comfort in knowing that it's perfectly OK for a sister or good friend to throw the engagement party instead.

In fact, with families and friends spread out all over the country these days, many couples have multiple engagement parties or pre-wedding parties, hosted by a variety of people. Keep in mind that an engagement party should be a low-key affair—like a wine tasting, Sunday brunch, or afternoon tea. You can save the big celebrating for the actual wedding.

Engagement Gifts

Having an engagement party may be the first of many pre-wedding celebrations where your family and friends may want to give you gifts. That's wonderful but it can be overwhelming for your guests. They may feel shopped out by the time the wedding rolls around. The two of you may be overwhelmed as well, with presents and all of the thank-you notes you need to write.

Since friends and family will likely want to shower you with gifts before your actual bridal shower, you two may want to register at a few stores. That way when guests call your parents for gift ideas, they can tell them which stores you're registered at.

If you don't want to have engagement party guests feel as if your party is just another fishing expedition for gifts, you or your parents (or whomever is hosting the affair) can put something on the invitation that asks for no gifts: "Please, no gifts at this time." You could also choose to designate a charity or good cause as the beneficiary of your engagement party. You can include something like this as an insert to your engagement party invitation: "In lieu of gifts, please make donations to Justine and Jim's favorite charity, the Capitol Area Society to Prevent Cruelty to Animals."

Broken Engagements

With all this happy talk about engagements, it's easy to forget that there are times or situations that may cause you to call off the engagement or to postpone the wedding. When this happens, and if you received any gifts during your engagement, you must return them. You should include a handwritten note that thanks the person for the gift but also informs them that the engagement has been called off. It's unnecessary to elaborate how, when, or why your engagement was broken.

While it's none of their business, you may want to have an excuse ready in case friends or family ask why you broke off your engagement. You can be vague, or even tell a little white lie just to appease them. Let your parents know your excuse so you can keep your stories straight.

Wedding Plans

Have you heard the term Bridezilla? That's the bride who becomes such a monster when she's planning her wedding that no one wants to be around her. If you mind your manners as you begin to plan your wedding, no one will be secretly whispering, "She's such a Bridezilla" behind your back.

Location, Location, Location

Decorum may dictate that the bride has first dibs on where she wants to hold her wedding, but that doesn't mean that you should automatically turn into a diva, demanding this and that about your wedding location. Sure, it's your prerogative to choose the chapel and the hall, but if you want to get along with everybody during the planning stages and to maintain their respect in the process, you need to keep an open mind. That means no hissy fits when you start discussing guest lists with your parents or menus with your fiancé.

Making a Guest List and Checking It Twice

One of the first things that you, your future spouse and your respective families need to discuss is your guest list. Keep in mind that each side should strive to invite 50 percent of the guests. So have everyone sit down and make their lists. Cross out any duplicates, and then compare the lists to see how the numbers add up. If the lists turn out to be more like 70 percent and 30 percent, see how you can even things up. Should you make your overall guest list smaller, and therefore cut from some of the 70 percent? Or should you expand your list overall—that is, if your budget can handle it?

Assume that 10 percent of your guests will R.S.V.P. that they can't attend. That's pretty much a constant with any event. Keeping this number in mind will help you plan for what kind of space you need to reserve for your ceremony and reception. Remember: you can always take away seats if not as many people show up but you can't always add seating in a too-small space.

If you want some flexibility with your guest list, designate some guests on the "A" list and others on the "B" list. You can then plan to send your invitations out in two waves. When people from the "A" list send their regrets, you can invite those from the "B" list in their place. If you decide to have an "A" and a "B" list of potential guests, plan your R.S.V.P. dates accordingly. Send out invitations to "A" guests super early so that as people begin declining, you can send invitations to "B" guests and still have plenty of time before the R.S.V.P. date.

E ALERT!

There's nothing ruder than receiving a wedding invitation that arrives with an R.S.V.P. date that's either already passed or is in a day or two. This tips the guest off to the fact that they were not on the "A" list and their inclusion on the guest list was an afterthought.

Keeping the peace is especially important when planning a wedding. If you find yourselves at a guest list crossroads, defer to the person or persons footing the bill for the affair. Traditionally, that has been the bride's family, meaning that they usually had the last say on who got invited or if it was OK to tip the guest-list scales in their favor. These days many couples plan and pay for their own weddings, meaning that the bride and groom should have final say. However, in the name of family harmony, it's always a good idea to be generous with your parents and your guest list, especially if you've got room and the budget to extend an invitation to the people they want to include. (You can always suggest that your parents pick up the tab for their extra invited guests, especially if you have a limited budget of your own money to spend.)

R.S.V.P.

To make guests lives easier, an engaged couple usually does one of two things with their wedding invitations: they include an R.S.V.P.-by date, and they send a separate R.S.V.P. card with its own self-addressed stamped envelope.

It is advisable not only for guests to reply in a timely manner but also for the bride and groom (or whomever is hosting the wedding) not to feel shy about following up with a guest who is tardy in replying. You should have no qualms about calling someone who has missed the R.S.V.P. date to see if that person is coming to the wedding.

FACT

The initials R.S.V.P. stand for *respondez s'il vous plait*, which is French for "respond, if you please." It is the height of rudeness for an invited guest not to respond to an invitation—either to accept or to decline. Unfortunately, too few people these days understand the importance of R.S.V.P.ing

Who Pays for the Wedding?

If you want to stick with the traditional straight and narrow when it comes to footing the wedding bill, then the bride's family should pay for and host the wedding and reception, and the groom's family should pay for and host the rehearsal dinner.

Before you get your heart set on having a free-ride wedding, with your parents picking up all the tabs, sit down and talk these things out with them. You may discover that the real world of finances prevents your parents from providing you with the seed money for your wedding. The two of you may have to pay for your own wedding. The good news is today's etiquette doesn't assign any strict rules to who pays for a wedding. So whichever financial route you decide to follow, you can rest assured that you're going to be behaving properly.

Wedding Attendants

You know your wedding will have a bride and groom in it, but will you also have a maid of honor and multiple bridesmaids? What about the groomsmen? Do you think you need to have as many men in your wedding as you do women? Also, when deciding on the size of your wedding party, keep the following in mind: if your out-of-town groomsmen or bridesmaids cannot afford their lodging or travel to the wedding, the bride and the groom should cover their costs. It's also your responsibility to make hotel reservations on behalf of your wedding party, if you're not paying for them.

Best Man

You might as well rename your best man your right-hand man, because that's really what he becomes during the wedding plans. Not only is he your legal witness when signing the marriage certificate but also the best man should make himself available to help with your wedding plans in any way he can.

The old adage that blood is thicker than water is especially true with wedding attendants. When in doubt always try to choose family before friends.

Most men choose a brother or close friend to be their best man, although if you're a Southern gentleman, you may select your father to stand by your side when you get married. Keep in mind that a best man should be someone close to you and someone who is reliable—because, in the end, it is the best man's first and foremost job to get the groom to his wedding on time. (Note to groom: Don't pick your perpetually late friend as your best man.)

These days best men do more than just drive the groom to the wedding. There are plenty of other assignments a best man can expect.

The Bachelor Party

You are the go-to guy for the bachelor party, and you can always enlist the other ushers' help in planning it, if party planning isn't your forte. Do the groom a favor and plan his party a few days before the wedding so you all have plenty of time for recovery, and, if you can, try to keep debauchery to a bare minimum (no pun intended).

Personal Assistant

You should make yourself the groom's de facto personal assistant before the wedding, and be sure he has everything he needs for his post-wedding plans, such as honeymoon tickets, luggage, car keys, and more. That includes bringing his clothes and suitcase to the reception so he's ready to leave on his honeymoon immediately after the celebration ends. You should also help him get dressed, if he asks for it, and be standing by with a handkerchief to mop his brow, should his nerves get the best of him.

You may also be called upon to hold the wedding rings (if your friend isn't using a ring bearer), pay the clergyman after the ceremony, and return any rented attire the day after the big event.

Gestures of Good Will

You should plan to be the gift-buying guy for a little something from the ushers and you to the groom, meaning that not only do you have to collect money from the group but you have to buy the gift, too.

Another gift you should expect to give your buddy is the first toast at the reception. Plan ahead of time what you're going to say—keep it clean—and you may want to hold off on consuming too much alcohol until after your toast is over.

Maid or Matron of Honor

The maid of honor (called a matron of honor if she's married) becomes your right-hand gal throughout your wedding plans, and you should make sure you choose someone who will enjoy being your personal assistant. Because when it comes down to it, the maid or matron of honor exists first and foremost to help the bride.

QUESTION?

What if I want to choose a man as my maid of honor?
It's becoming more and more commonplace for brides to choose a "male" of honor or a groom to choose a "best girl." If your best friend or closest relative is someone of the opposite sex, it's perfectly acceptable to include that person in your wedding—even as your right-hand man or woman.

Like the best man, the maid of honor will act as your legal witness for the wedding certificate, and she is likely to be a close friend or your sister.

If you've just been asked to be a friend or sister's maid of honor, get out your organizer because you're going to have a lot on your to-do list in the coming months. Those task include:

- Hosting a wedding shower on the bride's behalf.
- Collecting money from the other bridesmaids to buy the bride's gift.
- Acting as a liaison between the bride and the bridesmaids whenever wedding-related information needs to be communicated.
- Accompanying the bride on her dress-shopping excursions.
- Helping the bride get dressed before the wedding.
- Preceding the bride down the aisle and adjusting her train at the wedding ceremony.
- Standing in the receiving line after the ceremony to greet guests.
- Carrying the bride's purse or other personal effects on the big day.
- Bringing the bride's suitcase so that the bride can change clothes after the reception and in preparation for her honeymoon.

Groomsmen/Ushers

The main job of the groomsmen, also know as ushers, is to seat your invited guests at the ceremony. They should be your friends or siblings. You should think about choosing one usher for every four dozen or so guests—this will prevent any traffic jams at the church or synagogue door as guests arrive and wait to be seated. It would be nice if your wedding had as many male as female attendants, but don't spend too much time fretting over those numbers if you're off by one attendant. No one will notice.

If you've been asked to be an usher, you should expect to chip in for a gift for the groom and to pay for the rental of any specific clothing that he's asked you to wear at the wedding. If the bride and groom have chosen to have a head table with their attendants, you should expect to sit there—without your date. As far as the receiving line goes, you're off the hook—ushers don't participate in that.

Bridesmaids

Unlike groomsmen, your bridesmaids don't have many wedding-day responsibilities, except to walk in the procession and to stand up at the front of the ceremony with the rest of the wedding party. They are even excluded from standing in your receiving line and can join their spouse or partner immediately after the ceremony ends. However, you may want them to ride in the "bridal party" car from the ceremony to the reception, and they should oblige.

If your budget can handle it, do your female attendants a favor and pick up the tab for their outfits. You're asking them to wear dresses that you (not they) have handpicked, and you will avoid any arguments down the road about styles and colors if you can pay for their clothes upfront.

If you've been asked to be a friend or sister's bridesmaid, you should start saving up. You'll have to chip in for a gift for the bride, help the maid of honor put together the bridal shower, and pay for the clothing the bride wants you to wear at the wedding.

Flower Girls/Ringbearers

You can choose some of your youngest family members or the children of your closest friends to be your flower girl or ringbearer. (Just as maids of honor are no longer only women, so to with flower girls—or flower children—and ringbearers.)

The job of the flower child is to walk down the aisle ahead of the bride and scatter flower petals for the bride to walk upon. (Some ceremony sites restrict the scattering of flowers, so your flower child may have to blow bubbles or do something else instead.) The ringbearer uses a velvet cushion or silver tray (or some other special holder) to hold your wedding rings.

Ceremony

How your wedding ceremony occurs depends a lot on your religion, the location, and the formality of the affair. Also, if you choose to have a civil ceremony over a religious ceremony, then you're probably looking at a very different event.

A civil ceremony is one where a judge or justice of the peace presides, and these ceremonies are usually less ornate in nature than a religious ceremony. Such a ceremony can be held anywhere outside of a house of worship—a hotel, private club, restaurant, the reception location, a garden, or even at home. You should go for a civil ceremony if the two of you do not share a religion or aren't active in your current religion.

A religious ceremony will be held in a church, chapel, synagogue, mosque, or other religious setting and will include religious icons and traditions with an active clergyperson presiding. This kind of ceremony is perfect if you're a devout couple who shares the same faith.

If you are invited to a wedding of a denomination other than your faith, then you should try to follow along with the traditions as best as you can. For example, if the congregation bows their head or kneels at one point, it doesn't hurt to go along with the crowd.

Gifts for the Bride and Groom

You'll probably never see as many wrapped gifts gathered in one location as you will at your wedding. Because you'll have the potential to have a tower of gifts to deal with, you should always plan to have a gift table at your reception. Even in places like the Northeast, where money is the gift of choice, people will still arrive at your wedding bearing gifts. Make sure they have someplace to put them. Also, make sure you designate someone who will take the gifts to your home after the reception.

Registering on Time

Your wedding may be months away, but there are going to be plenty of occasions beforehand when people will want to buy you gifts. These occasions could be your engagement party, a bridal shower or even Christmas or Chanukah.

To make the lives of your well-wishers easier, you should register soon after you get engaged. Choose two or three stores where you can register your preferences and which most of your guests can easily access—either in person or via the Internet.

Besides registering in a handful of stores, you should also register for a variety of items in different price ranges so everyone can afford your gifts. Also, make sure you have enough gifts on your registry—you don't want your guests to attempt to buy something off your registry, only to discover that you've only selected ten things, and someone's already bought all ten of them.

Thanking Your Guests

Your guests have been extremely considerate in buying you a gift for your wedding, bridal shower, or other wedding-related occasion. Return the favor and show them some consideration by thanking them for their generosity. Try to get your thank-you cards written and mailed within two to four weeks of receiving a gift. Phone calls and e-mails aren't good enough—only a handwritten thank-you note counts.

Being a Good Wedding Guest

If your friends or family members are in their twenties and thirties, chances are you've been receiving a lot of bridal shower and wedding invitations lately. You need to keep in mind that there's more to being a good wedding guest than just sending your congratulations to the happy couple.

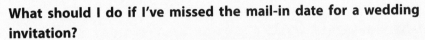

QUESTION?

What should I do if I've missed the mail-in date for a wedding invitation?

If you've missed the mail-in R.S.V.P. date for a wedding invitation, then at least call the couple. Let them know that, first, you're sorry that you're late in getting back to them and, second, whether or not you'll be attending their affair.

R.S.V.P. Rights and Wrongs

When you are invited to any wedding-related celebration, make sure that you R.S.V.P. on time. There's nothing more frustrating to a host or hostess than not knowing how many people will be attending their happy event.

Good Gift Giving

Most couples getting married register not to annoy guests but to help them when buying a gift. So when you go to shop for the happy couple, try to buy from the gifts on their registry. Then you'll be sure you're getting the couple something they really want.

If for some reason you cannot buy off the registry—or you found the same items from the registry for less at another store—then do the couple a favor: make sure you include a gift receipt with their package.

Dress the Part

One of your jobs as a wedding guest is figuring out how formal or informal a wedding is going to be—and then dressing appropriately. Typically, weddings held after sundown on a weekend are more formal than those held in the morning—the only exception being a Catholic high mass at noon, which is always formal.

So if you determine that the wedding you've been invited to is on the formal side, dress the part. That means a dark suit or tuxedo for the guy—the latter if the invitation reads, "black tie requested" or "black tie optional"— and a long dress for the gal. Of course, if you're unsure of a wedding's formality, call the bride and groom and ask. You'd be better off making the call than making a fashion faux pas.

Invited Guests Only

The inner envelope of the wedding invitation you receive tells you exactly who has been invited to a wedding. If it's your name only, then you are the person being invited. Not your kids, not your boyfriend, not your dog. Just you. If the inner envelope says your name plus guest, then you can bring your spouse or significant other. If the inner envelope says an entire family's names, kids included, then the kids are welcome to come to the wedding as well.

Of course, it is the bride and groom's prerogative to extend an invitation to others after invitations have gone out and R.S.V.P.s have been received. So if you were originally invited without your significant other, you may be pleasantly surprised to receive a verbal invitation to bring him or her with you at the last minute.

Delicately Dealing with Glitches

Most women dream about their wedding day from the time that they're little girls, but none usually anticipate the little glitches that can crop up from time to time with wedding plans. If you find yourself facing a snafu, don't worry: it's easy to save face if you know what to do.

Bad Weather

Mother Natures loves a wedding, and while she usually cooperates, you could be facing a downpour during your spring wedding or a snowstorm during your winter one. Either way you should have a bad weather plan in place.

If you're getting married during rainy season, make sure you tent any outdoor activities, and have plenty of umbrellas on hand for guests who didn't plan for the raindrops falling on their head.

For a winter wedding, make sure your ceremony and reception sites have plenty of salt on hand to melt ice—and people to shovel the walk, if necessary.

If you're worried that weather will be so bad that you'll have to cancel your wedding, such as a hurricane hitting, be sure to invest in wedding insurance. Also, keep your guest list handy so that if you do need to call everyone at the last minute to cancel or postpone the festivities, you won't have to scramble to alert everyone. And do make sure that if weather prevents you from having your wedding, that you do the right thing and alert all of your guests that you are postponing your celebration.

Adding Insult to Injury—and Illness

Believe it or not, brides and grooms have hobbled down the aisle on crutches or loaded up on anti-nausea medicine to make it through their wedding ceremony while dealing with a bout of the stomach flu. If either of you become ill before your wedding—and you think you'll be too sick to make it through the ceremony—then by all means cancel. (Don't forget to call everyone.) However, if you think you can tough it out, then go ahead and have your wedding. You may want to skip the receiving line, though, if you're contagious. You want your guests to leave your wedding having had a good time, not catching a virus.

If you're a wedding guest and you become ill suddenly, please call the bride and groom and let them know that you won't be able to make the wedding. Sure, they probably won't save any money on their already-paid-for affair, but at least they won't worry when you don't show up.

Warring Factions

One of the common glitches of modern life might be divorced parents who don't get along, even at their son or daughter's wedding. If you're the one faced with seeing your ex at the wedding, do your child a favor and put your differences aside for the day. A wedding is about two people getting married, not two people who used to be married and can't stand each other.

Children of divorce should think about seating their divorced parents away from each other. So as you plan your seating arrangements for both the ceremony and reception, be cognizant of where your parents end up. However, keep in mind that their behavior is their problem, not yours. It's polite to make things easier on them, but if they don't choose to be on their best behavior, there's nothing you can do about it.

Chapter 21

Dealing Delicately with Illness and Death

E ven the most verbose person can become tongue-tied when they find out someone near to them is sick or, worse, has died. It's never easy to deal with a tough situation like sickness or death, but deal with it you must.

The worst thing you can do when someone is grieving is to ignore or avoid that person, simply because you're not sure how to act. Imagine how you would feel if your friends and family members abandoned you during your darkest hour because they weren't sure what you needed or what to say to you. Sometimes just being there for a person, either physically or emotionally, is all you need to do to show good manners and to help this person get through a tough time in his or her life.

When Someone Is Sick

Everyone wants a mommy to take care of him or her when he or she is sick, even fully grown adults. That's why when you find out that someone close to you isn't feeling well or is somehow infirmed, you should offer to help them out in one way or another. It could be as simple as bringing them some chicken soup or taking in their mail until they're feeling better. They are sure to appreciate whatever it is that you can do to help.

Helping Out

Even though kids get sick all the time, it's easy for a mother or father to feel overwhelmed when a child is home sick. That's why you should always offer to help out a parent you know who is dealing with a sick kid, especially if the illness has been dragging on for sometime now. Maybe you can offer to take any other children she has off her hands one afternoon or to do grocery shopping for her. She will surely appreciate your kindness and generosity.

Terminal Illnesses

Things get a little trickier when someone you know or love is diagnosed with a terminal illness. That person may seem fine to you and be able to go about his or her daily business, but all the while you and everyone else knows that her time on earth is limited.

You need to stick by terminally ill people as much as you can, even if it's not easy for you to do so. Just like with death, sometimes it's easy to let your grief (or the knowledge of your impending grief) get the best of you when someone you care about is sick. Your immediate reaction may be to pull away, but don't—now more than ever this person needs your love, support, and assistance. Besides, giving it to her is the right thing to do.

A Death in the Family

When someone dies, it's very important that you designate someone or a few people either in your family or who are close friends to get the word out about the death. You never want to have someone hear that a person she cared about has died by overhearing another person talking about it in the supermarket checkout aisle.

As soon as you hear that someone has died, you should call the mourning family and share your condolences. You should also ask if they need any help making calls or arrangements for the upcoming funeral. It's likely that if the person has just died, they won't know yet what they're doing but the family is sure to appreciate your offer to help.

It is especially difficult when a child loses a parent or, worse, yet, a parent loses a child. In cases like this not only should you reach out to the grieving child or parent but also you should be sure to share your sympathy with the surviving spouse or any siblings.

Inquiring Minds

If this person's death was unexpected, it isn't polite to ask, "How did he die?" You can look to the person's obituary in the paper for hints on the cause of death—you'll usually find a clue if there is a hospital, charity, or health-related nonprofit organization to which the family would like people to send donations.

If you suspect the person killed himself, don't go fishing for details about his suicide. The family will probably refer to his death as happening "unexpectedly" (usually a euphemism for suicide), and it's their right to do so—and none of your business to know the truth.

Wakes and Funerals

In many religions, people in mourning find great comfort in having a chance to say "good-bye" to their deceased loved one and seeing that person one more time at the wake. The latter is especially true if the family decides to hold an open casket. They may also choose to have visiting hours at a funeral home, which gives family and friends the chance to pay their respects not only to the person who died, but also the living he left behind.

Viewing the Body

If a wake has an open casket, then you'll have the opportunity to view the body. Whether or not you actually go see the body up close and personal is entirely up to you. There are some people, especially children, who may find it frightening to get close to a dead body, and you should never force someone to go see the decedent if she doesn't want to. Regardless of whether you approach the casket, you shouldn't just hang out in the back of the room. If you've made it this far to the wake, then you've got to go over to the family members and share your sympathies with them.

ALERT!

Unlike Westerners who see black as the universal color of mourning, in Asia white is associated with death. If you happen to be going to an Asian funeral, choose white or light clothes over black or dark.

How to Dress

You need to dress for a wake or funeral as you would when going to church or synagogue—conservatively and respectfully. Women should wear long pants, skirts, or dresses. Men should choose a dark suit or a jacket and tie. Most people choose to wear dark colors as a sign of mourning. Children should also dress in a solemn color.

How to Behave

Everyone is sad when someone dies, and it's not up to you to try to cheer people up. This is not the time to crack jokes to lighten the mood or to act silly. It's a solemn occasion. On the other hand, if you feel as if it would make the mourners feel better to reminisce about happy times with the deceased, then go ahead and share your stories. If you just don't know what to say to the mourning family, a simple "I'm so sorry" or "My prayers are with you" will do the trick.

The Funeral Service

How a funeral progresses depends on how the family has chosen to remember the deceased. Some families have a service for the person at a church, synagogue, or funeral home, with a burial that follows immediately. If this is the case, then you should attend the service and then follow the funeral procession to the burial at the cemetery. Others have a graveside service before burial, and it would behoove you to attend the service and to stay for the burial.

Many children find the idea of burying someone in the ground disturbing. You can take your kids to a funeral service but you may want to skip the burial to avoid upsetting them.

Grief is a mysterious thing that affects people differently. Some people don't cry at funerals while others cry inconsolably. Now is not the time to judge others for their behavior, however normal or odd it may seem, at the funeral. Just make sure that you don't make a spectacle of yourself by doing something inappropriate, such as telling jokes, when you really ought to be bowing your head and praying for the deceased.

If you're asked to be a pallbearer at someone's funeral, try to honor that request. It is a great way to pay tribute to someone to be a pallbearer at his funeral.

The Funeral Procession

There is an expected etiquette of funeral processions from the service to the graveside. Here's what you should expect:

1. The first car in the funeral procession is the hearse, which carries the body.
2. Next, there is likely to be a private car that carries the family members of the deceased.
3. Mourners follow both cars to the cemetery.
4. En route all mourners turn their car headlights on and proceed in a line.

Before you leave for the procession, you may receive a flag or sign to put in your window that says "Funeral" or "Mourner." You may also receive a police escort from the service to the cemetery.

FACT

When you come upon a funeral procession on the road, you must give it the right of way. This is true even if you have a green light. State laws allow for funeral processions to break traffic laws, including running red lights. Sit patiently and eventually the line of cars will pass, and you can proceed.

Funeral Fees

As hard as it may be to consider, there are plenty of people who make a living off of other people's deaths. Nobody ever had a funeral for free, and you shouldn't expect to do so either if a loved one dies. There are always costs associated with funerals, and a funeral can cost anywhere from a few thousand dollars to tens of thousands of dollars. Some of the fees you'll incur include:

- Preparing the body
- The casket
- Rental of the funeral home for services, including hearse

- Car service for family members
- Use of clergy

Often, grief-stricken people can't deal well with the costs and responsibilities of planning and paying for a funeral. That's why it's always a good idea to have a trusted friend serve as your liaison between your family and the funeral home.

Sitting Shiva

Sitting Shiva is a Jewish tradition practiced mostly by Orthodox and conservative Jews that requires the family of the deceased to welcome mourners into their home for two days to a week after the funeral. (Although Shiva means seven in Hebrew for the seven days of mourning, today mourners may sit Shiva for only two or three days.) If you haven't been to someone's house when they're sitting Shiva, you might be surprised at what you might see.

1. Men do not shave during Shiva.
2. All the mirrors will be covered.
3. There may be a pitcher of water on the front step.
4. You may see shoes lined up by the door.

The first two traditions have to do with vanity—or the need not to have any during the week of Shiva. The idea is that all your thoughts should be about the person who died, not how you look. That's why people cover the mirrors and men don't shave. You're supposed to use the pitcher of water to clean your hands before you come in the house. This is simply a sign of respect. And people take off their shoes in the house to show how the loss of their loved one has humbled them so much that they can't even put on footwear.

FACT

If the person who died was Jewish, expect to go to his or her funeral within a few days. In the Jewish tradition, people bury their dead on the first non-Sabbath day following the person's death.

Announcing Someone's Death

There is always a process of letting people know that someone has died. You'll likely enlist friends and family members to make phone calls on your behalf. In addition, you may want to put something in the newspaper about your family member's death. Keep in mind, though, that obituaries and death announcements in the newspaper are not one and the same and serve different purposes in notifying the public of someone's death.

Death Announcement

A death announcement is what you see in the newspaper that looks a bit like a classified ad. In fact, families have to pay to have a death announcement put in the newspaper, just as they would an advertisement. Funeral homes also pay to announce the death of someone, which is why you sometimes see multiple death announcements for the same person. The funeral home announcement usually provides information on funeral services, burials, and where mourners should send their condolences. A death announcement may or may not include a photo of the deceased.

Obituaries

An obituary is actually an article that a newspaper runs when someone newsworthy dies. It usually talks more about the person's life and what he accomplished than the person's burial plans, although you may find this information at the end of the obituary. The decision to run an obituary rests with the individual newspaper. You can write an obituary and send it to the newspaper, and they'll often run it if there is space.

ESSENTIAL

The grieving family must acknowledge every sympathy card it receives. That means in the days and weeks after your loved one's death, you should set aside time to send a handwritten thank-you note to each person who sent you a sympathy card.

Offering Condolences

It is always wise to offer a grieving person your condolences via a phone call and a written card. You should call that person as soon as you hear about the death in her family, and then you should follow up with a sympathy card. If you'd like you may buy and send a preprinted sympathy card but never just sign it as is. You must always add a handwritten note to this card, even if it's just to say, "I'm so very sorry for your loss."

Beyond sympathy cards, there are many ways that you can offer someone your condolences. You can offer to help her with any funeral arrangements she has to make or little odd jobs that will make her life easier before, during, and after the funeral. This might be going grocery shopping for her, helping her to clean her home for the open house she's planning to have after the burial, or just making yourself available for a cup of coffee from time to time.

Sending Flowers

Sending flowers is another great way to offer condolences. You can send a traditional funeral wreath to the funeral home or you can send some kind of greenery to the person's home. Like with a sympathy card, you want to do more than just sign your name to the card that comes with the flowers. Again, all you need to do is add a personalized line, such as "We just wanted you to know that we're thinking of you."

ALERT!

Do not send flowers if the mourners have asked people not to send them. You need to respect their wishes. Consider sending a donation to a charity if that is what the family has requested in lieu of flowers.

Donations

Many people offer condolences by making a donation to a good cause in the name of the deceased, especially if the family asked for donations in lieu of flowers. If they didn't and you'd like to make this gesture, you can send money to that person's house of worship or favorite charity.

Mass Cards

In the Catholic religion, it's traditional to buy and send a Mass card to the deceased person's family. The church where you got the Mass card will say a Mass in that person's name in the near future, and devout Catholics often feel great comfort in attending the Mass said in their loved one's name. (The Mass card will provide the exact date.)

Funerals in Other Faiths

Each religion has its own way of dealing with someone's death and celebrating his life in the process. However, if you plan to attend the funeral of someone whose religion is different from yours, you may not know what to expect. Here are some basics to consider for what happens when a Hindu or Muslim dies.

Hindu Funerals

Hindus believe in cremation, which occurs the day the person dies. However, before cremation, family members go through an elaborate preparation process. This includes cleaning, anointing, shaving, and wrapping the deceased in a cloth. Then, they carry the body to the funeral pyre, where the body will be cremated. They put the body down so that the feet are pointing south (to the God of death, called *yama*), and the head is pointing north (to the God of wealth, called *kubera*).

Three to ten days after the cremation ceremony, the family will gather up the person's ashes and place them in a sacred location, such as a shrine.

Muslim Funerals

There is also a ritualistic cleaning of a dead body in preparation for a Muslim funeral. This is done while someone reads from the Koran, the Muslim holy book. Muslims do not embalm their dead as they want the body to be able to return to the earth in its original form. After the body is cleaned, they put it in a coffin and take it to the mosque.

This transport of the body to the mosque usually involves a funeral procession of some kind, with mourners either preceding or following the casket. This is usually done on foot. Because Muslims believe in the separation of sexes, funeral processions are often all male.

Despite the single sex nature of the funeral procession, the funeral service at the mosque should be open to everyone who wants to come and mourn. Once at the mosque you should place the deceased's head so that it points to Mecca, the holy site in Saudi Arabia.

Chapter 22

Miscellaneous Manners

There are certain day-to-day manners that don't fall into any one specific category, such as how to handle personal hygiene or how to deal with pests. Or what do you do when you find yourself in the middle of a social faux pas? Besides offering a quick and sincere apology, sometimes you aren't quite sure how to handle sticky etiquette situations. Read on for all you need to know about those miscellaneous manners that will come in handy at one point or another.

Personal Hygiene

Your mother probably told you to always go out of the house with clean underwear on, just in case you got hit by a car and needed to go to the hospital. She probably also told you that it's not polite to pick your nose in public. But what do you do when you meet up with a discourteous slob who really does act like he was raised in a barn? Do you ignore his bad behavior? Or is it wise to speak up? Well, when it comes to matters of personal hygiene, sometimes the answer is yes and sometimes it is no.

Spitting is never appropriate in public. If you find yourself with something in your mouth you need to get rid of, find a napkin or paper towel and use it to discreetly get rid of the offensive matter.

Bathroom Habits

It would be wonderful if everyone respected that cute little poem that you're bound to see in a restroom at some point in your life: "If you sprinkle when you tinkle, please be neat and wipe the seat." Whenever you're finished using a private or public toilet, you should always check to make sure that you haven't left any liquid gifts behind for the next person who uses the toilet.

Also, you must always double check that you've flushed the toilet when you're done using it. If you happen to come upon a toilet that someone's forgotten to flush, just flush it yourself. Don't find the person and scold her— it's one thing to recognize rude behavior, but it's even ruder to point it out to the offender.

If you notice that someone has just come from the bathroom and his zipper is undone, you've got to tell him. Don't shout it across the room, as that will only embarrass him. Instead, take him aside and say it directly: "FYI, your fly is open." He will surely appreciate you pointing this out before it leads to an even more embarrassing situation. Hopefully, if you're ever caught with your fly open, that person or someone else will return the favor.

Along the same lines, if you happen to notice that a girlfriend has spotted through her pants, thanks to her period, she will be eternally grateful if you tell her. Sometimes women's periods sneak up on them, and it's best to find out fast before things get ugly.

Most adults know how to hold their bodily functions in public. But every once in a while, one slips through. If this happens to you, don't make a big deal out of it. Just say, "Excuse me" and move on.

Embarrassing Spots

From time to time, you may find yourself dealing with embarrassing spots on your clothing, skin, or elsewhere. Ideally, someone else will alert you to this fact, and you can quickly save face by wiping the ketchup off your cheek or changing out of the shirt that has a big stain on it.

A good way to subtly let someone know that she's got something hanging out of her nose is to call her name, then pantomime wiping your own nose. This usually gets the message across loud and clear.

It's always a good idea after eating to do a quick teeth and face check in a mirror. You want to make sure you don't have anything between your teeth, or any remnants of lunch on your face or clothing. If you do, don't take out a toothpick and clean your mouth out. Instead, excuse yourself to the restroom and take a mouthful of water to swish out the stuck food. If that doesn't work, then you can try to pick it out, but only while you're in the privacy of the bathroom.

Personal Appearance

Freedom of expression may mean that you can leave the house wearing what you'd like, but the freedom to be well behaved does not. If you don't want to offend people or you're looking to make a good impression on others, you should keep your personal appearance in mind at all times. That means shower daily, don't forget to brush your hair and teeth, and make sure that you put on clothes that are reasonably neat looking. You don't have to go as far as to iron your t-shirts but try to avoid those with holes or stains on them.

If you favor baseball caps, try to wear them in casual situations only, such as when you go to or play in a baseball game. You can probably get away with wearing a baseball hat outside on a sunny day, if you've forgotten your sunglasses, or you woke up that morning with bed head.

However, regardless of whether or not you're having a good hair day, you should always remember that as soon as you go inside a building, you've got to take your hat off. The one time when you can get away with wearing something on your head indoors is if you're doing so for religious reasons or it's Easter Sunday, and you're showing off your new bonnet in church.

Backhanded Compliments

There are times when you may notice that someone you know seems to have changed her look. Maybe she's lost weight or colored her hair, or maybe he's shaved off his facial hair. While people always appreciate hearing compliments about their appearance, you've got to be careful about how you compliment them, lest you insult them in the process.

For example, if you notice that someone has lost weight, don't say, "Holy cow, you used to be such a porker!" Instead, you can gracefully broach the subject of someone's weight loss by saying, "Pardon my asking, but is there less of you now than there was before?"

If you notice other personal changes about a person, again proceed with any compliments carefully. Pointing out that someone has gotten her eyes done may not be a good idea, especially if she's self-conscious about having had cosmetic surgery. However, a good catchall way to raise the topic of someone's changed physical appearance would be to say, "I just can't put my finger on it but something about you is different, and you look wonderful." Again, this allows you to pay someone a compliment without blatantly pointing out that she really didn't look that great before she made whatever change in appearance it was that you noticed.

Pests and Other Problems

Along with many of life's conveniences come many inconveniences, such as telemarketers. It's hard to keep graciousness in mind when you're fending off telephone calls during dinner or trying to go to sleep when someone's car alarm is blaring in the distance. There isn't much you can do to prevent these nuisances from creeping into your daily life, but you can do your part toward polite society by making sure that you're not contributing to any of this pesky rudeness in your day-to-day dealings.

Nasty Noisemakers

There are two surefire ways to annoy your neighbors with noise that go beyond blaring music at all hours of the night. (That's a given.) The first is to install a car alarm that goes off with the slightest vibration. If you must have a car alarm, then at least make sure that it's designed to go off when someone is actually try to steal your car, not closing a car door next to you.

FACT

Some municipalities have passed laws that ban leaf blowers during certain hours or altogether. If you live in one of these places, be careful how you clean up your lawn clippings or autumn leaves. If you take the easy way out with a leaf blower, you may not only be considered rude, but you could also be breaking the law.

The second is to do yard work early on a weekend morning—and with a leaf blower, no less. This nifty cleaning-up tool may save you from sweeping your sidewalks but in the process, you're probably alienating everyone around you, thanks to the tool's deafening sound.

Beggars, Bigots, and More

Visit any big city, and you're bound to see beggars and panhandlers out on the street corner. You shouldn't feel bad about ignoring these people who come at you with an outstretched hand. And you shouldn't feel bad about saying, "No, sorry," when they ask you if you can spare any change, and you don't want to give them anything.

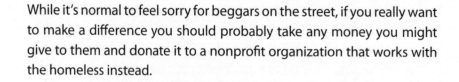

ALERT! While it's normal to feel sorry for beggars on the street, if you really want to make a difference you should probably take any money you might give to them and donate it to a nonprofit organization that works with the homeless instead.

You would also be wise to ignore bigots who start spewing racist, hateful things. Unfortunately, people like this tend to be very close-minded individuals. Don't waste your breath trying to argue with them or helping them to see the light of tolerance—it will likely be an exercise in futility. However, if you're fed up listening to them talk, it wouldn't be rude to say, "I don't want to hear this anymore" and to walk away.

The one excessive talker that you don't want to ignore is the insensitive jerk that insists on talking during a movie. It's true that many people are used to being able to talk while watching movies at home, but that doesn't give them carte blanche to add a running commentary to a movie that hundreds of others are trying to watch. If the guilty talking party happens to be sitting behind you, you can usually nip the talking problem in the bud by turning around and glaring at the person. A couple of loud "Shhs" also go a long way, too. If neither works, you may want to move to another seat or to get the theater management involved in shutting the offender up.

Now what do you do if the talking that's bothering you happens to be coming through the telephone, in the form of a telemarketer? For starters the "Do Not Call" lists that went into effect recently should have helped to cut down on unsolicited calls—that is, if you signed up. If you didn't, then don't just hang up when you get a call. Tell the person on the line, "Take me off your list." By law the telemarketer must respect your request, or he risks being fined by the federal government. You need to be patient, though, as it can take months for your number actually to be taken off of these call lists. In the meantime make "take me off your list" your mantra when dealing with telemarketers.

Don't get indignant with telemarketing calls you get from the companies you already do business with. Not only is the telemarketer just trying to do her job, but as an existing customer, you're fair game.

Annoying Habits

Everyone's got a habit that they're not even aware they're doing but which could be driving the people around them crazy. It could be cracking your gum or your knuckles or tapping your pencil incessantly on your desk.

If someone else's habit is bothering you, you need to decide ahead of time whether it's worth it to say something to the person or whether you simply need to take a chill pill and get over it. You could move away from the gum chewer or the pencil-tapper or try to tune them out.

If neither solution works, you need to speak directly to the person who is bothering you: "Could you please stop tapping your pencil? I can't concentrate on this test." Hopefully, she will apologize and stop immediately. However, there are times when people simply don't care that their behavior is bothering you, such as the lady in the cubicle next to yours who hums while she works or cracks her gum when she's concentrating. You can try asking her to stop but chances are she won't. Then all you can hope is that you get promoted soon so you can move your office to another part of the building.

Always share gum with others when you decide to go for a chew, and keep your mouth closed once you start chewing. Cracking and bubble popping are surefire ways to annoy those around you.

Discourteous Comments

When it comes to discourteous comments, probably the best way to sum things up is to borrow from Britney Spears and say, "Oops, I did it again." Sometimes you just can't help yourself, and you let something slip. Then, after it's out there, you wish you could take it back.

You should try to develop what some people call an edit function, which is like the five-second delay in live television. You need to stop and think about what you're about to say before you say it. That way if it is inappropriate, you can shut your mouth before it's too late. There are many instances in life when an edit function would come in handy, including the following.

Age-Related Questions

Unless you work in a bar or liquor store, you probably shouldn't come out and ask someone her age. This is especially true of women who may be sensitive about aging and are apt to celebrate multiple twenty-ninth birthdays. At the same time you never want to ask someone his age in a job interview or you risk setting yourself up for an age-discrimination accusation.

There are times when you may be discussing trivia or pop culture, and you're curious to establish how old the person you're talking to really is. You can get to that information in a roundabout and perfectly polite way. Instead of asking, "How old are you?" you could say, "I hope you don't mind my asking, but what year did you graduate from high school?" This will help place this person on a timeline, and you won't have asked them to reveal their real age. It's clever and courteous.

Braggers

Everyone has something to brag about at one time or another, and usually good friends and family members are happy to hear about your good fortune. It's when you never stop talking about yourself and your good fortune that you risk turning people off.

If you find yourself cornered at a cocktail party or in a conversation with a braggart, the most polite and effective way to deal with that person is not to respond to his outrageous claims at all. Silence is an amazing way to humble people. If that doesn't work, you can always try to change the topic.

But if this braggart is like most, he'll eventually find a way to bring the conversation back to being all about him. At that point, you can politely excuse yourself and walk away.

Delicately Dealing with Disabilities

If your children happen to see someone who is disabled, they're probably going to ask you about it—usually in a loud enough voice that the person they're asking about can hear them. Sometimes, your children can get a good lesson in tolerance from the person with the disability himself, who may answer their questions for you. Otherwise, it's up to you to handle their questions as matter-of-factly as possible.

When a child asks why someone is sitting in a wheelchair, say, "That person's legs probably don't work as well as yours and mine, and he needs that wheelchair to get around." A simple, straightforward answer should help satisfy their curiosity and teach them a little something about people's differences.

Never scold your child for noticing someone with a disability and asking about him. He's just being curious, and it's your job as a parent to educate him on people's differences.

The other kind of disability that you may have to delicately deal with is when someone doesn't speak as clearly as everyone else, either because he's had a stroke or he stutters. If you're with your child and he asks about why someone is speaking oddly, again deal with the matter directly. Tell your child that sometimes people are born a certain way and can't speak as well as they'd like to, or they get sick later in life, and it affects their speech.

Besides being upfront and honest with your child, you need to be polite to the person as well by listening closely to what he has to say and being patient while he finishes his thoughts. Never assume the part of translator and finish this person's sentence for him. He's likely had years of practice in how to communicate with others, and with a little patience, he will surely get his idea across.

Unintended Insults

Occasionally, you may have a slip of the tongue that results in your insulting someone unintentionally. This could be asking someone who has put on a bit of weight if she's expecting or inquiring about someone's husband, who just left her or recently passed away. Both situations result in your having egg on your face—and the need for you to save face fast.

If you find yourself saying something you wish you could take back, the best way to make amends is with a simple, clear, and unqualified apology: "Oh, dear, I'm dreadfully sorry. There's nothing I can say to excuse myself and my behavior, and I hope you can forgive me."

Bad Manners in Public

In a perfect world, everyone would behave beautifully when they're going about their business, but in reality that perfect world exists only in a dream. Chances are that on any given day, you're going to see people displaying bad manners in public. Sometimes it will behoove you to say something; other times you're just going to have to deal with the fact that not everyone is as well behaved as you are.

Cutting in Line

Back in elementary school you and your friends probably handled cutting in line in a very efficient fashion: when someone tried to sneak in the line, everyone yelled, "No cutsies," and the person skulked off to the back of the line. While the no cutsies rule applies in the grown-up world, not everyone abides by it.

If you happen to see someone cutting in front of you in line, such as at the movies or at the register in a store, you can say, "Excuse me, but I was ahead of you." Usually, most people will tell you that they weren't paying attention, they're sorry for cutting in front of you, and they'll move to the end of the line. However, what do you do if the person shrugs and says, "So what are you going to do about it?" In that instance, he's just threatened you, and there's no need to push the point. Manners are all good and fine, but you should never risk your safety and well being by trying to one-up someone on politeness.

QUESTION?

What do I do if I see someone littering?

If the litter isn't too dirty, you can subtly make your point by picking it up, handing it to the person and saying, "Excuse me, but you dropped this." Otherwise, you can watch silently as that person displays bad behavior and swear that you'll never duplicate it.

Problems at the Checkout Counter

The sign in the supermarket checkout line clearly says, "Ten items or fewer," but you notice that the guy in front of you easily has twenty items. What do you do? First and foremost, don't take it on yourself to point out this discrepancy. It's the cashier's problem. Second, if you're in a hurry, don't stand there and huff and puff while the other person checks out. If you need to get somewhere fast, go to another checkout line.

Finally, make sure that you never ever end up in an express line with more items than is allowed. Always do a quick count of your cart before you choose your checkout line and that way you'll never be one of those supermarket hogs who everyone hates.

Appendix 1

How to Write It

A big part of being polite is sending handwritten notes to people for a variety of occasions. Despite the need for note writing, not everyone feels comfortable putting his or her ideas on paper. That's where this Appendix steps in to help you out.

In this section you'll find an outline and/or boilerplate that you can use when you need to send a thank-you note, message of congratulations, or even an invitation for a bridal shower you may be throwing in a friend's honor. With this helpful information at your fingertips, you'll never have any excuse for not using good manners in written form.

Thank-You Notes

There are a number of occasions that warrant your sending a handwritten thank-you note. These include (but are not limited to) when you receive a gift for a birthday, wedding, anniversary, or baby shower. You should also send a thank-you note after you've been invited to someone's house for dinner, you've met with a client for business purposes, or someone did you a favor, such as taking in your mail when you went away on vacation.

Thank-You Formula

Writing a thank-you note for a gift or favor follows this simple formula:

1. Start your note by greeting the person by name.
2. Thank the person—by name—for the gift or good deed.
3. Tell the person briefly how you might use this gift or why this gift or favor meant so much to you.
4. Thank him again.
5. Sign your name.

Here are two examples of this formula for thank-you notes for gifts and favors:

Dear Jane:

Thank you so much for the one-of-a-kind piece of pottery you gave me for my birthday. I've already added it to my collection, and it looks fabulous. Thanks again for such a great gift.

Best wishes,

Lisa

Dear Jane:

Thank you so much for keeping an eye on our house while we were on vacation. Knowing that the house was well taken care of gave us terrific peace of mind while we were away. Thanks again for your generosity, and please let me know if we can ever repay the favor.

Best wishes,

Lisa

When thanking someone for a business meeting, invitation to dinner, being a houseguest, or some other social occasion in which you were included, you can use the above formula as your guide. All you have to do is tweak lines two and three.

So a real-life example of such a thank-you note for a business meeting would read like this:

Dear Jane:

Thank you for taking time out of your busy schedule to meet with me today. I enjoyed speaking with you about this new project we may be working on together, and I look forward to speaking with you more about it in the future. Thanks again, and let's touch base soon.

Sincerely,

Lisa Miller

A real-life thank-you note for a social occasion, such as dinner at someone's house, might read like this:

Dear Jane:

Thank you so much for having Tom and me over for dinner last night. The food was fabulous, and the company was even better. I look forward to treating your family to a meal at our home in the near future, and I'll call you soon to set up a date. Thanks again for a great evening.

Best wishes,

Lisa Miller

Notes That Convey Condolences

It's never easy when someone you love dies, and that's why it's so important for people to show support for the grieving parties by sending them a sympathy card. Even if you choose a store-bought card, you should always add a few personalized lines to it before signing your name. Saying something like "I'm so sorry for your loss" or "I'm keeping your family in my prayers during this difficult time" would suffice.

How to Write a Condolence Card

Sometimes a mass-market card simply can't convey how sad you are about someone's passing. In times like this, it's best to send a handwritten note to the grieving parties.

Here's a way to write a sympathy note that's sure to mean a lot to the recipient:

Dear Jane:

I was saddened to learn of your father's death. I hope that the love and support of family and friends will help get you through this difficult time. I just wanted you to know that you are in my thoughts.

Fondly,

Lisa Miller

If you know the family very well and feel like you want to share some personal memories of the deceased in your sympathy note, you can do so. Here's how a more detailed sympathy note might read:

Dear Jane:

I was saddened to learn of your father's death. Football Sundays are never going to be the same without your dad rooting for the Packers, and I'll drink a beer in his memory the next time the Packers play. I hope that the love and support of family and friends will help get you through this difficult time. I just wanted you to know that you are in my thoughts.

Fondly,

Lisa Miller

Acknowledging Sympathy Cards

No matter how distraught you may be over the loss of your loved one, it's good manners to acknowledge those who sent their sympathy wishes to you. Many funeral homes provide preprinted thank-you notes that grieving parties can send, and they are an acceptable choice only if you add a personalized line before signing your name. Saying something simple should suffice, such as "Thank you for remembering Jack in your kind note."

If you choose to handwrite every acknowledgement card, you can use the basic formula of a thank-you note but with the body of it tweaked to reflect the solemn occasion:

Dear Lisa:

Thank you for sending the sympathy card after my dad's death. It made me feel a little bit better during this sad time to know that friends were thinking of me. Thanks again for your thoughtfulness.

Fondly,

Jane Smith

Notes of Congratulations

Friends and family are sure to appreciate your good manners if you send them a note of congratulations when something good happens to them. This could be the birth of a child, a promotion at work, the purchase of a new home, or any other occasion when people typically celebrate in some fashion.

It's easy to pull together a note of congratulations. Here's how one would read for your friends, the new parents:

> *Dear Jane and John:*
> *Congratulations on the birth of your daughter, Ashley. We were so excited to hear the good news and can't wait to meet your bundle of joy. You guys are going to be great parents.*
> *Fondly,*
> *Lisa and Tom Miller*

If you're sending congratulations after seeing something in the newspaper, alumni newsletter, or other print media about someone, try to enclose a copy of that mentioned in your note of congratulations. Your note would read something like this:

> *Dear Jane:*
> *Congratulations on your job promotion. I read about your becoming vice president in the local paper, and I've enclosed a copy of the article, in case you haven't seen it yet. I know you're going to be great in your new position, and congratulations again.*
> *Best,*
> *Lisa Miller*

Spreading the News About a Wedding

You have a number of options for announcing that you're getting married. You can send out engagement announcements to friends and family soon after you get engaged, and later on, before your wedding date, you can send a wedding announcement to the local paper as well.

Engagement Announcements

An engagement announcement follows a pretty simple formula. Here are the basics: The bride's parents announce their daughter's engagement and include not only the bride's and the groom's full names but also their educational background and employment status. The announcement also includes the groom's parents' names and when the wedding will occur.

Most engagement announcements are printed on invitation-quality paper stock. The type is always centered on the page. When sending your engagement announcement to the local paper, you can send a picture of the bride-to-be only or you can send a picture of both of you. A sample engagement announcement would read like this:

Mr. and Mrs. Adam Claypool of Hillandale, Maryland, announce the engagement of their daughter, Miss Justine Ann Claypool, to Mr. James Brendan Danielson of Dallas, Texas. Mr. Danielson is the son of Dr. and Mrs. Roger Wakefield Danielson, also of Dallas.

Miss Claypool is a graduate of the University of Maryland and is a development officer at National Public Radio in Washington, D.C. Mr. Danielson is a graduate of the Rochester Institute of Technology and is a television producer at KXAS in Dallas. A November wedding is planned.

Wedding Announcements

Usually, you would only send out a wedding announcement so it can be printed in your local paper. Here's how it would read:

Miss Justine Ann Claypool, daughter of Mr. and Mrs. Adam Claypool of Hillandale, Maryland, was married yesterday, July 5, 2004, to Mr. James Brendan Danielson of Dallas, Texas. Mr. Danielson is the son of Dr. and Mrs. Roger Wakefield Danielson, also of Dallas. The Reverend William Smith officiated at the United Methodist Church of Bethesda, in Bethesda, Maryland.

Miss Claypool, 29, is keeping her name. She is a graduate of the University of Maryland and is a development officer at National Public Radio in Washington, D.C. Mr. Danielson, 32, is a graduate of the Rochester Institute of Technology and is a television producer at KXAS in Dallas. After honeymooning in the Cayman Islands, they will reside in Dallas.

If the couple elopes, you would send a wedding announcement to alert all the people you might have invited to the wedding about the nuptials that have already occurred. It would read:

Mr. and Mrs. Adam Claypool of Hillandale, Maryland, announce the marriage of their daughter, Miss Justine Ann Claypool, to Mr. James Brendan Danielson of Dallas, Texas, on September 15, 2004. Mr. Danielson is the son of Dr. and Mrs. Roger Wakefield Danielson, also of Dallas. The couple will now reside in Dallas.

Wedding Announcements with Bells and Whistles

In some social circles, the wedding announcements that appear in the paper not only include the basics of the wedding but also the names of all the wedding attendants and details of the bride's gown. If this best describes how people in your family write their wedding announcements, then make sure that you collect all those details so you can include them.

Your extended wedding announcement might read something like this:

Miss Justine Ann Claypool, daughter of Mr. and Mrs. Adam Claypool of Hillandale, Maryland, was married yesterday to Mr. James Brendan Danielson of Dallas, Texas. Mr. Danielson is the son of Dr. and Mrs. Roger Wakefield Danielson, also of Dallas. The Reverend William Smith officiated at the United Methodist Church of Bethesda, in Bethesda, Maryland.

Miss Claypool, 29, is keeping her name. She is a graduate of the University of Maryland and is a development officer at National Public Radio in Washington, D.C. Mr. Danielson, 32, is a graduate of the Rochester Institute of Technology and is a television producer at KXAS in Dallas. After honeymooning in the Cayman Islands, they will reside in Dallas.

The bride's sister, Judith Claypool, was the maid of honor. The groom's brother, Michael Danielson, was the best man. The bridal attendants were Sally Smith, Missy Danielson, and Janet Nelson. The groomsmen were Steven Danielson, Daniel Danielson, and Mark Wilson. Lorraine Danielson was a junior bridesmaid, Ashley Danielson was the flower girl, and Daniel Danielson Jr. was the ring bearer. The bride's gown was by Vera Wang.

Wedding Invitations

The United States long ago ceased to be a British property, but when it comes to wedding invitations, the wording and spelling is still very British. For example, when you request the honor of someone's presence at your wedding, you'll actually write "honour" on the invitation. Also, you'll always spell out the time—half-past noon instead of 12:30—and the year. So the year 2004 would read two thousand four. (Some folks prefer two thousand and four. Either way is acceptable.) Finally, like an engagement announcement, all the type on a wedding invitation is centered on the page.

Here is how a basic wedding invitation would take shape:

Mr. and Mrs. Adam Claypool
Request the honour of your presence
At the marriage of their daughter
Justine Ann
To
Mr. James Brendan Danielson
Son of Dr. and Mrs. Roger Wakefield Danielson
Saturday, the eighteenth of September
Two thousand four
At half-past noon
United Methodist Church of Bethesda
Bethesda, Maryland

If either the bride's or the groom's parents are divorced, you should list them separately on the invitation:

Mr. Adam Claypool and
Mrs. Marie Claypool
Request the honour . . .
Son of
Dr. Roger Wakefield Danielson and
Mrs. Denise Danielson . . .

If the bride and groom were paying for their own wedding, their names would come first on the invitation:

Miss Justine Ann Claypool
And
Mr. James Brendan Danielson
Request the honour of your presence
At their marriage . . .

If the bride and groom are paying for their wedding and the parents are helping out as well, you would write the invitation this way:

Miss Justine Ann Claypool
And
Mr. James Brendan Danielson
Together with their parents
Mr. and Mrs. Adam Claypool
And
Dr. and Mrs. Roger Wakefield Danielson
Request the honour of your presence . . .

Wedding Shower Invitations

There is less formality surrounding wedding shower invitations than there is with actual wedding invitations. So you have a lot more leeway in how you word your invitations.

See the two examples below for different ways you can convey the same message:

Janet Nelson and Sally Smith are hosting a bridal shower for
Justine Claypool at the Red Robin Restaurant, 1000 Bethesda Pike
in Bethesda, Maryland, on Sunday, August 3, 2004, at 4:00 P.M.
Please R.S.V.P. to either Janet (301-555-5555) or
Sally (301-555-5556) by July 26th.
Justine and James have registered at Crate and Barrel, and Target.

A different bridal shower invitation might read:

Justine Claypool is getting married, and we're
throwing a surprise bridal shower.
Join us at 4:00 P.M. at the Red Robin Restaurant,
1000 Bethesda Pike in Bethesda, Maryland, on Sunday, August 3, 2004.
Don't be late—Justine will be getting there at 4:30 P.M.
R.S.V.P. to bridesmaids Janet (301-555-5555) or
Sally (301-555-5556) by July 26th.
Remember: don't spill the beans.
Justine and James have registered at Crate and Barrel, and Target.

Baby Showers and Birth Announcements

There are usually two reasons for sending out written material when someone is pregnant. Either you're throwing her a baby shower, or you're the new mom, and you need to send out birth announcements.

Baby Shower Invitations

Like bridal showers there is no strict etiquette about how you write a baby shower invitation. In fact, it could read just like a bridal shower invitation, except for the pertinent details. Here's an example of how you might word a surprise baby shower invitation:

Justine Claypool is having a baby!
Come celebrate with the expectant mother at a surprise bridal shower.
Sunday, August 3, 2004, at 4:00 P.M.
Red Robin Restaurant, 1000 Bethesda Pike in Bethesda, Maryland
Don't be late—Justine will be getting there at 4:30 P.M.
We'll be playing a game with baby pictures, so please
be sure to bring one of yourself as a baby.
R.S.V.P. to Janet (301-555-5555) or Sally (301-555-5556) by July 26th.
Remember: don't spill the beans.
Justine has registered at Target's Lullaby Club

Birth Announcements

It's always a good idea to send out birth announcements, whether you've given birth to a child or adopted one from somewhere else. Here's how a typical birth announcement, for both scenarios, would read:

Justine Claypool and James Danielson
Welcomed their daughter
Charlotte Ann
Six pounds, ten ounces
Twenty inches
On March 25, 2006

Charlotte Ann Danielson,
Together with her parents,
Justine Claypool and James Danielson
Is delighted to announce the arrival of her
Baby brother
Matthew Michael
Seven pounds, seven ounces
Twenty-one inches
On February 14, 2008

Justine Claypool and James Danielson
Are delighted to announce the adoption of
James Michael
June 28, 2007

Birthdays and Anniversaries

When it comes to most celebrations these days, you may think that you can get away with a phone call to your guests. While a phone call does work in a pinch, to be truly proper, you should send a written invitation. Here's how to handle invitations to birthday celebrations and anniversary parties.

Birthday Parties

With an invitation that is going to a child, you don't have to be tremendously formal. Just make sure you provide all the details that the child (and parent) will need to know to R.S.V.P. and to attend.

Please come to Shelley's Fifth Birthday!
Saturday, April 19, at 4:00 P.M.
At Chuck E Cheese
2000 Bethesda Pike
Bethesda, Maryland
R.S.V.P. to Shelley's Mom (Winnie), 444-555-6666
We'll enjoy pizza, cake, and video games.

Anniversary Celebrations

Most families hold a big celebration when you pass a marriage milestone such as twenty-five years (silver anniversary) or fifty years (golden anniversary). In instances like this, when you've planned an elaborate anniversary party, you should send invitations that are formal in nature—especially if you've planned a black-tie affair.

You should always commemorate the years that the couple has been married on the top of their anniversary party invitation.

If you're throwing the party for yourself, this is how you should word your invitation:

1979-2004
Mr. and Mrs. Paul Frederick
Request the pleasure of your company
At a reception honoring their
Silver wedding anniversary
Saturday, October 18, 2004, at 7:30 P.M.
Bombay Yacht Club
3601 Connecticut Avenue NW
Washington, D.C.
R.S.V.P. by September 20: 202-555-5555

If your children are throwing you an anniversary party, this is how the invitation should read:

1954-2004
Buddy Frederick and Celia Frederick Collins
Invite you to honor their parents
Mr. and Mrs. Paul Frederick
On the occasion of their golden wedding anniversary
Saturday, October 18, 2004, at 7:30 P.M.
Bombay Yacht Club
3601 Connecticut Avenue NW
Washington, D.C.
R.S.V.P. by September 20: 202-555-5555 (Buddy)

Appendix 2

Manners School

No matter how hard you try to act politely or instruct your children on how to be well mannered, sometimes you need to call in reinforcements. In this instance, those reinforcements would be the etiquette doyennes at manners' schools, who know how to teach people, both young and old, how to behave.

Manners Classes in North America

Teaching adults and children how to behave properly in the classroom, in the boardroom, and in the dining room is a growing industry across North America. Whether you're interested in signing up a child, an employee, or yourself for some lessons in proper protocol, check out this sampling of schools, listed state-by-state.

California

The AML Group, Etiquette and Protocol Consultants, 1927 Jackson Street, San Francisco, 94109, 415-398-3229, *www.amlgroup.com*

Founder Lisa Mirza Grotts offers two seminars in which any smart businessperson would want to partake: Business and Social Etiquette, which covers gift giving, introductions, and international clients; and Business and Social Entertaining, which provides everything you need to know to be a proper host to business acquaintances as well as friends.

Ready for Media, 18842 Pacific Coast Highway, Malibu, 90265, 310-456-6857 *www.readyformedia.com*

While the focus of this company is prepping people for interactions with the media, this communication-centered business offers etiquette instruction that's appropriate for business settings. From meet and greets to impressing clients worldwide, these unique workshops teach you how to better conduct yourself in business.

Canada

The Protocol School of Ontario, P.O. Box 248, Zurich, Ontario, N0M 2T0, 519-871-4374, *www.psoo.com*

It is the boardroom and the dining room where Pamela Bedour, founder and director of The Protocol School of Ontario, focuses her energy. Her classes for adults help improve people's communication skills and their confidence, and she preps executives on how to behave when traveling abroad. She also helps tomorrows CEOs learn proper behavior through her children's and teen's etiquette programs, which cover everything from table manners to thank-you notes.

Connecticut

The Connecticut School of Etiquette, P.O. Box 2163, Darien, 06820, 888-283-6586, *www.morethanmanners. com*

According to founder Michele O'Reilly, proper etiquette is the key to success. No wonder she likes to start her students young, with a "Courteous Kids" class for youngsters ages four to seven. This school also offers classes for older children, teens and adults, and if your manners really need help, you can hire her for private coaching.

Georgia

Personal Best, Inc., 735 Langford Lane, Atlanta, 30327, 404-252-2245, *www.personalbest.net*

Founder Peggy Newfield focuses her fine skills on helping the employees of Fortune 500 companies act their best in all situations, including taking a client out to dinner or traveling abroad. In addition to on-site classes, you can purchase Personal Best seminars on tape for at-home study.

Maine

The Protocol School of Washington, P.O. Box 970, Yarmouth, 04096-0970, 1-877-766-3757, *www.psow.com*

Despite its name, the Protocol School of Washington conducts all its classes in Portland, Maine. Not only does the founder and director Dorothea Johnson offer etiquette classes to adults working in industries such as government, education, and entertainment, but also she has a mail-order program on manners for children.

Massachusetts

Protocol Advisors, 241 Beacon Street, Boston, 02116, 617-267-6950, *www.protocoladvisors.com*

Fortune 500 companies turn to Protocol Advisors for instruction on everything from dressing well to dining well. In addition, you can sign up for seminars on such esoteric topics as golf etiquette.

New Jersey

Corby O'Connor Business Etiquette & Protocol, 163 Fells Road, Suite B, Essex Falls, 07021, 866-249-7494, *www.corbyoconnor.com*

Manners may make you appear polite, but to etiquette guru Corby O'Connor, it's all about gaining the competitive edge. That's why her corporate protocol seminars focus on how both your behavior and your attire affect your business success.

New York

RASolutions, P.O. Box, Chenango Bridge, 13745-0471, 607-648-4243, *www.rasolutions.net*

Where this upstate New York firm succeeds is in giving courses on business dining etiquette, a must for any person serious about getting ahead these days. The company specializes in working with those employed at colleges and chambers of commerce.

Ohio

The Etiquette Institute, P.O. Box 340042, Columbus, 43234, 888-677-9346, *www.magnificentmanners.com*

It's no surprise that former elementary school teacher Cathi Fallon offers many protocol programs for the youngest students. One such program is called "Pretty As A Picture," which teaches social graces to elementary school girls. The Etiquette Institute even offers special programs for Girl Scout troops and birthday parties.

Pennsylvania

The Madison School of Etiquette and Protocol, 1444 Old Welsh Road, Huntingdon Valley, 19006, 215-938-1178, *www.etiquetteconsult.com*

Gail Madison is bringing manners to the masses with her etiquette classes for folks of all ages. From camps to company workshops, she teaches children, teens, and adults everything from dining instruction to corporate and international etiquette.

South Carolina

Charleston School of Protocol and Etiquette, P.O. Box 41113, Charleston, 29423, 843-207-1025, *www.charlestonschoolofprotocol.com*

Master manners maven Cynthia Grosso offers a summer camp and school-year finishing program for children ages nine to thirteen that help them to develop social and cultural skills. Her corporate-level training runs the gamut, from proper dining etiquette to how to behave when traveling abroad.

Tennessee

Flora Mainord Enterprises, School of Etiquette, 10238 South River Trail, Knoxville, 37922, 865-966-6057, *www.floramainord.com*

These etiquette classes vary from in-person seminars to interactive instruction to one-on-one tutorials on how to make a good first impression. Brides-to-be should find the class in wedding etiquette to be of particular interest.

Manners and Protocol, P.O. Box 3446, Brentwood, 37024-3446, 615-661-6313, *www.mannersandprotocol.com*

Manners and Protocol offers traveling seminars throughout the state on corporate etiquette and how having good manners can make you a more successful person. There are also a few classes geared toward children and manners.

Texas

Social Graces Perfected, 1807 Hwy. 183-S, Leander, 78641, 512-259-1053, *www.socialgracesperfected.com*

Not only does this school teach about such tried-and-true etiquette topics as how to behave while doing business, but also it ventures into some interesting social territory. Students of Social Graces Perfected, which also has a location in Wyoming, can learn how to be well behaved at their wedding or holiday events, and your children can improve their social graces for birthday parties and school gatherings.

The Texas School of Protocol, 909 Reinicke, Houston, 77007, 713-864-9841, *www.m-do-m.com*

This business's tag line is "manners do matter," and owner Karen Groussard Marlow works hard to bring this message to folks living and working in and around the Houston area. Her traveling workshops for all ages not only teach you the proper protocol of communication and dining, but also how to dress yourself professionally and appropriately at all times. In addition, she instructs people on art, music, theater and dance appreciation.

Washington

The Polite Child, 13110 NE 177th Place, Suite 123, Woodinville, 98072, 866-485-4089, *www.thepolitechild.com*

While the ultimate goal in sending your child to manners class would be to improve his behavior in social situations, the folks at The Polite Child hope to improve his self-esteem as well. Working with school districts on the West Coast, The Polite Child offers classes for preschoolers, grade-schoolers, tweens and teens, in topics ranging from party manners to polishing up for the prom.

Appendix 3

Recommended Books for Children

Sometimes the easiest way to instill good manners in your children, beyond daily drills, is to make manners a topic for nighttime reading. That's not to say that you should be reading chapter and verse from Emily Post as a bedtime story, although there is a nifty book from Post on kids' manners. It is possible to find age-appropriate reading matter for your kids that will help drive home the message that manners really do matter.

Here is an age-by-age breakdown of appropriate books that will help your children learn manners.

Infants, Toddlers, and Preschoolers

Just because your little one can barely speak or doesn't even know how to spell "please" or "thank you," it's never too early to teach him the basics of being polite. These books will help you in that task:

Ricci, Christine. *Dora's Book of Manners.* (Simon Spotlight, 2004).

Samuel, Catherine. *Elmo's Book of Manners.* (Random House, 1999).

Szekeres, Cyndy. *Toby's Please and Thank You.* (Little Simon, 2001).

Young Elementary School Students

Now that your child is going to school full-time, she can probably handle some detailed books on manners. You can start off reading these suggested titles to her. Then when she's a bit older, she'll enjoy reading them herself.

Berenstain, Stan, and Jan Berenstain. *The Berenstain Bears Forget Their Manners.* (Random House, 1985).

Marciano, John Bemelmans. *Madeline Says Merci: The Always Be Polite Book.* (Viking Children's Books, 2001).

Josyln, Sesyle. *What Do You Do, Dear?* (Harper Trophy, 1986).

Ziefert, Harriet. *Someday We'll Have Very Good Manners.* (Putnam, 2001).

Older Elementary/Middle School Students

As children ages eight to twelve become the social animals that the tween years promise, they'll find these books on manners quite helpful:

Barnes, Bob, and Emilie Barnes. *A Little Book of Manners for Boys.* (Harvest House, 2000).

Holyoke, Nancy. *Oops! The Manners Guide for Girls.* (American Girl Library, 1997).

Post, Peggy, and Cindy Post Senning. *Emily Post's The Guide to Good Manners for Kids.* (HarperCollins Children's Book, 2004).

Teenagers

Historically, teenagers have been the most defiant demographic. Do your teen a favor and give her one of these books that offer review lessons on manners. She'll surely need to know how to act politely if she wants to succeed in high school, college, and beyond.

Eberly, Sheryl. *365 Manners Kids Should Know.* (Three Rivers Press, 2001).

Packer, Alex J. *How Rude! The Teenagers' Guide to Good Manners, Proper Behavior, and Not Grossing People Out.* (Free Spirit Publishing, 1997).

Thompson, Robin. *Be the Best You Can Be.* (Robin Thompson Charm School, 1999).

Index

A

Addresses, 66–67
Adult-only parties, 56–58
African countries, 164
Age-related questions, 266
Airplane etiquette, 129–31
Anniversaries, 205–6, 281–82

B

Babies, 27–39. *See also* Children,
    raising; Pregnancy
    announcements, 13, 19–20,
        280–81
    bathing, 32–33
    car seats/strollers for, 35–36
    crying, 33–34
    diaper dealings, 30–32
    with fevers, 36
    gifts for, 8–9, 12–13, 20–22
    naming, 10–11, 23–24
    naps for, 25, 34
    new parents' life with, 17–18,
        24–25
    nursing, 28–30
    rituals for, 23–24
    showers for, 7–10, 279–80
Beggars, 264–65
Birthday celebrations, 50–51,
    202–4, 281
Birthday wishes, 225–26
Braggers, 266–67

Bus behavior, 131–32, 146–47
Business behavior, 101–12. *See also*
    Technology
    assistants and, 112
    cubicle conduct, 102–5
    cultural differences, 111–12
    dress codes, 105
    e-mail, 104–5
    entertaining after hours, 107
    in-office celebrations, 109
    international. *See specific country*
        names
    meals/paying checks, 106–7
    meetings, 106
    pursuing promotions, 110
    sexual harassment, 110–11
    solicitations/gifts, 108–9, 209

C

Canada, 153
Caribbean countries, 164
Cars
    being pulled over, 144
    driving courtesies, 140–44
    gas station manners, 149
    heavy traffic, 146
    parking lot protocol, 145
Cell phones/pagers, 122–24, 142–43
Central/South American countries,
    162–63
Checkout counter courtesy, 269

Children, raising, 37–51
    bad words and, 47–48
    birthday celebrations, 50–51,
        202–4, 281
    chores, 54
    discipline, 46
    fashion/clothing and,
        48–50
    feeding and, 39
    manners books for kids, 286
    naps and, 25, 34, 38–39
    parties with adults, 54–56,
        177–78, 179
    public behavior, 40–45
    receiving gifts graciously,
        204–5
    school behavior, 45–46
    toddlers, 38–40
China, 159–60
Common courtesies, 68
Commuters, 145–47
Complaining considerately,
    73–74
Compliments, backhanded,
    262–63
Congratulations, offering, 226–27,
    274
Cruise ship protocol, 126–29
Cultural differences, 59–61, 111–12,
    197–98, 256–57. *See also specific*
        country names
Cutting in line, 268–69

THE EVERYTHING SERIES!

BUSINESS & PERSONAL FINANCE

Everything® Budgeting Book
Everything® Business Planning Book
Everything® Coaching and Mentoring Book
Everything® Fundraising Book
Everything® Get Out of Debt Book
Everything® Grant Writing Book
Everything® Home-Based Business Book
Everything® Homebuying Book, 2nd Ed.
Everything® Homeselling Book, 2nd Ed.
Everything® Investing Book, 2nd Ed.
Everything® Landlording Book
Everything® Leadership Book
Everything® Managing People Book
Everything® Negotiating Book
Everything® Online Business Book
Everything® Personal Finance Book
Everything® Personal Finance in Your 20s
    and 30s Book
Everything® Project Management Book
Everything® Real Estate Investing Book
Everything® Robert's Rules Book, $7.95
Everything® Selling Book
Everything® Start Your Own Business Book
Everything® Wills & Estate Planning Book

COOKING

Everything® Barbecue Cookbook
Everything® Bartender's Book, $9.95
Everything® Chinese Cookbook
Everything® Cocktail Parties and Drinks
    Book
Everything® College Cookbook
Everything® Cookbook
Everything® Cooking for Two Cookbook
Everything® Diabetes Cookbook
Everything® Easy Gourmet Cookbook
Everything® Fondue Cookbook
Everything® Gluten-Free Cookbook

Everything® Grilling Cookbook
Everything® Healthy Meals in Minutes
    Cookbook
Everything® Holiday Cookbook
Everything® Indian Cookbook
Everything® Italian Cookbook
Everything® Low-Carb Cookbook
Everything® Low-Fat High-Flavor Cookbook
Everything® Low-Salt Cookbook
Everything® Meals for a Month Cookbook
Everything® Mediterranean Cookbook
Everything® Mexican Cookbook
Everything® One-Pot Cookbook
Everything® Pasta Cookbook
Everything® Quick Meals Cookbook
Everything® Slow Cooker Cookbook
Everything® Slow Cooking for a Crowd
    Cookbook
Everything® Soup Cookbook
Everything® Thai Cookbook
Everything® Vegetarian Cookbook
Everything® Wine Book, 2nd Ed.

CRAFT SERIES

Everything® Crafts—Baby Scrapbooking
Everything® Crafts—Bead Your Own Jewelry
Everything® Crafts—Create Your Own
    Greeting Cards
Everything® Crafts—Easy Projects
Everything® Crafts—Polymer Clay for
    Beginners
Everything® Crafts—Rubber Stamping
    Made Easy
Everything® Crafts—Wedding Decorations
    and Keepsakes

HEALTH

Everything® Alzheimer's Book
Everything® Diabetes Book
Everything® Health Guide to Controlling
    Anxiety

Everything® Hypnosis Book
Everything® Low Cholesterol Book
Everything® Massage Book
Everything® Menopause Book
Everything® Nutrition Book
Everything® Reflexology Book
Everything® Stress Management Book

HISTORY

Everything® American Government Book
Everything® American History Book
Everything® Civil War Book
Everything® Irish History & Heritage Book
Everything® Middle East Book

HOBBIES & GAMES

Everything® Blackjack Strategy Book
Everything® Brain Strain Book, $9.95
Everything® Bridge Book
Everything® Candlemaking Book
Everything® Card Games Book
Everything® Card Tricks Book, $9.95
Everything® Cartooning Book
Everything® Casino Gambling Book, 2nd Ed.
Everything® Chess Basics Book
Everything® Craps Strategy Book
Everything® Crossword and Puzzle Book
Everything® Crossword Challenge Book
Everything® Cryptograms Book, $9.95
Everything® Digital Photography Book
Everything® Drawing Book
Everything® Easy Crosswords Book
Everything® Family Tree Book, 2nd Ed.
Everything® Games Book, 2nd Ed.
Everything® Knitting Book
Everything® Knots Book
Everything® Photography Book
Everything® Poker Strategy Book
Everything® Pool & Billiards Book
Everything® Quilting Book
Everything® Scrapbooking Book

All Everything® books are priced at $12.95 or $14.95, unless otherwise stated. Prices subject to change without notice.

Everything® Sewing Book
Everything® Test Your IQ Book, $9.95
Everything® Travel Crosswords Book, $9.95
Everything® Woodworking Book
Everything® Word Games Challenge Book
Everything® Word Search Book

HOME IMPROVEMENT

Everything® Feng Shui Book
Everything® Feng Shui Decluttering Book,
 $9.95
Everything® Fix-It Book
Everything® Homebuilding Book
Everything® Lawn Care Book
Everything® Organize Your Home Book

EVERYTHING®
KIDS' BOOKS

All titles are $6.95

Everything® Kids' Animal Puzzle & Activity
 Book
Everything® Kids' Baseball Book, 3rd Ed.
Everything® Kids' Bible Trivia Book
Everything® Kids' Bugs Book
Everything® Kids' Christmas Puzzle
 & Activity Book
Everything® Kids' Cookbook
Everything® Kids' Crazy Puzzles Book
Everything® Kids' Dinosaurs Book
Everything® Kids' Gross Jokes Book
Everything® Kids' Gross Puzzle and
 Activity Book
Everything® Kids' Halloween Puzzle
 & Activity Book
Everything® Kids' Hidden Pictures Book
Everything® Kids' Joke Book
Everything® Kids' Knock Knock Book
Everything® Kids' Math Puzzles Book
Everything® Kids' Mazes Book
Everything® Kids' Money Book
Everything® Kids' Nature Book
Everything® Kids' Puzzle Book
Everything® Kids' Riddles & Brain Teasers Book
Everything® Kids' Science Experiments Book
Everything® Kids' Sharks Book
Everything® Kids' Soccer Book
Everything® Kids' Travel Activity Book

KIDS' STORY BOOKS

Everything® Fairy Tales Book

LANGUAGE

Everything® Conversational Japanese Book
 (with CD), $19.95
Everything® French Phrase Book, $9.95
Everything® French Verb Book, $9.95
Everything® Inglés Book
Everything® Learning French Book
Everything® Learning German Book
Everything® Learning Italian Book
Everything® Learning Latin Book
Everything® Learning Spanish Book
Everything® Sign Language Book
Everything® Spanish Grammar Book
Everything® Spanish Practice Book
 (with CD), $19.95
Everything® Spanish Phrase Book, $9.95
Everything® Spanish Verb Book, $9.95

MUSIC

Everything® Drums Book (with CD), $19.95
Everything® Guitar Book
Everything® Home Recording Book
Everything® Playing Piano and Keyboards
 Book
Everything® Reading Music Book (with CD),
 $19.95
Everything® Rock & Blues Guitar Book
 (with CD), $19.95
Everything® Songwriting Book

NEW AGE

Everything® Astrology Book, 2nd Ed.
Everything® Dreams Book, 2nd Ed.
Everything® Ghost Book
Everything® Love Signs Book, $9.95
Everything® Numerology Book
Everything® Paganism Book
Everything® Palmistry Book
Everything® Psychic Book
Everything® Reiki Book
Everything® Tarot Book
Everything® Wicca and Witchcraft Book

PARENTING

Everything® Baby Names Book
Everything® Baby Shower Book
Everything® Baby's First Food Book
Everything® Baby's First Year Book
Everything® Birthing Book
Everything® Breastfeeding Book
Everything® Father-to-Be Book
Everything® Father's First Year Book
Everything® Get Ready for Baby Book
Everything® Get Your Baby to Sleep Book,
 $9.95
Everything® Getting Pregnant Book
Everything® Homeschooling Book
Everything® Mother's First Year Book
Everything® Parent's Guide to Children
 and Divorce
Everything® Parent's Guide to Children
 with ADD/ADHD
Everything® Parent's Guide to Children
 with Asperger's Syndrome
Everything® Parent's Guide to Children
 with Autism
Everything® Parent's Guide to Children with
 Bipolar Disorder
Everything® Parent's Guide to Children
 with Dyslexia
Everything® Parent's Guide to Positive
 Discipline
Everything® Parent's Guide to Raising a
 Successful Child
Everything® Parent's Guide to Tantrums
Everything® Parent's Guide to the Overweight
 Child
Everything® Parent's Guide to the Strong-
 Willed Child
Everything® Parenting a Teenager Book
Everything® Potty Training Book, $9.95
Everything® Pregnancy Book, 2nd Ed.
Everything® Pregnancy Fitness Book
Everything® Pregnancy Nutrition Book
Everything® Pregnancy Organizer, $15.00
Everything® Toddler Book
Everything® Tween Book
Everything® Twins, Triplets, and More Book

All Everything® books are priced at $12.95 or $14.95, unless otherwise stated. Prices subject to change without notice.

PETS

Everything® Cat Book
Everything® Dachshund Book
Everything® Dog Book
Everything® Dog Health Book
Everything® Dog Training and Tricks Book
Everything® German Shepherd Book
Everything® Golden Retriever Book
Everything® Horse Book
Everything® Horseback Riding Book
Everything® Labrador Retriever Book
Everything® Poodle Book
Everything® Pug Book
Everything® Puppy Book
Everything® Rottweiler Book
Everything® Small Dogs Book
Everything® Tropical Fish Book
Everything® Yorkshire Terrier Book

REFERENCE

Everything® Car Care Book
Everything® Classical Mythology Book
Everything® Computer Book
Everything® Divorce Book
Everything® Einstein Book
Everything® Etiquette Book, 2nd Ed.
Everything® Inventions and Patents Book
Everything® Mafia Book
Everything® Philosophy Book
Everything® Psychology Book
Everything® Shakespeare Book

RELIGION

Everything® Angels Book
Everything® Bible Book
Everything® Buddhism Book
Everything® Catholicism Book
Everything® Christianity Book
Everything® Jewish History & Heritage Book
Everything® Judaism Book
Everything® Koran Book
Everything® Prayer Book
Everything® Saints Book

Everything® Torah Book
Everything® Understanding Islam Book
Everything® World's Religions Book
Everything® Zen Book

SCHOOL & CAREERS

Everything® Alternative Careers Book
Everything® College Survival Book, 2nd Ed.
Everything® Cover Letter Book, 2nd Ed.
Everything® Get-a-Job Book
Everything® Guide to Starting and Running a Restaurant
Everything® Job Interview Book
Everything® New Teacher Book
Everything® Online Job Search Book
Everything® Paying for College Book
Everything® Practice Interview Book
Everything® Resume Book, 2nd Ed.
Everything® Study Book

SELF-HELP

Everything® Dating Book, 2nd Ed.
Everything® Great Sex Book
Everything® Kama Sutra Book
Everything® Self-Esteem Book

SPORTS & FITNESS

Everything® Fishing Book
Everything® Golf Instruction Book
Everything® Pilates Book
Everything® Running Book
Everything® Total Fitness Book
Everything® Weight Training Book
Everything® Yoga Book

TRAVEL

Everything® Family Guide to Hawaii
Everything® Family Guide to Las Vegas, 2nd Ed.
Everything® Family Guide to New York City, 2nd Ed.
Everything® Family Guide to RV Travel & Campgrounds

Everything® Family Guide to the Walt Disney World Resort®, Universal Studios®, and Greater Orlando, 4th Ed.
Everything® Family Guide to Cruise Vacations
Everything® Family Guide to the Caribbean
Everything® Family Guide to Washington D.C., 2nd Ed.
Everything® Guide to New England
Everything® Travel Guide to the Disneyland Resort®, California Adventure®, Universal Studios®, and the Anaheim Area

WEDDINGS

Everything® Bachelorette Party Book, $9.95
Everything® Bridesmaid Book, $9.95
Everything® Elopement Book, $9.95
Everything® Father of the Bride Book, $9.95
Everything® Groom Book, $9.95
Everything® Mother of the Bride Book, $9.95
Everything® Outdoor Wedding Book
Everything® Wedding Book, 3rd Ed.
Everything® Wedding Checklist, $9.95
Everything® Wedding Etiquette Book, $9.95
Everything® Wedding Organizer, $15.00
Everything® Wedding Shower Book, $9.95
Everything® Wedding Vows Book, $9.95
Everything® Weddings on a Budget Book, $9.95

WRITING

Everything® Creative Writing Book
Everything® Get Published Book
Everything® Grammar and Style Book
Everything® Guide to Writing a Book Proposal
Everything® Guide to Writing a Novel
Everything® Guide to Writing Children's Books
Everything® Guide to Writing Research Papers
Everything® Screenwriting Book
Everything® Writing Poetry Book
Everything® Writing Well Book

Available wherever books are sold!
To order, call 800-258-0929, or visit us at *www.everything.com*
Everything® and everything.com® are registered trademarks of F+W Publications, Inc.